D1137728

DIS-ORIENTING RHYTHMS

DIS-ORIENTING RHYTHMS

The Politics of the New Asian Dance Music

EDITED BY

SANJAY SHARMA, JOHN HUTNYK

AND ASHWANI SHARMA

ZED BOOKS

London & New Jersey

Dis-Orienting Rhythms was first published in 1996 by
Zed Books Ltd, 7 Cynthia Street, London N1 9JF, UK, and
165 First Avenue, Atlantic Highlands, New Jersey 07716, USA

Editorial copyright © Sanjay Sharma, John Hutnyk, Ashwani Sharma, 1996
Copyright © individual contributors, 1996
The moral rights of the authors of this work have been asserted by them
in accordance with the Copyright, Designs and Patents Act, 1988

Typeset in Monotype Bembo by Lucy Morton, London SE12
Printed and bound in the United Kingdom by Redwood Books Ltd,
Kennet House, Kennet Way, Trowbridge, Wilts, BA14 8RN

A catalogue record for this book is available from the British Library
US CIP data is available from the Library of Congress

ISBN 1 85649 469 1 (Hb)
ISBN 1 85649 470 5 (Pb)

CONTENTS

Introduction
Sanjay Sharma, John Hutnyk and Ashwani Sharma   I

PART ONE SPACE AND ARTICULATION

I Sounds Oriental: The (Im)possibility of Theorizing
Asian Musical Cultures
Ashwani Sharma   I5

2 Noisy Asians or 'Asian Noise'?
Sanjay Sharma   32

PART TWO EXPRESSIVE STYLES

3 Asian Kool? Bhangra and Beyond
Rupa Huq   61

4 Remixing Identities: 'Off' the Turntable
Shirin Housee and Mukhtar Dar   81

5 Psyche and Soul: A View from the 'South'
Koushik Banerjea and Partha Banerjea   105

PART THREE ENGAGEMENTS AND ENTANGLEMENTS

6 Re-Sounding (Anti)Racism, or Concordant Politics?
Revolutionary Antecedents
Virinder S. Kalra, John Hutnyk and Sanjay Sharma   127

7 Repetitive Beatings or Criminal Justice?
John Hutnyk   156

PART FOUR PHANTASMAGORIC TERRAINS

8 Versioning Terror: Jallianwala Bagh and the Jungle
Koushik Banerjea and Jatinder Barn   193

9 New Paths for South Asian Identity and
Musical Creativity
Raminder Kaur and Virinder S. Kalra   217

References   232

About the Contributors   242

Index   243

ACKNOWLEDGEMENTS

The editors would like to thank all the contributors, and especially Raminder Kaur and Virinder S. Kalra, for their overall work on this book. Thanks also to Barnor Hesse, Bobby Sayyid, Rajinder Kumar, Louise Murray and the crew at Zed, Esther, Aki and Simon at Nation, Apache Indian, Bally Sagoo, Radical Sista, the Transl-Asia Project folk and the Charterhouse reading group in Manchester. (John Hutnyk would like to thank the International Centre for Contemporary Cultural Research and the Economic and Social Research Council. Lal salaam.)

Lyrics to Kaliphz, 'Hang 'Em High' are published by kind permission of Perfect Songs. Lyrics to Apache Indian, 'Movie over India' reproduced by kind permission of MCA records. Lyrics to Asian Dub Foundation, 'Jericho', 'Journey', 'Strong Culture' 'Rebel Warrior'; and Hustlers HC, 'Big Trouble in Little Asia', 'Vigilante' all reproduced by kind permission of QFM publishing and the artists themselves. Lyrics to Fun^Da^Mental, 'Dog-Tribe' and 'President Propaganda', reproduced by kind permission of D. Watts and M. Uddin, and M. Uddin and D. Webb, respectively.

*This book is dedicated
to the memory of Ved Parkash Sharma,
and all the other South Asian settlers who
struggled and remade their lives in Britain*

INTRODUCTION

Sanjay Sharma, John Hutnyk and Ashwani Sharma

> Now we're Nomads
> That stay in one place
> Not a country
> Not a face...
> This is a journey from
> Loneliness to pride
> No longer any need to hide...
> ('Journey', Asian Dub Foundation)[1]

'Saris', 'vindaloo' and 'Ravi Shankar' are perhaps some of the less offensive ethnically marked objects that define a South Asian cultural presence in multi-racist Britain. So why should we complain? Ethnicity is in. Cultural difference is in. Marginality is in. Consumption of the Other is all the rage for late capitalism. Finally, it appears that the 'coolie' has become cool. Yet in congruence, racial violence continues to soar as Fortress Europe further secures its borders. You may wonder how this is related to a book about the new Asian dance music, which seeks to reflect critically upon an exponentially rising youth culture vying for a legitimate place in contemporary British popular culture.

This book does begin the process of writing in the presence of an emergent Asian youth culture in Britain. However, the reader will discover that many of the questions raised in these chapters are not answered. We like it like that. We recognize that an increasing heterophilia found in Cultural Studies feeds this expanding discipline's voracious appetite for all that is labelled 'hybrid'. It makes this book a risky project. Our intention has not been an exercise in meticulous description, or authoritative ethnography, or insider 'native' accounts and explanation of vibrant forms of Asian cultural expression in Britain. These cultural forms continue to be imbued with an exoticized, othered status in the West, and our primary goal has been to break out of the Orientalist tradition of simply making knowable these cultural productions for an ever-eager academic audience and other agencies of control. The imperative to provide a conclusive report on the current state of play of the children of the diaspora strikes us as a compromise that cannot be countenanced. We recognize interest in a sociology of South Asian culture in Britain, and especially youth cultures, as having close ideological connections with the disciplines of command that police inner-urban neighbourhoods, close down Black clubs, collude in immigration control, and so on – and all this is part of the same spectrum as an interest in what happens with Britain's ethnicized populations in the generations after migration.

Dis-Orienting Rhythms opens up a series of critical debates and tensions concerning the production of the new Asian dance music as an object of knowledge for academic consumption. We are interested in both diversification and consolidation of the possible points of resistance to such imperatives of disciplinary control, and in a critique of the celebration and substitution of 'difference' for ensuing socio-economic inequalities and racial terror. First of all, our aim is to explode the possibilities of simply writing about such cultural production; we are *for* a new sociology, cultural studies, politics, or whatever, that does not rehearse Orientalist and exoticizing scholarship, but opens space for insights, creativity, and intervention. In extension of this, we are interested in the political project of making spaces within the public sphere for these cultural processes, for the flourishing of a wild creativity, for alliances and collaboration against oppression at all levels, and so for an expressive culture unbound from the conventions and clichés of hegemonic order.

This is one of the first books on contemporary Asian popular culture in the UK, so why focus on music? The book explores, in various ways, the crucial role that contemporary Asian dance music has played in the formation of an urban cultural politics in Britain. We have charted, but not exhausted, possible responses to questions that come out of this cultural politics.

In writing the chapters that make up this volume, we asked the contributors to keep in mind a tripartite code: against simplification, against anti-politics, against victimologies. What unites all the contributors is a perspective that includes opposing an ethnic identity politics that is absolutist or essentialist, that offers only management of identity by singularly empowered individuals – self-appointed, state, media, or academic-approved vanguards – with vested interests in maintaining boundaries of identity and in closing down openings and dispersals. Why is it that political aspirations and articulations have regressed (to the point where an ethnographer such as Marie Gillespie [1995] can claim that Apache Indian's hybrid musical style is 'subversive', as if being hybrid is all there is to being subversive)? For many nowadays, to offer a radical politics that challenges anything much seems too difficult. These closures of political aspiration, the decline of 'politics' in favour of gesture, identity, and liberal multiculturalism, and the disappearance of critical questioning are all to be challenged across the line of music and politics.

This book has been organized into four parts. However, each chapter engages with a multiplicity of debates and contentions and cannot be wholly confined under our organizing rubric. To insist on this ordering would prematurely close down other possible conjunctions and readings. Each of the chapters is a specific engagement with the different dimensions and political imperatives of diasporic Asian musical cultures.

The first part of the book begins with an introductory chapter by Ashwani Sharma. By juxtaposing a critique of the term 'World Music' with an interrogation of the academy's recent attention to cultural difference and ethnicity, he exposes the Eurocentric limits of the celebration of hybrid Otherness. This opening intervention marks and makes visible the limits of theorizing Asian musical cultural production at this historical conjuncture in which both epistemic and racial violence exist conterminously with the fetishization of marginality. Next, in Chapter 2, Sanjay Sharma builds upon and closely details how mainstream academic accounts of Asian music, in particular Bhangra and post-Bhangra, are framed within an authenticity problematic of cultural difference. In deconstructing the category 'Asian' from its ethno-cultural determinations, the chapter attempts to produce a new theoretical understanding of Asian cultural representation that moves beyond the essentialist 'race'-orientated discourses and overdetermined accounts of ethnicity in the academy. By creating an interrogative dialogue with noted post-Bhangra Rap artists, Sanjay Sharma points towards more productive ways of undertaking cultural study: to a pedagogy committed to the construction of forms of political engagement that do not reduce popular culture to the scrutinized Other. Moreover, this practice blurs the boundaries between academic production and cultural expression. This approach exemplifies a concern of the book as a whole: to engage in discursive work that disrupts and challenges the conventions of the theorizing of South Asian musical cultural production. Chapters 1 and 2 together attempt to map out provisionally the contours of a critical space within which different forms of intervention are able to be articulated. The chapters that follow continue to locate and reproduce the poetics of this enunciated space.

Part Two narrates the formation of an Asian expressive culture in Britain. Rupa Huq in Chapter 3 focuses upon the diversification of Asian musical forms, providing a detailed and well-informed account of how groups and individual artists themselves reflect on their musical productions. She undertakes some close analysis of the mainstream media representation of these Asian dance musics. By concretely illustrating the problematic media discourse that governs how these musics are located, Huq brings to the surface the forms of negotiation and struggle that cultural producers have to undertake in order to work within the commercial environment. In Chapter 4, this cultural history is further explored in the discussion by Shirin Housee and Mukhtar Dar with one of the foremost producers of Asian dance music, Bally Sagoo, and the innovative DJ Radical Sista. These artists not only renarrate their experiences and intimate involvement in the formation of an Asian dance music culture in Britain, their accounts also resonate with the experiences of Asian youth itself. These experiences, especially as voiced by Radical Sista, include the struggle of many young women in the creation of, as well as their unrecognized presence in and engagement with, the new dance music. The discussion form allows for a dialogic style of exposition, enabling other stories to be told, other histories to be narrated, new, unforeseen and unexpected connections to be made.

Many of our chapters pursue a project of narrating and recovering unwritten histories. Koushik Banerjea and Partha Banerjea in Chapter 5 eloquently write back an Asian presence into the Soul movements of the late 1970s and 1980s Britain – a crucial venture given that Soul/Black dance music has been a central element in the subsequent developments of Asian dance music. Through an imaginative poetic style and semantic play, Banerjea and Banerjea interrupt the too neat, Manichean bifurcation of black and white, which inevitably renders Asians invisible and marginal to the practices of (sub)urban culture. By consciously drawing from their specific and personal histories, these authors bear witness to the importance of a politics of space and of the *location* of cultural struggles. They stress how particular geographies – real and imagined – are crucial to the formation of subjectivities in everyday political engagements. Their invocation of 'an alternative public space' is further suggestive of a politics that this book in part is attempting to chart.

In Part Three, from an imperative that shares interests in historical recovery, Virinder S. Kalra, John Hutnyk and Sanjay Sharma in Chapter 6 explore the antecedents of political Asian musical performance and anti-racist/anti-imperialist struggles, and reconnect and contextualize these with the contemporary musical output of Rap groups such as Hustlers HC, Kaliphz and Fun^Da^Mental. By plotting the lineage of the poetic songs of the Indian Workers Association in the 1970s to the new dance music of the 1990s, this chapter stresses the crucial importance of culture to all forms of political action. John Hutnyk in Chapter 7 reviews the music television reception of Asian self-defence mobilization, interweaving censorship issues and Asian involvement in campaigns against the racist Criminal Justice Act in the UK – as read alongside the failures of academic and parliamentary anti-racist 'initiatives'. Inspired by the track 'Dog-Tribe' and the work of Asian Dub Foundation, Hutnyk inflects the need to seek new alliances within the Left and within anti-racist formations through Antonio Negri's reading of Marx. These two chapters in different ways offer very explicit instances of how musical cultures have been intertwined with direct political engagements, marking out the strengths and limitations of these forms of cultural politics.

What is particularly significant about many of the chapters in the book is their claim that contemporary struggles can only be addressed through the renarration of histories, not only in Britain, but, very important, in relation to the South Asian subcontinent. The two chapters in Part Four engage with the movements and translations of cultural productions across the world. They both innovatively seek to conjoin the disparate fragments of a global culture (Appadurai 1990). In Chapter 8, Koushik Banerjea and Jatinder Barn argue loquaciously – through an innovative Jungle-inspired, antiphonal mode of address in and around the metaphor of space – for the recovery of an anterior colonial moment in the reproduction of contemporary practices of racism. They mark out the insidious forms that the fear of the encounter with racial terror produces across the (post)colonial divide. Through their juxtaposition of imperial masculine violence and everyday practices of white working-class terror, their reading of the dissonant music of Jungle highlights its trangressive potentialities in the fractured spaces of a postcolonial Britain in decline.

The final chapter, by Raminder Kaur and Virinder S. Kalra, revisits some of the concerns of the book and considers, through the artist

Apache Indian, the need to develop a more appropriate conceptual language in order to grasp the cultural significance of the multiple global musical flows of communication and identity production. In dialogue with Part One and the present limitations of cultural theory, they attempt to introduce new concepts in the engagement with Asian musical culture. Their introduction of the deconstructive term 'Transl-Asia' offers a new discursive framework for the work that this book has begun to undertake. This chapter then needs to be read not as a conclusion but more as a point of departure.

This book represents one of the few sustained attempts to situate popular South Asian culture within the study of the politics of 'race' and nation in Cultural Studies and related disciplines. In spite of important developments in the 1980s and 1990s with regard to questions of cultural difference, South Asian culture in Britain (and also in North America), has been marked by its virtual absence from the field of study. Our intention has been to highlight the point that these Asian dance musics are legitimate and 'autonomous' diaspora musical forms worthy of attention, particularly in their capacity to implode both the ubiquitous imperialist centres of the West and contemporary cultural racisms constituted through exclusionary narratives of nationhood. In particular, Banerjea and Barn allude provocatively to the invisibility of whiteness in much of Cultural Studies discourse on popular culture. Why is it that writings about Techno and Rave erase their Black antecedents and continued Black influence through deracialized accounts of trance dance tribalism and the shamanic disappearance of the body? Conversely, how is it that Jungle is simultaneously dismissed for being 'too black' or not 'black enough'. It follows also that the perceived cultural specificity of Bhangra, which often cannot but be reduced to the status of a World Music, is no more than a code of its cultural impenetrability for white consumption. The othered status of Asian dance musics is not only resistive of being rewritten with whiteness as its unstated centre, but exposes the operations of power–knowledge that ingest these othered musics in making them 'truly British'. More specifically, Ashwani Sharma not only raises the difficulty of theorizing Asian musical culture, but also argues that the master's contemporary theoretical tools, neatly made discernible by the limits of hybridity talk, are in need of radical rethinking or jettisoning. Furthermore, the more insidious and synergistic projects of the academic exegesis, and capitalist devouring, of cultural difference in order to expand further the limits of the West need to be made visible and resisted.

Nevertheless, the intervention of the study of the cultural politics of 'race' and black cultural forms has been disruptive of the ethnocentricity of Cultural Studies (for example, Chow 1993; Gilroy 1987, 1993a; Hall 1992; hooks 1991 and Mercer 1994). Whilst acknowledging the advances made in theorizing black representation and representational practices, we contend that questions concerning the specificities of South Asian cultural representation continue to be theoretically undeveloped and marginal in the field of Cultural Studies. The turn to questions of identity in the mid-1980s in Britain, with the emphasis on the politics of representation, opened up the space for new forms of cultural politics and practices. Sanjay Sharma, by evoking the notion of a de-centred Asian identity as a political category entertains the possibility of political struggles mobilized around the signifiers 'Asian' *and* 'Black',[2] arguing that the terms are not mutually exclusive but can be articulated together. This question of the continued viability of the political signifier 'Black' and its relation to the cultural politics of Asian dance music is an issue that, at least implicitly, concerns many of the contributors to this book. The unique British anti-racist moment of 'Black' in the 1970s and 1980s appears to be in decline if we are to believe the cultural critics – compare the differing perspectives and political projects of Tariq Modood (1994) and Stuart Hall (1995), who both seem to drift towards the same conclusion. The 1990s have witnessed the return to ethnicity (however reconstituted) as a positionality for grounding political being and action. Some contributors to this book, for example Kaur and Kalra from the perspective of complex globalized identity formations, have called for an autochthonous naming of an Asian identity that takes account of the cultural specificities of and ways of being silenced by the signifier 'Black' in Britain. Moreover, as Sanjay Sharma suggests, we do not wish to return naïvely to an uncritical notion of Black, but any premature closure of this debate is liable to reproduce the historical amnesia of the postmodern condition. The valency of 'Black' as a political positionality that strategically unites disparate groups against increasingly organized and vicious manifestations of Euro-racism remains a project worth struggling for and remaking, especially given the possibility of forging new alliances and self-determinations, as argued for crucially by Hutnyk. The legitimate entry of the term 'Asian' into contemporary and popular politico-cultural discourses should not necessarily be read as the disappearance of 'Black' or as the impossibility of making newer alliances – rather, it is to be understood as the contestation and renegotiation of these identifications and positionalities.

The book secures a precarious and contingent identity by tagging syncretic musical genres of Bhangra through to Jungle as 'Asian'. Yet we are seeking to make connections across these divergent musics beyond the supposed ethnicity of the artists and crowds involved in their production and reception, and in the global liminal sites of their creation. One of our specific tasks, as pursued in several chapters, has been to explore how these musics may be identified or (re)claimed as being 'Asian' in Britain, though never contained by this contested signifier (for example, as Huq has pertinently asked, where does the music of Echobelly, Cornershop or Voodoo Queens fit into our schema?). The affirmative moment of Bhangra has undoubtedly constituted a diasporic South Asian music that is here to stay and further mutate. But this does not deny the pre-Bhangra Asian youth their participation in Soul or Punk, or their post-Bhangra involvement in Techno, Grunge, Metal and everything else on offer. By struggling over the master signifier 'Asian', the book attempts to develop productively, as well as to challenge, the assumptions underpinning the essentialist discourse on ethnicity and popular culture. We see this book engaging with the important work that is being undertaken in African-American, Chicano(a), Latino(a) and East Asian Studies (for example, Chow 1993; Gates 1988; Rosaldo 1993 and West 1989). The development of a theoretically informed political analysis of the cultural politics of the underground emergence of South Asian dance music and club culture is considered an imperative project. It is to be viewed not only as a corrective impulse to the ethnocentrism of Cultural Studies, but as a move that further pushes beyond the discipline's present boundaries.

Paul Gilroy (1993a) has made the timely assertion that Cultural Studies remains inflected with ethnocentric dimensions and is limited by the analysis of culture within homogeneous national units. Here, we would like to propose, informed by Spivak (1993), a transnational cultural studies approach, as implied in a variety of ways by many of the chapters in the book, and particulary by Kaur and Kalra in their provocative concept of Transl-Asia. This approach operates beyond exclusionary national concerns, and engages with the globalized and diasporic nature of South Asian cultural formations and textual practices. We imagine this approach only as a beginning, requiring further mapping out and locating of the social and historical emergence of these formations and representations.

In particular, how are we to rethink the notion of diaspora? It has become a fashionable theme for 'post-colonial' studies, but what do we specifically mean when we speak of the South Asian diaspora in relation to music and other cultural productions outside the subcontinent?

Perhaps we should be more interested in circulation and flows? In this respect, the workings of diaspora with regard to Apache Indian and bands like Fun^Da^Mental are in need of further study. Likewise the notion of the (re)circulation of Bally Sagoo's Bollywood remixes 're-turning back home' raises a series of questions, not only about the flows of global capital and commodities or the kinds of narratives that constitute and sustain notions of the homeland in the first place, but also about the indigenization of cultural productions that are simultaneously 'Western' and 'non-Western', and the problematizing of these very terms. Perhaps the new Asian dance music can be read as a cultural form that narrates diasporas, dynamically affirming, transforming and mutating both imagined and material linkages. Diaspora then may be considered as a site in which music provides opportunities to formulate new alliances beyond national boundaries, rather than only as a fantasy of home affirming 'tradition' or 'origins'. A useful formulation by Gilroy summarizes work yet to be done:

> The [tele-technological] means of distribution are capable of dissolving distance and creating new and unpredictable forms of identification and cultural affinity between groups that dwell far apart. The transformation of cultural space and the subordination of distance are only two factors that contribute to a parallel change in the significance of appeals to tradition, time and history (Gilroy 1993a: 194).

However, as has already been stated, this book project is not intended to be only located within the discursive spaces of the academy, but attempts to move beyond and create new terrains for political intervention. We are cautious not to celebrate the hyper-syncretic quality of the new Asian dance music naïvely as a ready-made vehicle for realizing a necessarily progressive kind of politics of difference. We would need to ask, first, what are the productive and unproductive registers of music? For example, how is it that music can become a 'space' that is open to the articulation and deployment of identities in ways that other media and popular cultural forms seem more to police and close down? Musical cultures can mobilize, but often don't, in ways that lead to a politics that can be integrated into a popular cultural form providing successful points of identification with politics. More critically, is music compromised by its imbrication with capitalism, Music television (MTV), Star, the big production houses like Sony and BMG? Is music a cultural holding pen diverting energies from more confrontational politics? Is music the forum through which the appropriation of Black expressive culture is most easily achieved by the hegemonic white culture of Britain (Blues into rock'n'roll, Rastafari into Police-type Reggae, Hip-Hop and House into Euro-Beat and Dance-Pop)? There are no simple answers to these many difficult questions. However, crucial to what is at stake is a recognition that the site of popular culture is a place of struggle that not only can be won (Hall 1992) but also can redefine and rupture the institutional boundaries that separate artists, activists and academics. This book has attempted to bring these cultural workers into mutual dialogue. In various ways, all the chapters attempt to interrogate and forge productive relationships and linkages across the formal sites of music and politics, and to generate alternative languages of cultural politics framed beyond the myopia of ethnic identity politics or the confines of the nation-state.

The book has been brought to fruition through intense debate, unrelenting intellectual and ideological dissension, collaborative writing, a commitment to social transformation, *and* a passion for Asian dance music on the part of all those involved. As the editors, we have loosely organized this text into overlapping sections only to highlight the connections between and across the individual chapters. Our intention has not been to make apologies for, or to suppress, the multifarious argument, the disparate writing styles, the non-translation of vernacular expression, the multiplicity of competing and sometimes discordant voices that leap out from each of the chapters. More important, this book is unique in that it arises from a collective of writers who effectively reside at the margins of what continues predominantly to be a white and racist academy in Britain. The making of this book itself signifies a new space and recognition being claimed for and by emergent Asian academics and cultural critics operating both inside and outside British universities. This book aims not only at disrupting the institutional boundaries and stifling conventions of academia, nor only at the exploration of alternative modes of writing and argumentation, or the refusal simply to tell exotic stories of Asian musical rituals in Britain. Rather more incisively, our project may pose a challenge and even a threat to white academia which persists in ethnicizing Asian communities and continues remarkably to cast its anthro-gaze in total ignorance or disavowal of Said's seminal critique of Orientalism. This book attempts to innovate alternative projects for the study of South Asian popular culture. Undeniably, the book will engender new regimes of truth about South Asian cultural practices in the academic mainstream. We clearly distance ourselves from any desire for *Dis-Orienting Rhythms* to become *the* definitive account: on the contrary, it represents new openings and beginnings. Nevertheless, we do hope it has initiated the process of making available an unbounded, creative and politically committed academic practice for future research attempting to explore diasporic South Asian cultural productions. Play that funky music white boy? We don't think so.

NOTES

1. Nation Records, 1995. Words by Dr Das, Pandit, Savale, Zaman. Published by QFM/Warner Chappell Music.

2. In the book, the usage of the term 'Black' necessarily shifts within the context of argumentation made in the particular chapter. Where appropriate some contributors still adopt the term 'Black' as the anti-racist category that has represented the common experiences of colonialism and contemporary racism for African-Caribbean and South Asian communities in Britain. However, identity terms remain contested. In the 1990s, it has become protocol to distinguish 'black' (that is, African-Caribbean) and 'Asian' groupings in Britain.

PART ONE

SPACE AND ARTICULATION

SOUNDS ORIENTAL:

THE (IM)POSSIBILITY OF THEORIZING

ASIAN MUSICAL CULTURES

Ashwani Sharma

We always impute to the 'other' an excessive enjoyment: he wants to steal our enjoyment (by ruining our way of life) and/or he has access to some secret, perverse enjoyment. In short, what really bothers us about the 'other' is the peculiar way he organizes his enjoyment, precisely the surplus, the 'excess' that pertains to this way: the smell of 'their' food, 'their' noisy songs and dances, 'their' strange manners, 'their' attitude to work (Žižek 1993: 203).

The 'new orientalism' views 'the world as immigrant' (Spivak 1993: 64).

The constitution of debates is the dominant mode of pacification employed by the university: the validation of certain manageable conflicts within the context of institutionalisation, moderation, and the indefinite deferral of consequences. What is transcendental to academic debate is submission to socio-economic power (Land 1992: 11).

NOISY SECRETS

Along the Soho Road in Birmingham, there is a small music shop, a place of 'excess' and a place perhaps even beyond the Orientalist gaze, in which signs of 'South Asian culture' circulate chaotically, hidden from, but deep inside, the body of the imperial beast. The corrosive hybridity of post-colonial Asian dance music ruptures the ordered silence of contemporary Britain. As you enter this shop, waves of polyphonic rhythms and melodies struggle for aural ascendancy: sounds of Bombay clash with the religious shubads of Punjab; or Apache Indian is being drowned out by the frenzied poetry of the great Qawwal Aziz Mian. The image-saturated walls are swamped with lurid posters of scantily dressed Bombay film stars juxtaposed against the iconography of Hindu gods, Sikh gurus and Islamic insignia. Second-hand Mills and Boons, and copies of *Reader's Digest* compete alongside *Das Kapital* for your attention. Heavily thumbed South Indian 'erotic' novels hide behind ageing copies of *Stardust* and *Cineblitz*. Pirated Bally Sagoo tapes lie discarded in a bin of cheap offers, the syncopated drum'n'bass of Jungle interrupts...

I could continue in this tone that revels in an ordered chaos providing the possibility of an infinite configuration of signifiers – but why begin with this representation of an obscure shop in the middle of England? In the fashionable language of contemporary academia, this is a space where 'migrant Asian' culture is literally constructing and re-constructing itself. A space of knowledge, in which local and global identities are being continually negotiated, where histories and memories are being re-narrated. Nevertheless, what is the desire on my part to make this space intelligible? Why write about music? And who is reading?

This chapter marks the dangers and the (im)possibility of grafting 'Asian' onto the edges of legitimate cultural study, as well as critical reflection upon the limits of the politics of musical populism. In particular, I will highlight the dangerous workings of a neo-Orientalism as it pertains to the question of contemporary Asian musical cultures. The potential emergence of Asian popular culture, especially 'diasporic' Asian dance music, as an object of study in the metropolitan universities, suggests that the task of making some intellectual noise is imperative. This Othered music becomes a deterritorialized site in which liberal notions of cultural diversity and difference are incorporated within the terroristic violence of 'racialized capitalism'. For this study, music provides an explicit example of the cultural arena in which transnational capitalism and racialized power relations are embedded. Moreover, it provides a point of entry into the seductive workings of the contemporary study of ethnicity, in particular the valorized discourses of marginality, diaspora and migrancy.

An adequate explication of these transnational political concerns requires an engagement with the economic and cultural modalities of contemporary forms of (post)modern knowledge and relations of power. A significant body of work that has interrogated the 'postmodern condition' has been profoundly Eurocentric, and has largely focused on the West and Western modernity (see Boyne and Rattansi 1990). Nevertheless, I would contend that these problematic conceptualizations of postmodernity are an (early) attempt to map the changing dynamics of power in the commodified global relations of the new world order.

Furthermore, any attempt to study these new cultural objects has to interrogate and intervene in the workings of hegemonic cultural industrialism, so that when we turn the music up, the violating rhythms of this (nascent) transnational politics in and outside the academy become audible.

MARGINAL SOUNDS?

Recent developments in the metropolitan university and its dependent publishing sector – especially in the ever-expanding and now formally institutionalized discipline of 'Cultural Studies' and the related field of 'Post-colonial Theory' – have led to questions of cultural difference, ethnicity and identity coming to the foreground. The theoretical interest in the 'Other' has also resulted in increasing attention being paid to 'marginal' cultures, and it could be claimed that 'the margins' are moving to 'the centre'. This focus on marginality is not exclusive to the academy, but reflects the wider interests of triumphantly multiproduct(ive) Western culture. The introduction to a recent collection of essays addressing marginalization clearly articulates the political dangers of this turn to marginality:

> Counter narratives of all kinds do enter 'mainstream' culture. One of the great strengths of the existing structure is its capacity to absorb a constant flow of new elements. In any system based on consumption, new products and new styles must be perpetually supplied. Such a flow is essential to its health and survival.... The vital, independent cultures of socially subordinated groups are constantly mined for new ideas with which to energise the jaded and restless mainstream of a political and economic system based on the circulation of commodities. The process depends on the delivery of continual novelty to the market while at the same time alternative cultural forms are drained of any elements which might challenge the system as a whole (Ferguson et al. 1990: 11).

As the authors of *Out There* point out, there is a notable danger that theoretical work interrogating the processes of marginalization, which draws heavily upon post-structuralism and particularly deconstruction, will be incorporated into the liberal project of academia. Concomitantly, this occurs without challenging the dominant structures of power that produce the marginalization of cultures, either in the context of nation-states in the West, or significantly in relation to global cultural politics. As a corollary, the theoretical deconstruction of the power relations inherent in the production of the 'Other' masks the oppressive socio-economic structures in which marginal cultures are situated. The debate about marginality itself is becoming a politics, and not a discursive site from which to intervene into the functioning of cultural violence. Instead, the margin is the place from which dominant structures exercise their disciplinary control. We are in the midst of the marginalization of the centre: the de-centred dominant is displaced from within the margins, but the power relations between the centre and margin remain intact. Ferguson et al. continue by posing the question: 'But although this structure is strong and flexible, it is also inherently unstable. How much can the centre really absorb without having its own authority called into question?' (Ferguson et al. 1990: 11). More than likely, this would depend upon the ability of the dominant structure to reconfigure and re-divide the margins, with the effect of constituting new marginalities, while at the same time producing new centrings. The exercise of power produced by the invisible centre has to continually appear to de-centre itself, by appearing at the margins, whilst allowing the margins to become visible, but controlled.

These somewhat abstract formulations can be partially grasped if we keep our gaze firmly upon the operations of contemporary neo-colonialism in the form of powerful global cultural industries, and if we simultaneously pay attention to the enthusiastic turn to post-coloniality, ethnicity and migrancy in the metropolitan university. Iain Chambers in his poetic writings in *Migrancy, Culture, Identity* suggests:

> The migrant's sense of being rootless, of living between worlds, between a lost past and a non-integrated present, is perhaps the most fitting metaphor of this (post)modern condition. This underlines the theme of diaspora, not only black, also Jewish, Indian, Islamic, Palestinian, and draws us into the processes whereby the previous margins now fold in on the centre (Chambers 1994: 28–29).

It would be difficult to deny the importance of the theoretical engagement with new forms of identity formation that Chambers so evocatively addresses. Nevertheless, his use of migrancy as a metaphor (typical of cultural writing especially in post-colonial theory), as *the* postmodern or post-colonial condition, is however deeply problematic. This universalization of a specific and undifferentiated category of a subject renders the violence endemic in the production of migrancy invisible. The problem lies in how the migrant is decontextualized out of her socio-economic and historical situation, and becomes the transcendental subject of subalternity and/or of *the* postmodern subject, outside the workings of contemporary neo-colonialism. Furthermore, in the context of a contemporary transnational globality, Spivak warns of this 'new orientalism':

> Today the old ways, of imperial adjudication and open systemic intervention, cannot sustain unquestioned legitimacy. Neo-Colonialism is fabricating its allies by proposing a share of the centre in a seemingly new way (not a rupture but a displacement): disciplinary support for the conviction of authentic marginality by the (aspiring) elite (Spivak 1993: 57).

For Spivak, this 'new orientalism' reproduces neo-colonialism by incorporating into the centre, in the guise of elite academic work, elements of migrant culture at the expense of the 'Third World'. This focus on migrancy or diaspora as *the* post-colonial condition, with the resultant erasure of the Third World, is evident in much of the work that focuses on migrant or diasporic cultures. That is, the migrant or diasporic culture is seen as a supplement of the Third World national culture within the dominant national culture.[1] This formulation fails to address the specific location of cultures in both national and transnational formations. The increasing focus upon marginal cultures in the rhetoric of contemporary theory, without situating this academic work within the flows of global commodity capitalism and the international division of labour, reduces the potential political effectivity of academic work only to a manageable rhetoric and, more seriously, renders the subaltern without agency (see Spivak 1988).

This desire to centre so-called 'migrant' cultures, to deconstruct difference, can also be understood as the strategic management of the radical disruptive potential threat that 'Otherness' poses to the late modern project of Western liberalism. To understand the Other is no more than a stratagem for the containment, mastery and exploitation of cultural difference. Contemporary Western liberal culture, exemplified by the relations of power–knowledge in the academy, has turned to migrant culture as a tactic for accommodating and pacifying the threat of difference. The threat to the legitimacy of narratives of dominant white masculine bourgeois Western culture that difference may engender has been assuaged by the denial of difference and by the violent exclusion of the Other as racially subaltern. However, in postmodernity, ethnic difference as the master trope of politics has been inscribed into the workings of the heterogeneous fields of power–knowledge that circulate in the new world order.

The turn to ethnicity, as Stuart Hall has potently suggested, offers some productive avenues for thinking through a new politics of representation and identities. He argues:

...what is involved is the splitting of the notion of ethnicity between on one hand the dominant notion that connects it to nation and 'race' and on the other hand what I think is the beginnings of a positive conception of the ethnicity of the margins, of the periphery. That is to say, a recognition that we all speak from a place, out of a particular experience, particular culture, without being contained by that position.... We are in a sense all *ethnically* located and our ethnic identities are crucial to our subjective sense of who we are. But this is also a recognition that this is not a ethnicity which is doomed to survive, as Englishness was, by only marginalizing, dispossessing, displacing and forgetting other ethnicities. This precisely is the politics of ethnicity predicated on difference (Hall 1988: 29).

Hall understands ethnicity as a divided concept and explicitly signals in his essay the dangers of the 'closed, exclusive and regressive' uses of the notion. The danger is that within the contours of everyday culture and politics, division becomes conflated and the essentialist notions of ethnicity masquerade as pluralistic ones on the blurred terrain of contemporary cultural formations. The fixing of ethnicity that Hall alerts us to is partially achieved by appealing to one of the key terms in cultural theory: hybridity. His notion of ethnicity implicitly carries the idea of hybridization:

The final point which I think is entailed in this new politics of representation has to do with an awareness of the black experience as a diasporic experience, and the consequence which this carries for the process of unsettling, recombination, hybridization and 'cut-and-mix' – in short, the process of cultural diasporization ... which it implies (Hall 1988: 29–30).

This focus upon 'new ethnicities' within the cultural paradigms of diaspora and migrancy has, then, subsequently invited greater interrogation of the concept of hybridity. The powerful redefinition of ethnicity evoked by Hall (and others) through the concept of hybridity enters the dynamic of popular cultural politics to be incorporated, reterritorialized and reworked by hegemonic structures to produce new marginalized and essentialized identities, keeping in place and perpetuating the violence of now 'postmodern' culture.

More specifically, within the paradigms of post-colonial theory and Cultural Studies generally, hybridity is inevitably being conceptualized as the encounter of a 'Third World' culture with the West. The consequence is that hybridity is understood as part of the project of Western modernity and modernization, and in spite of the critique of modernity the underlying assumption is that hybridity produces new and more progressive cultural formations (see Bhabha 1994).[2] Post-colonial theory not only privileges the colonial encounter, but marginalizes the complexity of so-called 'traditional cultures'. Under the guise of a critique of the violence of Western modernity, postmodernity is invoked through the concept of post-coloniality to valorize the encounter with Western culture. In privileging the tropes of diaspora, migrancy and hybridity, this encounter of Third World cultures with the West becomes the framework through which 'non-Western' cultures are interpreted. In the particular case of South Asian cultural formations, those Asian cultural productions marked as hybrid are celebrated and valorized as being enlightened and politically emancipatory, as well as being universalized as the metaphoric condition of late modernity.

This cultural logic parallels very much the marketing practices of transnational entertainment corporations, promoting global music stars through a skilful deployment of the rhetoric of ethnicity and hybridity (Hutnyk 1996a). The global domain of cultural capital in the form of so-called World Music presents us with an illuminating example of the workings of neo-colonialism.

'WALKING AWAY WITH THE MUSIC'[3]

The label 'World Music' emerged in the eighties as a record industry category to promote and sell 'non-Anglo-American' popular music to Western consumers. However, this label conflates distinct forms of musics from different places around the globe into effectively a single 'non-Western' musical genre. Chambers has raised some key theoretical questions about the World Music phenomenon:

> Youssou N'Dour and Ruichi Sakamoto playing together in New York; Cheb Khaled at the Place de la Bastille in Paris; Les Têtes Brûlées in Naples: are these simply examples of the centre pillaging the periphery, bringing home exotic sounds from the edges of the empire? Are we merely passive witnesses to the structures of capital imposing their institutions and organisation on new territories: the final triumph of the commodity as it takes over our ear? Or is there also something more subtle, more complex involved? The second perspective would suggest the need to overcome the limits of a simple dualism, and to think in terms of the extensive consequences of historical and cultural differences that are increasingly drawn into the coeval frame of common time (Chambers 1994: 79).

Nevertheless, as Chambers's subsequent comments suggest, he rejects (as is typical of much post-colonial theory) the importance of global socio-economic power relations. He continues:

This would be to propose that the sounds of 'World Music' function not as a stereotypical 'other' that confirms and closes the circle of ethnocentric identification: exotic embellishments requested for refurbishing the rock track. It would be to suggest that such sounds also offer a space for musical and cultural differences to emerge in such a manner that any obvious identification with the hegemonic order, assumed monolithic market logic, is weakened and disrupted by the shifting, contingent contacts of musical and cultural encounters. This represents the instance of a musical and cultural conversation in which the margins are able to reassess the centre while simultaneously exceeding its logic. It is this complex, asymmetrical, structuring of the field of power that is masked in the simple hierarchies imposed by the centre-periphery distinction (Chambers 1994: 79).

Contrary to Chambers, we may ask whether these 'more subtle, more complex suggestions' are not the very terrain upon which the global capitalist market operates, rather than reserve that question for the 'monolithic logic' he assumes. I would agree that 'the shifting, contingent contacts of musical and cultural encounters' may offer a disruption to hegemonic ordering, but who is doing the disrupting, and for whom? It is not accidental that the places where we can hear these 'World Music' stars are in the metropolitan centres of the West (and we should ask who is this 'we'?). The deconstruction of the 'simple hierarchies' cannot avoid how these musics are commodities of 'ethnic Otherness' for ever-hungry, relatively affluent Western consumers. Furthermore, instances of 'musical and cultural conversation' validated under the sign of World Music too easily mask the exploitative labour relationship of the very powerful transnational corporations with the 'Third World' musicians, let alone with those of the Third World with only their photogenic poverty to sell.

The rise of World Music in the 1980s is undoubtedly part of the emergence of a notion of 'ethnicity' as a master-signifier of marketing and advertising. Ethnicity now appears in a diverse range of market sectors: from fashion, design, food and tourism to advertising, but also specifically in the entertainment cultural industries such as publishing, cinema, theatre, dance and music.

The introduction to the *Directory of World Music* articulates starkly the cultural politics of this consumer culture:

'The objective was ... to boost sales of the increasing numbers of records being issued, as the boom in interest in African Music continued and extended to other parts of the world. One of the obstacles to persuading record shops to stock much of the new international product was reported to be the lack of an identifying category to describe it, record shop managers didn't know whether to call it 'ethnic', 'folk', 'international', or some other equivalent.

After a great deal of discussion the term chosen was 'World Music', other contenders such as 'Tropical Music' being judged too narrow of scope (Sweeny 1991: ix).

The World Music labels, with their selling of cultural 'Otherness' in the form of specific ethnic musics, have continuously had to position the variety of heterogeneous musical forms into specific ethnic categories. Crucially, as in the selling of 'exotic' holidays, or 'Third World' films, ethnicity is coded in terms of nation and national cultures. Therefore, within the genre of World Music, particular musics and artists are divided by their national origin. The diversity of these very different musical forms, often belonging to specific localities that either have little to do with the hegemonic national culture or cross the boundaries of nation-states, is nevertheless subsumed into these units of national culture. In World Music marketing practices, a pervasive strategy has been to promote specific artists as representations of authentic ethnic national musical cultures.[4] This has inevitably led to the valorization of artists who play 'traditional' (non-electric) instruments and sing in indigenous languages. For example, sub-Saharan Africa is especially celebrated, because of the perceived lack of contact with the technological culture of the West. This desire for tradition and primitivism is of course hardly novel and has been formative to Western modernity. In the 1980s, however, we witnessed the large transnational entertainment corporations integrating 'ethnic Otherness' on a global scale.

The (un)critical celebration of World Music in the West also needs to be read in the context of the changing nature of Western pop/rock music. It is not coincidental that the category of World Music emerges as a musical form at the same time as the perceived demise of (white) rock (and bland nostalgia for 1960s white pop), its emergence being also related to the increasing impact of (Black) dance music. World Music, in an increasingly vacant white liberal culture, has become an attempt to search for what is considered to be 'authentic', 'human', and 'real', against the emergence of highly technologized and, in places, highly articulate and politically militant musical genres, such as Hip-Hop (which had posed a challenge to the racist structures of the music industry and wider Western public culture). This differentiation between 'black music' and World Music is also an attempt to firmly bifurcate the syncretic metropolitan cultures from the authentic Third World. That musics labelled in the unitary World Music genre are firmly placed within Third World national categories poses problems, however, for the World Music labels, as some of the most celebrated artists are highly influenced by musical developments in the West, using technology and

Western instrumentation quite freely. Similarly, these so-called 'traditional' artists and their music, of course, are dynamically adapting and mutating in relation to socio-cultural and economic changes in their own localities.

The ideological resolution to the problematic of cultural 'integrity and authenticity' for the discourse of World Music is found in the celebration of musical hybridity, although this hybridity takes a particular form in which the nature of 'ethnic authenticity' is recomposed. World Music promotions often position exceptional artists rooted in their specific musical cultures, and re-work their music through the encounter and fusion with Western technology and production. This meeting with the West is seen as enhancing the music. The valorization of particular musical artists as global 'ethnic' stars also has the effect of marginalizing and ignoring the vast body of musical forms that have not had the 'fortune' of encountering the West. The national label is crucial in placing these global stars within particular imagined, but fixed ethnicities and so limiting the possibility of the artists being considered anteriorly as displaced, marginal or transcending their own cultural particularity, and permanently disrupting the binary logic of the centre–periphery.

A good example of the elevation of a music and an artist to global stardom in the World Music scene is the music of Qawwali and the artist Nusrat Fateh Ali Khan. Qawwali is a very popular syncretic musical form in Pakistan and north India, as well as across the South Asian diaspora. Although Nusrat Fateh Ali Khan is a major figure in Qawwali, he has been promoted as '[t]he extraordinary voice of the world's greatest exponent of Qawwali – the expression of mystical Islam' (on the cover of the album *Shahen-Shah* (1989) for Real World Records). Although Nusrat Fateh Ali Khan has produced vast numbers of albums for small independent Asian labels, it was only after working with Real World that he emerged as a major global star. The Nusrat marketing discourse has relied upon both celebrating his unique singing skills and emphasizing the importance of Western technological production.[5] Rather unsurprisingly, Real World has virtually ignored the crucial religious and socio-critical elements of the music, and has attempted to reduce the music to an aesthetic form. As the sleeve notes on the *Must Must* (1990) album indicate, there 'are only two songs with actual lyrics: the rest are classical vocal exercises in which the words have no meaning but are used for the quality of their sound'.

However when the sleeve notes eventually do acknowledge a key problem in working with cross-cultural musical productions, the contradictions are reconciled by appealing to an essentializing hybridity:

A lot of the tracks were much longer, we had to shorten things, cut phrases out, move the voice around, repeat sections and join sections together. This is where the problem arose. We made some edits that were not acceptable to Nusrat, because we'd cut a phrase in half – sometimes there were lyrics that we made nonsense of.... Sometimes even though they were just singing Sa Re Ga we had interfered with the meaning of the phrase. A compromise was achieved – important lyrical phrases were restored without losing the musical structure Michael [the producer] had developed. So a halfway point was reached between East and West in song writing, in performance, and in attitude.

This brief sample of the elevation and erasure of Nusrat Fateh Ali Khan's Qawwali music suggests the contradictory ways particular cultural forms can be celebrated and authenticated as hybrid within the logic of difference in global commodity capitalism. The recent major industry promotion and distribution of Asian artists located in the West such as Bally Sagoo (Columbia, Sony) further illustrates how concepts within the discourse of ethnicity, such as 'migrant' and 'diaspora', are articulated alongside the expansion of new consumer markets around the world. The 'new' politics of hybridity as manifest in the discourse of migrancy does not only essentialize Asian culture, it further ignores the exploitative relations of power between the overdeveloped West and the underdeveloped zones of capital. In this way the politics of hybridity tends towards the erasure of the workings of highly differentiated global capitalism and racism. Moreover, the erasure of the specificity of South Asian cultural productions results in the subaltern subjects of the 'Third World' having no position or location to speak from. The limits of the West and the anonymous simplification and commodification of content are expanded to the point that only by the process of Othering do these musics exist in the flows of global production.

Sagoo's 1995 album *Bollywood Flashback* is a significant event in the global commodification of Indian music and can be used to illustrate how this new Asian dance music in the West, through the discourses of migrancy and diaspora, comes to be privileged as the Asian global music. Prior to this album release, Sagoo had been a major figure in the British Bhangra scene, producing a number of very popular Bhangra remix albums for small independent British Asian record labels. Although hugely popular amongst South Asians in Britain, his music has been virtually unknown to a wider public. The appearance of Bally Sagoo on Sony is not, however, an attempt by this corporation to capitalize upon the massive but largely autonomous market for Bhangra in Britain, or a move for a global Bhangra dance music market. Rather,

Photo: Columba

BALLY SAGOO

it is an attempt to exploit a huge potential market for Hindi film music across the globe.[6]

As contended earlier, the discourse of World Music operates by bifurcating it from Black dance music cultures found in urban localities in the West. Sagoo's own Black dance music roots (Chapter 4) and the already syncretic musical form of Bhangra should pose World Music marketing problems for major Western record companies. As an urban musical culture that articulates the heterogeneity of expressive cultures in metropolitan cities, Bhangra has continually absorbed various elements from global musical genres and forms, whilst developing its own distinctive sound. The recent emergence of Asian dance music has been a development of Bhangra as part of the vibrant Black music cultures of the UK, and is inseparable from the local urban spaces that provide the crucial context for the formation of its sounds.

In contrast, the consumption of Bombay film music has been in-visible in the West, its production has been located outside the West, and until recently its products have been largely inaccessible to Western markets outside the kinds of stores described at the beginning of this chapter.[7] It is only with the emergence of the practice of remixing Bombay film music with dance beats and heavy bass lines, that major Western labels have expressed an interest in this new form of Asian dance music. *Bollywood Flashback* is an album of remixes of celebrated Bombay Hindi film songs. The album is heavily reliant upon the technologies of sampling and remixing, with different sounds, rhythms, melodies being juxtaposed and combined to produce new versions of very popular film songs. The significance of the Sony deal is the way that Bally Sagoo's mixing of Bollywood music has been (re)packaged for potentially new, middle-class consumers – in the West, but also importantly in the Indian subcontinent.[8] Although the publicity for Sagoo valorizes the fusional and dynamic nature of his work, this is neither unique nor unexpected. Bombay film music has always drawn heavily from various musical genres in India and from the West. From the beginning, this film music has contained strong elements of Western orchestration, as well as Western pop music, in its songs, as well as drawing from various Indian folk and classical genres. Post-colonial Indian film music has continually adapted to musical changes in the West. Sagoo himself has recently been producing music for Bombay cinema. One could understand the new forms of remixes as a development of this tradition (but the appearance of Western and 'indigenous' mixes in recent films such as *Mohra* and *Kalnayaak* makes it increasingly difficult to locate the 'origins' of this new dance music). The marked difference now has been the interest shown by large entertainment corporations in the music – and this interest also extends the penetration of Western cinema into India with the dubbing of major Hollywood films such as *Jurassic Park* into Hindi for box office success.

The increasing availability of this Western-produced Bombay music in South Asia through satellite and record deals in India is producing new forms of musical cultures in the subcontinent, which in turn is having an impact upon the Asian urban music in the West. However, the specific selection and promotion of Bally Sagoo as the representative of a new wave of remixed Bombay film music exemplifies the arguments around the privileging of migrancy in post-colonial discourses and by global capitalism. Sagoo is positioned as the 'migrant subject' who supposedly draws simultaneously upon his 'ethnic traditions' and Western knowledge of technology to produce a new hybrid music, and thus make it accessible for Western and other emerging global markets. The specific promotion of Sagoo as a hybrid post-colonial migrant demonstrates how a cultural form such as Bollywood remix is presented as a *new hybrid* (Third) World Music genre, conflating the differences between the politics of race and ethnicity in the West (Sagoo's location), and the politics of culture and nation in the Third World (as with the role of Bombay film music in the subcontinent).

BEYOND THE GAZE OF ORIENTALISM?

The logic of contemporary global racialized capitalism is to (re)produce new forms of exploitative social relations, at the local, national and transnational levels. The recent turn, in the avant-garde sectors of the Western academy, to the study of marginal culture, has failed to engage adequately with the oppressive dynamics of this mode of reorganized capitalism. The importance of theoretical insights into the struggle in popular culture, along with the significance of representation and language in the constitution of identity and subjectivity, has been reduced to an uncritical celebration of the texts of consumer culture (see McGuigan 1992). Little attention has been paid to construction of programmes of radical or revolutionary social change, however problematic and conflictual these may (need to) be. Moreover, the important debates about cultural difference, ethnicity, 'race', gender, sexuality and identity circulating in the metropolitan universities have neither seriously attempted to engage with the 'Third World', where the politics and economics of neo-liberalism and the new world order are producing new forms of exploitation and social suffering, nor have they seriously linked struggles against correlate problems within the West – such as inner-urban over-policing, racism, underemployment – with a necessary anti-imperialist perspective. At best the privileged intellectuals of the West gaze impotently at the commodified horrors of new imperialism; at worst, they perpetuate the exploitative global relations of power–knowledge by conflating the politics of post-colonial textual reading and a weekender anti-racism with the dynamics of the Third World social situation.

We may ask, is the fascination with the 'Other', inside the academy as well as outside, part of the process that Žižek has identified as the perceived 'theft of enjoyment' that is at the centre of the new racism and Orientalism? In the context of the reactionary politics of academia, the recent but belated enthusiasm for marginal cultures needs to be understood as part of the process of the latest phase in the normalizing, controlling and exploitation of 'Otherness' for the reproduction of hegemonic culture. Devoid of any progressive political agendas, the project of celebrating hybrid 'ethnic' cultures obscures the epistemic violence of Western intellectual knowledge and the ever more stark and sharp violence of racial terror and neo-colonial exploitation. This violence reduces 'Other' cultures to essentialist and 'traditional' fixities – as 'victims' of progress, as objects of tourism, as the labour of migration and the colours of multiculturalism – and then valorizes hybridity as their encounter with the emancipated West. Under the rhetoric of hybridity, new forms of ordering have emerged with their own implicit liberal value judgements of cultural hierarchy.

What forms of new cultural politics are needed to intervene into the workings of the present culture of racism, capitalism and Orientalism, without being incorporated into the mutating devouring machine? It has not been the aim of this chapter to provide immediate answers to the enormous challenges that face the committed cultural worker. Nevertheless, I will signal three recent events that possibly deconstruct the scenarios I have been presenting. The first is the presence of a 'Nusrat' Qawwali track in the Hollywood film *Natural Born Killers* (Stone 1995). This can be read, via the arguments I have been positing, as the management of Otherness in the play of difference within a centred hegomonic discourse. But at the same time, in the context of the narrative of the film and its self-reflexive posturing, the excess of the track undermines the economy of a misanthropic whiteness – as if the music is 'too Other' for absolute cultural containment. The Qawwali track, with its haunting lyrical harmony and deep, violent bass line, has an uncontrollable 'alien' presence within the anarchic play of the film. Is this 'radical Otherness' of the music, its near-'demonic' presence, one of the ways that the hegemony of the West is being imploded?[9] The second event, and possibly another insidious challenge to the machinations of an essentialist politics of ethnicity, is the sudden appearance of Jas Mann, the lead singer of the pop group Babylon Zoo, at the top of the British music charts. Is the presence of this 'Asian' artist an undermining of the certainties of the discourse of Asian identity within popular culture? Is his bodily play with Indian ethnic markers, and queer masculine performance, an example of the de-centred Asian subjectivities being interrogated in this book? Has the speed of his rise (and probable quick demise) 'returned the Orientalist gaze', or is this the latest form of the commodification of ethnic difference? Possibly the ambiguity in his music and image offers a 'line of flight' away from the pervasive ideologies underpinning the reterritorialization of alterity.

My third and final, more surreptitious, example of potential subversion is the recent performance of the Qawwal Aziz Mian with the

Rap group Fun^Da^Mental. This encounter between two very different modalities of musical expression disrupts any easy exegesis of Asian dance music: the ecstatic poetics of Mian counterpointed with the militant rhetorics of the rappers enable alternative forms of cultural imaginings. This musical entanglement, and its challenge of producing new configurations at the edges of commodity culture, exemplifies literally and metaphorically the critical interventions that the contributors in this book are undertaking.

However, the detour of theory does not prevent the desire to return to the little shop – a dissonant place transforming the centres of postcolonial Britain. The question remains, under what conditions will it be possible to narrate these Asian sites whilst 'hiding in the light'?

NOTES

A special thanks to John for his help in pulling this chapter together. A big respect to Sanjay for making this chapter happen, and of course Sangeeta for her critical insights especially when times were tough. And finally I dedicate this piece of the writing to Kashif who makes it all worthwhile.

1. There has been an increasing body of work that privileges the concept of diaspora as a framework for understanding culture. See, for example, Gilroy (1993a), Clifford (1992) and issues of the journal *Public Culture*.

2. Bhabha's work perhaps represents the most advanced and compelling theorizations of hybridity. Bhabha clearly indicates that all cultures are hybrid at their very inception. Nevertheless, there remains a tension in his work that appears to imply that the condition of hybridity (for example through the migrant figure of author Salman Rushdie) varies in the encounter of 'Western' and 'non-Western' cultural formations. There is a danger that Bhabha's formulations may be read as suggesting that a migrant hybridity is more emancipatory than that of a 'traditional' culture.

3. This is the title of a video documentary made by Shafeeq Valani (n.d.), which provides a sustained critique of the World Music scene.

4. One only has to go into any major record shop in Britain to see how the music is placed under national labels.

5. As a result of the dance remixes of Nusrat Fateh Ali Khan by Massive Attack as well as by Bally Sagoo, Qawwali has become popular with Asian youth in Britain. The tradition of Qawwali from which Nusrat Fateh Ali Khan emerges is very important for understanding its specific popularity with vast numbers of people in Asia. The World Music discourse virtually ignores the wider context of the musical culture and the vast number of other Qawwali musicians. Qawwali music is a form of Islamic Sufi music centred upon the ecstatic celebration of Islam and Allah. But, crucially, within the music there is a strong tradition of criticism of the social formations it was embedded in. This includes, whenever appropriate, criticism of religion and social injustices. Drawing upon and being

situated in the spiritual and sometimes heretical Sufi tradition, it challenges the corruption and hypocrisy in society. Drawing heavily on the hedonistic tradition of Persian and Urdu poetry, it elevates love, drink and at times debauchery, in the montage of the music. It is in part this subversive history that has made the music very popular with working-class South Asian audiences.

6. Hindi/Bombay film music not only has a huge market within the Indian subcontinent. It is listened to throughout the Third World, the Caribbean and the Americas.

7. Bombay film music provides distinctive South Asian musics to the Asian communities in Britain and North America. Bombay film culture, largely unknown outside Asian communities, has played a very powerful role in organizing South Asian popular culture, and in particular music. This immense industry has largely been dominated by a number of big companies in South Asia. Crucial to the development of Bhangra in Britain has been the local retail music shops that began primarily selling Bombay film music in the 1970s.

8. Bollywood remixes in the Indian subcontinent have now locally been described as 'Bally Sagoo music'. Private conversation with Mambo, manager of Bally Sagoo, July 1995.

9. 'Radical Otherness' needs to be understood as a strategic positionality responding to the essentialist discourses of absolute difference and cultural assimilation. Thanks to my friend Sunnie Arshi for this provocative insight.

2

NOISY ASIANS

OR 'ASIAN NOISE'?

Sanjay Sharma

Bhangra … music was important in that it gave us something that we could be nationalistic about – because I never had this as a teenager.… [It] gave back something for ourselves, it had nothing to do with English people or white society. It consolidated the debate about whether we are Black, British or Asian.

Gurinder Chudha (interviewed in Bhuchar 1989: 9)

There are certain categories that detract from whether you're actually good at what you do: 'Asian rap' is one of them, because people look at you and say 'not bad for a bunch of Pakis'.

2Phaan Da Alien, Kaliphz

My favourite Indian instrument is the bass guitar.

Dr Das, Asian Dub Foundation

Any attempts to map out or explicate the 'New Asian Dance Music' immediately encounters the freaky act of cultural categorization, as well as the poverty of established musical classification. An aimless wander into one of those unavoidable shopping-mallesque mega-recordstores anticipates a lengthy search under the classificatory schemes of 'Indian', 'South Asia', 'Folk' or 'Soul/Dance', 'Rap', 'Reggae', 'Rock/Pop' … if all else fails, under that innocuous label 'World Music'. Moreover, the fact that the sutured term 'Asian' remains largely a contested ethno-cultural category in Britain further alerts us to the unstable and multi-farious nature of this form of musical cultural production. Nevertheless, for the sake of brevity, the totalizing phrase 'New Asian Dance Music' can be retained, but will not escape further critical interrogation and delineation. In this chapter my aim is not simply to chart out the histories of the song and dance genre of Bhangra or to present genealogies of what has been dominantly conceived to be a musical genre of Punjabi–South Asian origins fused with Western/black dance musics (see Banerji and Baumann 1990; Baumann 1990, 1994; Back 1994). Also, the more recent surfacing of musical movements that may be termed 'post-Bhangra', and which denote shifts towards more specific and intentional fusions of Bhangra beats and South Asian instrumentation with other contemporary (dance) music genres, are traced out in more detail in Chapters 3 and 4. Whilst these musical surfacings have given rise to even more labels such as 'Bhangramuffin' (Bhangra with Ragga, for example, Apache Indian), 'Acid Bhangra', 'Bollywood remixes' (Bally Sagoo), or 'Asian Rap and Jungle', there has been an emergent scene behind these labels which has a significant cultural politics. There has also been the emergence of a dynamic club culture (for example, Hot 'n Spicy at the Limelight nightclub in London, similarly at Shankeys Soap in Manchester), and a sound system culture (for example, Hustlers HC, and Joi arising out of the Joi Bangla youth movement in the East End of London). This club culture, whilst organized mainly around South Asian participation, expresses a process of musical cultural hybridization and syncretism that moves beyond a straightforward juxtaposition of dance music genres.

Such complexity cannot be exhaustively mapped out within the confines of a single text. My interests are less ambitious and lie more specifically in exploring some of the (dis)continuities and key political generative capacities of Bhangra dance music and post-Bhangra Rap, in relation to the emergence of an 'Asian' identity discourse during the 1980s and 1990s in Britain. The term 'Asian' marked as an ethnocultural category in both popular and academic discourses has so far been confined to the simplistic describing and subsuming of specific national, ethnic and religious identities. Those accounts that have attempted to explore the category 'Asian' in more political terms have only served to reassert an essentialist and culturalist understanding of Asian identity formation (see especially Hazareesingh 1986 and Modood 1988, 1990 and 1994). It will become clear that my intentions centre on deconstructing the signifier 'Asian' and reclaiming it against prevailing culturalist notions and regressive shifts towards ethnic particularisms that close down political opportunities over the contestation of this signifier. Any anti-essentializing move to deconstruct the notion of Asian identity encounters the danger of sliding into an endless postmodern play on difference or, more disturbingly, the erasure of a subaltern subjectivity. In contrast, my reading of the New Asian Dance Music and the development of an Asian subject position is motivated by taking Hall's (1992) argument over the site of popular culture almost literally. That is, the musical sites of Bhangra/post-Bhangra – a major though still remarkably invisible form of popular culture in Britain – are spaces to be struggled over and won in our understanding that the signifier 'Asian' can be one of many temporary positionalities that offer us strategic places from which to speak in this racist Britain. (The contestation over these positionalities has become important, especially since the perceived decline of the anti-racist political location of 'Black' in the 1990s). In particular, an engagement with the ambiguous pedagogy of post-Bhangra Rap will demonstrate how the struggle over the signifier 'Asian' not only disarticulates it from its putative culturalist moorings, but also reveals how 'Asian' continues to be intimately tied to rethinking the possibilities of the Black anti-racist project. It is the hybrid and contradictory spaces of the New Asian Dance Music that this unfinished project takes as its point of departure. Such a beginning seeks to avoid a naïve valorization of this dance music in order to make a series of disingenuous claims, but will argue that these very debates open up alternative political positionalities and ways of being in their de-centring of normative notions of 'Asianness'.

WHAT'S IN A NAME?
BHANGRA, ASIAN IDENTITY AND THE
SEARCH FOR AUTHENTICITY

As a consequence of the scant academic attention paid to the emergence of Asian dance musics in Britain, the few mainstream accounts that do exist have hegemonized our understanding of these popular forms of Asian-specific expressive culture. Writings around Bhangra perhaps suffer the most, no doubt symptomatic of its perceived Otherness and ritualistic exoticism, for example as found in Gillespie (1995). A stable-mate, Baumann (1990; 1994), is another of those modern 'ethnically sensitive' white ethnographers still directing the anthro-colonial gaze on to Black folks' cultures. He appears to present an informed account of the historical emergence of this fusion-based music and its Punjabi cultural roots. Whilst highlighting importantly that the relationship of Bhangra and other musical genres such as Reggae, Dub, and Soul with the black sound system culture were significant in the development of Bhangra during the early 1980s, he fails to comprehend fully these complex musical processes and cultural exchanges. Baumann (1994) is all too anxious not to characterize 'Asian culture' in a unitary or uncontested manner (in his study of multiracial Southall), but nevertheless produces an account underwritten by a problematic of cultural authenticity that suppresses other possible narratives of Bhangra. For example, he transparently presents an account of Bhangra and Asian identity formation through the comments of one of the lead singers in the east London group Cobra:

> I can remember going to college discos a long time ago, when all you heard was Reggae, Reggae, Reggae. Asians were lost, they weren't accepted by whites, so they drifted into black culture, dressing like blacks, talking like them, and listening to Reggae. But Bhangra has given them their music and made them feel that they do have an identity. No matter if they are Gujuratis, Punjabis or whatever – Bhangra is Asian music for Asians (quoted in Baumann 1994: 18).

Baumann recognizes the huge internal cultural diversities and diverse histories of South Asian migrants and their children in Britain, but the notion of the 'reinvention' of Bhangra from its Punjabi folk origins putatively signifies the development of a specifically Asian 'cultural consciousness' and identity amongst Asian youth. His interpretation of the above passage negates other narratives of syncretic Asian youth identity formations negotiated and made actively with modes of black cultural expression. He too simplistically essentializes what has remained a nebulous, relationally defined and situated identificatory category of 'Asian' for these youth. It is interesting to observe that Back (1994: 6), working from a more developed theoretical perspective, nevertheless employs the same quote to assert comparably that '[t]he emergence of Bhangra in the 1980s signalled the development of a self-conscious and distinctively British Asian youth culture which expressed the primacy of an Asian identity'.

Both these authors do interpret correctly the emergence of Bhangra as an articulation of an 'Asianness' in alternative public spaces, which previously had a limited means of expression. The music journalist Dil Neiyyar (1988: 6) has stated eloquently:

> Bhangra ... the music, clothes and dances are the medium through which the otherness of British/South Asian experience is articulated .... it is both a form of cultural resistance and an affirmation of the lives we lead ... it is perceived as something distinct, belonging to us.... It is a definite break from tradition, but its reference points are rooted in tradition.... The Bhangra beat is a pulse, a soundtrack, a distinct manifestation of the South Asian urban experience.

Bhangra does signify *one* of the processes for some Asian youth positioning themselves in British society. The cultural space created by

Bhangra suggests a means for Asian youth to assert their 'Asianness' and locate themselves firmly in their contemporary urban surroundings. Dominant forms of cultural resistance for Asian youth have more often been based on opposition to racial violence, racist practices (Sivanandan 1982), and, more widely, against a white British culture that attempts to negate and deride Asian cultural expression. Nevertheless, Bhangra is suggestive in enabling Asian youth to affirm their identities positively within a dominant cultural formation that 'offers' either an acculturating process of assimilation into the British nation, or exclusion from it.

The problem with Baumann's account especially is its overly culturalist reading of Bhangra, endowing it with a unifying impetus in the creation of a unitary Asian youth identity. By contrast, Back is more concerned with pursuing the project of what he terms (borrowing from Deleuze and Guattari) an 'intermezzo culture', by focusing on the musical and performative aspects of Apache Indian's more complex fusions of Reggae and Bhangra. Back argues that in the alternative public sphere of the dance, liminal ethnicities are produced which link together different social collectivities. The development of an intermezzo culture is one 'of interbeing that cannot be confined within unitary definitions of the "Subject" or identity'(1994: 19). His theoretical contentions are appealing yet remain underdeveloped in a worthwhile attempt to move beyond the either/or of identity discourse (for example, black or white subject positions) and towards thinking of identity formation in terms of a multiplicity, see Deleuze and Guattari 1980/ 1987). In making his claims of an intermezzo culture, Back also encounters the danger of over-valorizing antiphonal musical strategies, and what are in actuality transitory and contingent spaces of the dance floor. However, my main point is that to some extent Back unintentionally reproduces Baumann's reading of Bhangra as engendering a discourse of Asian youth identity that ultimately flattens out differences and contestations across class, caste, ethnicity and gender. In contradistinction to Bhangra, Back characterizes the more recent musical developments of (post-Bhangra) Apache Indian, as more productive in the creation of new intermezzo cultural subjectivities.[1] The Otherness of Bhangra as perceived by both Baumann and Back, and its attendant 'cultural inaccessibility' for (white) enthnographers, locates their reading of this expressive culture squarely within an authenticity problematic that sustains a neo-Orientalist understanding of anterior Asian youth cultural formations. There is a danger of temporally equating Bhangra with an Asian cultural essentialism, and post-Bhangra as a more politically emancipatory musical site.

It is worth taking Gilroy's observation (1993a) seriously, that two confrontational perspectives dominate in understandings of black music: (a) an exceptionalist position which identifies music with cultural continuity and tradition; and (b) a 'postmodern' position which rejects the supposed racial/cultural essentialism of the former, and champions the totally contingent, plural nature of identity formation. Gilroy rightly does not wish to reject the power of racial subjugation in shaping the lives of Black people, which the latter position implies. Though equally, he is opposed to the former position which ignores the internal fragmentation and differentiation of Black cultures. In an attempt to transcend this binarism he proposes an 'anti-anti-essentialism': to resist the postmodern dissolution of the Black subject but recognize the exercise of power involved in the contingent processes of identity production.

> Black identity ... is lived as a coherent (if not always stable) experiential sense of self. Though it is often felt to be natural and spontaneous, it remains the outcome of practical activity: language, gesture, bodily signification, desires (Gilroy 1993a: 102).

Gilroy privileges the *performative* aspect of (musical and antiphonal) interactions between the performer and the crowd which 'produces the *imaginary* effect of an internal racial core or essence by acting on the body through the specific mechanisms of identification and recognition' (Gilroy 1993a: 102, my emphasis).

One of the logics of Gilroy's contention points to the performative situatedness of musical exchange in the discursive production of identities. In mainstream writings on Bhangra, the focus on the racial/ethnic bodies of the artists and crowds results in an abject failure to take into account the processes of musical performance and the context of its reception. The playing of Bhangra at an Asian community event such as a Punjabi wedding would not necessarily share an equivalence with its take-up by, say, the London-based Asian gay and lesbian support group Shakti at their dance nights. Similarly, the question of how females negotiate and derive pleasure in the masculine performative spaces of the dancefloor, and from gender-suspect Bhangra lyrics, demands attention.[2]

The problem with the accounts of Bhangra of both Baumann and Back is that they largely function within a perspective that operates in terms of cultural continuity and tradition. Their reductive reading of Bhangra sublimates its South Asian origins and leads to the positing of a culturalist notion of Asian identity formation disassociated from wider socio-political contexts and youth cultural movements. The lack of appropriate attention paid to the hyper-syncretic and fusional musical qualities in Bhangra, particularly in relation to black dance music genres, fails to recognize sufficiently that the 're-invention' of Bhangra in Britain has taken place in constant dialogue with these other musical sources. This does not preclude Asian youth from non-identification with Bhangra (Chapter 3), as its linguistic and musical instrumentation is predominantly associated with a Punjabi cultural specificity. But Bhangra has experienced dialogic mutation with other dance musics, more intensively since its arrival in Britain. It should be stressed that musical exchanges have not been unidirectional. As pointed out by a member of the Rap group Hustlers HC (*Eastern Eye*, 6 June 1995), Reggae music contains a *bhangara* rhythm related intimately to the dholak drum patterns present in Bhangra music. (This is helpful in explaining how Bhangra and Reggae rhythms have been so easily musically fused.) The earliest Bhangra bands such as Alaap or Heera, and more recent groups such as Achanak or XLNC, have been adapting constantly and dynamically with new and different musical influences, making it perverse to identify an essential Bhangra sound.

I do not wish to imply that the naming of Bhangra by Asian youth themselves as an Asian expressive culture is an inauthentic act. I am not concerned so much with the historical origins of Bhangra but with how it comes to be named as exclusively 'Asian' (or Punjabi). It is useful to make a very brief theoretical detour to an argument put forward by Sayyid (forthcoming) and Žižek (1989) in relation to the act of 'naming'. At the risk of gross simplification, they argue that the maintenance of the relationship between an object and its name is a contingent operation, and that the act of naming is a retroactive process which attempts to secure an immutable connection with the properties that are said to constitute it as such.[3] This means that the 'primal baptism' that associates the object Bhangra with exclusively 'Asian properties' is constantly renewed in the subsequent articulations of Bhangra. The issue at stake is not then questioning the authenticity of the identity of Bhangra – given that it is a truly hybrid musical genre in Britain – but the (hegemonic) operations that secure Bhangra with a particularist Asian identity.

This move in displacing the authenticity problematic liberates us from thinking of Bhangra as a cultural essentialism, and disrupts the perpetuation of an exclusively culturalist notion of Asian identity supposedly realized through Bhangra. Equating an unmediated Asian youth identity formation contiguously with Bhangra not only overstates the 'cultural domain', but also fails to consider the contingent nature of these identity productions. This is particularly significant in relation to the emergence of a pervasive 'Black' political identification in the early 1980s. All this can point to a more nuanced consideration of the emergence of Bhangra as an *affirmative moment* in the formation of an Asian identity discourse in the early 1980s, a site for Asian youth culture acquiring a sense of identity and visibility in the public domain, and negotiating an ambivalent positionality in relation to a culturally hostile and exclusionary British nation.

However, it is crucial to locate these developments in relation to a wider Black anti-racist identity discourse.

> The demand for black representation could be heard in the early 1980s ... [t]he shift from 'ethnic minority' to 'black' registered in the language of political discourse demonstrated a process in which the objects of racist ideology reconstituted themselves as subjects of social, cultural and political change (Mercer 1992: 55).

Mercer highlights the heyday of British anti-racism, the birth of the political Black subject, its rearticulation from a racial category to a political category, forming a new symbolic unity primarily between African-Caribbean and Asian people in Britain. It need not be emphasized that the political category 'Black' has undoubtedly been a vital focal point for forming the basis of autonomous anti-racist community struggles in Britain in the late 1970s and during the 1980s. But Mercer's account of the rearticulation of 'Black' is limited within the political domain, and does not choose to recognize the parallel intertwined processes of youth articulating and affirming their Asian identities in alternative but equivalent cultural spaces.

Hall (1991: 56) has made a timely statement in his reflections on the Black cultural politics of the 1980s in Britain:

> The question of Black, in Britain ... has its silences. It had a certain way of silencing the very specific experiences of Asian people. Because though Asian people could identify, politically, in the struggle against racism, when they came to using their own culture as the resources of resistance, when they wanted to write out of their own experience and reflect on their own position, when they wanted to create, they naturally created within the histories of the languages, the cultural tradition, the positions of people who came from a variety of different historical backgrounds. And just as Black was at the cutting edge of a politics vis-à-vis one kind of enemy, it could also ... provide a kind of silencing in relation to another. These are the costs, as well as the strengths, of trying to think of the notion of Black as an essentialism.

The attempts towards de-essentializing the 'innocent Black subject' instigated by theorists such as Hall, Mercer and hooks are crucial for engendering new projects of cultural politics that resist subsuming other differences and emergent positionalities under the hegemony of 'Black'.[4] The Asian dance musics of Bhangra (and, as Back (1994) implies, post-Bhangra) represent a medium through which the non-exhaustive identifications of 'British and Black' (Hall 1992: 29) *and* 'Asian' become politically available to Asian youth. These musics enable Asian youth to articulate and deploy a sense of 'Asianness' that is not necessarily in opposition to notions of being Black, and, though more problematically, even British. These dance musics may, then, act as a site for the *translation* between diasporic Asian, Black and British identifications, (Chapter 9). This presents an alternative route for Asian youth, as opposed to the choice of either resisted assimilation or the search for 'tradition' and 'authenticity'.

In desiring to de-essentialize Bhangra from its ethnic markers and shake off accompanying culturalist notions of Asian identity formation, I do not simply seek to assert that the term 'Asian' can operate innocently as a progressive political category. In comparison to the rearticulation of 'Black' as a signifier enabling anti-racist politics, the identificatory term 'Asian' does not share an equivalent political and cultural history. This does not imply that 'Asian' has been ineffectually used for doing anti-racist politics, but its commonsense and hegemonic invocations connote a narrow ethno-cultural category in Britain. This may easily slide into a conservative politicization of the term within the stifling paradigm of ethnicity – as especially prevalent in the work of Modood (1988, 1990 and 1994). In a rather bizzare account of Asian identity formation, he argues that 'Black' should be replaced with 'Asian' as the preferred description of groups from the Indian subcontinent:

> What I mean by an 'Asian' identity is some share in the heritage of the civilizations of old Hindustan prior to British conquest. Roughly, it is those people who believe that the Taj Mahal is an object of their history (Modood 1988: 397).

Modood fails to acknowledge the huge internal diversities and cleavages of the multiple histories of South Asian people, and also the influences of contemporary diasporic cultural conditions and practices in Britain. He simply substitutes 'Black' with an even more culturalist category of 'Asian'. Similarly, Modood (1990) naïvely contends that the 'mode of experience' as opposed to the 'mode of oppression' (racism) should determine identity, and this leads him to over-emphasize an already essentialized construction of Asian ethnicity. His regressive misreading of recent critiques of an anti-racist Black identity results in positing an absolutist notion of 'Asianness' and ignores the political valency and productivity of what he terms 'political Blackness'.[5]

Nevertheless, just as 'Black' has become a contested signifier, similarly the category 'Asian' (and its particular 'ethnicities') whilst offering places for us to speak from is something to be struggled over, radically politicized, and reclaimed against any of its culturalist moorings. The need to de-centre normative notions of Asian identity has affinities with Hall's ambitious project of reappropriating the term 'ethnicity' outside narrow multiculturalist conceptions and racialized nationalist discourses. As a strategic move, Hall has attempted to reclaim ethnicity from the essentializing discourses of identity by proposing a shift towards what is termed the 'new ethnicities', which '... speak from a particular place, out of a particular history, out of a particular experience, a particular culture, *without being contained by that position*' (Hall 1988b: 258, my emphasis).

POST-BHANGRA SOUNDS: AN-OTHER STORY ABOUT RAP

My contention has been that the politico-cultural space opened up by the pleasures of Bhangra music is a site in which an affirmative moment of Asian identity formation has been enunciated in relation to other (political) positionalities. The continuance and multiplication of this project is also present in the 'post-Bhangra' dance musics. The deployment of this term is more for its heuristic purchase than as an empirical, descriptive label. In one sense it signifies that contemporary developments in the new Asian dance musics may be associated with Bhangra instrumentations but are not necessarily dependent or contained by Bhangra, and often operate musically more in terms of other dominant genres, of Ragga, Rap or Jungle for example. Rather, just as Bhangra has been in constant dialogue with other (Black) dance genres, post-Bhangra carries this through more incisively and intentionally. Nevertheless, post-Bhangra musics should not readily be divorced from the 'affirmative moment' induced by Bhangra. This does not suggest that all subsequent musical developments have a founding originary moment in Bhangra, nor are artists such as Apache Indian or the Kaliphz contained within the label of post-Bhangra, or even necessarily Asian dance music. I do want, however, to hold on to the possibility of being able to read them (non-reductively) as offering the potential for further radically de-centring notions of 'Asianness'.

It is hardly coincidental that many post-Bhangra artists such as

Hustlers HC, KK Kings, Fun^Da^Mental, Det-Ri-Mental, and Asian Dub Foundation (ADF) have effortlessly fused South Asian instrumentation and lyrics with the dominantly conceived black music genre of Rap. Rap music emanating from the sub-culture of Hip-Hop has been originally associated with the South Bronx in New York, and arose in the 1970s as a medium that expressed the political outlook of a dispossessed generation of urban black/African-American and Latino youth. Today Rap has a transnational impact, both in its highly commercialized form and as a 'global protest music' (Lusane 1993).

The enormous global output of Rap makes it difficult for anyone to know 'what the totality of its hypercreativity looks like' (Gilroy 1992: 309). Nevertheless, a dominant (popular and academic) discourse of Rap primarily associates it with artists of the African diaspora, and invariably defines it as a black art form that reflects the culture of 'blackness' (Stephens 1992). Rose's excellent insider account of Hip-Hop, *Black Noise*, states early on that 'Rap is a black cultural expression that prioritizes black voices from the margins of urban America' (1994: 2). She is cautious of the excessive anti-essentializing streak of postmodernist thought that readily disarticulates the emergence of Rap away from its socio-historical location and cultural priorities. In particular, Rose is legitimately critical of the mimicry of Rap stylistics by some (commercially orientated) white artists.

> Although the terms dilution and theft do not capture the complexity of cultural incorporation and syncretism, the interpretation has more than a grain of truth in it. There is abundant evidence that white artists imitating black styles have a greater economic opportunity and access to larger audiences than black innovators (Rose 1994: 5–6).

However, it is noticeable that the authenticity debate surrounding Rap music as a black art form predominantly operates within the black/white divide (which is curious given that Hip-Hop emerged historically from the 'hybrid multicultural' spaces of urban America). Similarly, the intelligent monthly British fanzine *Hip-Hop Connection* reproduces this logic in its highly readable letters pages, which over the last few years have consistently fuelled a raging debate over racial authenticity and the political validity of white participation in Rap. What is notable is that skilled Rap artists of South Asian descent remain absent from this debate – if they are subsumed under the label 'black' this is not at all apparent. But the intervention of Asian performers in this 'black art form' does challenge an essentializing racial discourse of blackness found in Rap, especially given that many South Asians share comparable racial and class locations and potential audiences alongside African-Caribbean groupings in Britain. Numerous theorists have pointed to the antiphonal processes of Rap enabling mutually created languages to surface that redefine the boundaries of racial identification (Lipsitz 1994; Stephens 1992; West 1989). Rap groups such as Hustlers HC, Fun^Da^Mental and ADF are important because they signify a potentiality in the disruption of essentializing racial/ethnic boundary formation and identification, and mark the possibility of a transcendence in the normative representations of both 'blackness' *and* 'Asianness'. ('Rap is a *Black* thing" compared with 'Why are *Asians* into Rap?'). As a corollary, the culturally hyper-syncretic musical modality of these groups also registers a certain excess to Rap, that may appear to be more generative of alternative discursive interstitial identity formations.

I would be naïve to celebrate these post-Bhangra musical developments as a path towards whatever kind of utopian transracial or culturally 'hybrid' identity. This is not only because the intermezzo cultural spaces of the dancefloor are transitory and contingent, but also that Rap music is a key expressive site through which the antinomies between racial/cultural essentialism and pluralism are actively being played out; and neither do post-Bhangra Rap groups escape sufficiently from these tensions. As Swendenburg has remarked:

> rap is a crucial political–cultural phenomenon which confounds many hegemonic notions about the nature of oppositional expressive cultures ... Rap practitioners assert an identity politics that often seem essentialist, separatist and even supremacist, while simultaneously working effectively to forge new transracial identities and solidarities (1992: 64)

One of the trajectories of post-Bhangra music can be described by the identification of Rap groups such as Hustlers HC, Fun^Da^Mental and ADF as 'consciousness rappers' (Decker 1992), to whom political–racial pedagogic modes of address are central. Whilst acknowledging that much of their diverse musical output operates outside Asian identity discourse, we can also understand these groups more specifically in relation to the articulation of a *strategic identity politics*.[6] The term and practice of 'identity politics' have rightly been much maligned, and the compelling critique of identity politics made by Bourne (1987) remains relevant.[7] She argues that identity politics is reactionary in fostering an apolitical, amaterialist and subjectivist point of view, and that it produces a personalized politics that is inward-looking. Although overstated somewhat, Bourne's tract is pertinent because it highlights the hazards of a politics based on identity alone and the essentializing closures it engenders. Contrary to what Modood (1994) has mistakenly suggested, we cannot assume that an Asian identity necessarily constitutes particular kinds of anti-racist or otherwise progressive politics.

Nevertheless, one way of engaging productively with this music is to recover – against both Modood and Bourne – a *strategic* Asian identity politics articulated by these Rap groups that is concurrently neither essentializing nor dissolutive into a deconstructive play on difference. As Fuss (1989: 105) maintains, whilst 'identity' may be continually assumed, it is constantly being called into question. It should be acknowledged that it is 'fictitious', potentially disruptive, and 'is a radically destabilizing force and not at all a stable guarantee of a coherent politics'. Similarly, I am carefully using the word 'strategic' in Spivak's sense (1993), which does not denote a totalizing theory, but is apposite for a situation. The notion of a strategic identity politics forces us to think through issues of how identity is being deployed and where its effects are. What I am attempting is to argue that the identity discourse articulated by these Rap groups recognizes that Asian identity cannot be predicated on experience alone or exist outside representation (Hall 1992). Such a discourse is also resistive of hegemonic culturalist definitions, and it is through such forms that a radical opening up of the signifier 'Asian' to further politico-cultural contestation is being actively made. These groups' Rap music is a contradictory site (in common with some other Asian popular cultural forms), which offers the possibility of simultaneously invoking/affirming/de-centring a politicized category of 'Asian' or its particular ethnicities in a racist British social formation.

In order to substantiate some of these claims, we can go on to examine the lyrical content of a few tracks by these Rap groups. A brief exploration of some of the performative aspects of undoubtedly one of the most dynamic British Rap groups today, Fun^Da^Mental will also be made. First, however, I should qualify what follows by observing that I am often left frustrated with attempts to undertake textual analysis of Rap lyrics, as this is often accomplished in a realist narrative mode and in isolation to the performative musical experience. (The forthcoming analysis does not entirely escape from this criticism either).[8] More specifically, the political content of the lyrics cannot simply secure their reception: as with any text, multiple readings and positionalities are possible, though contingent upon numerous 'determining' situational and discursive factors. And more concretely, we should take the complaint from Hip-Hop fans seriously, that the lyrics of Rap in themselves are not sufficient – *what about the beat?* (But this does not mean that Rap lyrics are not also constitutive in the production of identities and subjectivities, as is any relationship between a reader and a text). What I will do here is offer a particular set of readings of these lyrics, in relation to the previous theoretical remarks made in locating this music at a specific juncture of Asian youth identity formations in Britain.

Hustlers HC: stirring up trouble

The two-man Rap group Hustlers HC offers a blend of Hip-Hop incorporating Gangsta Rap narrativity and stylistics with more chilled-out, jazz-influenced phat beats. Their track 'Big Trouble in Little Asia' is one of the first to articulate directly some significant dimensions of Asian cultural and political life in Britain. A haunting melodic guitar riff and jazzy Hip-Hop beat carry the listener, and the rising tempo – syncopated by Reggae breaks – increasingly intensifies the message. Read as a narrative, it begins at the point of the colonial encounter between Britain and India and moves on to explore an array of cultural complexities and internal and external social antagonisms experienced by people of South Asian descent living in Britain:

> Hey yo I see big trouble down in Little Asia,
> For an Asian growing up things get crazier and crazier,
> For my culture does not fit in with yours,
> Your corrupt culture makes my rich culture look poor,
> I'm trying to learn more about my past,
> I'm fighting to make my culture last
> But the clock keeps ticking tocking
> Knocking down the walls, so people fall
> Down into the deep deep well
> Where you close your ears to the stories that they tell
> Of India in the days gone by
> The civilization that cause such frustration
> That it had to be captured and controlled
> Made to fit the mould
> A jewel in the Empire made of gold
> Now it's raped and left out in the cold
> So come to the land of opportunity
> Be a street sweeper, a factory worker
> So many came and worked the bum jobs hard
> Educated people treated like retards
> But the land of opportunity needs a business community
> So the factory worker made good, like he always knew he would
> But what about me, this ain't my country 'gee'

I have no loyalty I'm here as long as it suits me
It wasn't my intent or my idea
Sometimes I wish I was born a million miles from here
'cos born I am a child without a home
Homeless I've grown up, Homeless I will roam
A citizen of the world, with Asia on my mind
My culture's all I have, My culture I will find
I hope you're sitting comfortably I'm gonna burst your bubble
Tell you much stories about big trouble in Little Asia.

> (Hustlers HC, 'Big Trouble in Little Asia', Nation Records, 1994.
> Words by Paul Arora and Mandeep Walia of Hustlers HC.
> Published by QFM/Warner Chappell Music)

The beginning of the rap invokes 'Asian culture' as a resource, some-thing to be struggled over and defended in the face of destructive racist colonial forces both in the 'homeland' and in Britain. In common with many consciousness rappers, Hustlers HC narrate and reclaim suppressed histories of (enforced) colonial displacement, capitalist work relations and racial oppression. But there is no innocent celebration of an Asian cultural identity in this track: dissonance is expressed against an emergent and assimilatory middle-class Asian business community, in addition to a deep-seated ambivalence in belonging to the British nation. The affirmation of cultural identity, 'My culture is all I have' is not simply something to be summoned from the past; it is to be actively recovered, remade and transformed in the present: 'My culture I will find.'

As expressed by the title, 'Big Trouble in Little Asia', the heart of the song explores the internal fragmentations and multiple antagonisms of an Asian cultural formation existing within a hostile and racially violent Britain. (The song title is also a parodic play on an Orientalist Hollywood film with a similar name). The track moves on to critique sharply the rise of gang cultures organized along ethno-religious lines amongst Asian communities.

Listen to the life in a day
Of an Asian struggling to live
Fighting the oppression learn each a little lesson
Christmas day they're smoking crack on brick lane
Santa Claus never came or maybe he's ashamed
That his own colour his own creed
Treats another colour like an inferior breed
Gangster life fast becoming an element
Religion and culture becomes a white elephant
For once white denotes negativity
Black denotes a racial relativity

Religion breaking up the community
Asian man the storm coming and we need unity
The Hindu, the Muslim and the Sikh
United we stand, divided we are weak
Weakened the most by the coconut
The sell out to the white the coward in the fight
But the Judas must learn together we will burn
Every dog has his day and he will have his turn
Big trouble come I wish I never see the day
I challenge the BNP to march on Southall Broadway
Big trouble comes and by any means
The Blood will stain it and it ain't easy to clean
I know I'm telling you this story
And it may not phase ya
But it causes Big Trouble down in Little Asia.

(Hustlers HC, 'Big Trouble in Little Asia')

In this track Hustlers HC are concerned more widely with the
divisions caused by particularist religious and ethnic affiliations, and
urge a political unity in fighting racial oppression. They also reserve
their hostility for the 'totally assimilated' Asian, denouncing him (*sic*) as
a cultural traitor and sell-out. This is denoted by the popular term
'coconut' (brown on the outside but white on the inside), which
directly refers to the racial/cultural authenticity of an Asian in relation
to white identity. It is notable that the term is not concerned with the
question of Asian authenticity in relation to the signifier 'Black' ('denotes
a racial relativity'), but marks the limits of racial assimilation into a
dominant racist white culture, 'together we will burn'. Near the end of
the track, the meaning of the title 'Big Trouble...' is radically altered,
the shift from intra-group antagonisms to a provocative challenge to
the racist British National Party (BNP) is made: Asians will unite and
fight back! The song's closure does not simply mimic the realist 'ghetto
tales' present in much of Gangsta Rap, but self-reflexively suggests that
whilst its story may not register with the listener, its dialogic narrative
nevertheless is of social significance and deserves contemplation.

Asian Dub Foundation: lyrical warriors

The group Asian Dub Foundation (ADF) is better described as a
collective arising from a community music project. The label 'Rap
group' disguises the multiplicity of musical styles the group exhibits,
ranging from toasting, dub, funky guitars in addition to South Asian
instrumentations, and not forgetting the dope Hip-Hop beats that drive

the music. In their track 'Strong Culture', the pedagogic intent centres on the affirmation of an Asian identity in relation to cultural invisibility, and the reassertion of political agency.

> I grab the mic
> To commence
> with the mic check
> Supply rhymes, man
> you've never heard yet
> you've never thought
> an Asian could do this
> Well you're wrong
> Wrong again
> Hardcore!
> That's what I wanna be
> All over the white world
> Yes they'll remember me
> Don't look at me as an
> Innocent bystander
> Because I'll scare you after dark
>
> (ADF, 'Strong Culture', Nation Records 1995.
> Words by Dr Das, Savale, Zaman, Uddin.
> Published by QFM/Warner Chappell)

In grabbing 'the mic' ADF cogently assert the significance of knowledge ('rhymes') from an Asian positionality and the legitimacy of their participation in Rap, challenging any claims to the inauthenticity of their involvement in Hip-Hop. In particular, they counter the supposed onlooker status and passivity of Asians in a white-dominated music industry, and Asians' marginality in popular cultural spaces, declaring menacingly their latent disruptive musical intentionality ('I'll scare you after dark').

The song moves on to ground ADF's project more specifically, by invoking a diasporic notion of 'Asianness' in the imagined community of their 'homeland'.

> Another critical rhyme
> Make you wanna look
> Observe it
> It's like a comic book
> Coming from the place
> With a capital B
> I'll let you guess –
> No let me tell you:
> The B and the A and N and

Photo: Clare Godfrey

ASIAN DUB FOUNDATION

The G and the L and the A
With the word called Desh
Sums up the country
The word and the place
Called Bangladesh
So you never contest
Yes you thought
I couldn't do it
I'm not a Black man
This time it's an Asian
Some fear the white man
Some fear the Ku Klux Klan
But they ain't up to no good...
Listen up to this rap
It's Asian guys coming correct

(ADF, 'Strong Culture')

The rhythmic spelling out of B-A-N-G-L-A to a repetitive accelerated dub beat punctuates its tropological appellation and lyrical coupling
with 'Desh', producing the sign 'Bangladesh' which signifies both a local
and diasporic community of place and temporality. The stress on the
production of this sign ('you thought I couldn't do it') accentuates its

particularity in a wider social formation that neither redefines it as a narrow ethno-cultural identity, nor erases it under the racist term 'Paki' (as referred to in a previous verse). The desire to strategically recapture a specific Asian political agency against the hegemony of 'Black' is also expressed. The invocation of an Asian 'strong culture' that permeates the track insists on the possibility of Asian cultural specificities and priorities in wider anti-racist struggles and political dissension.

The politicization of the category 'Asian' is pursued further in the track 'Rebel Warrior'. The back cover of this single declares that the song was inspired by the poem 'Bidrohi' written in India in the 1920s by Kazi Nazral, who was incarcerated for his anti-colonial sedition and advocacy of Indian independence.

> Ami Bidrohi
> I the Rebel Warrior
> I have risen alone
> With my head held high
> I will only rest
> When the cries of the oppressed
> No longer reach the sky
> When the sound of the sword
> Of the oppressor
> No longer rings in battle
> Hear my war cry!
>
> (ADF, 'Rebel Warrior', Nation Records, 1995.
> Words by Dr Das, Savale, Pandit. Published
> by QFM/Warner Chappell Music.)

The track recovers this heroic figure erased from Western history, and attempts to recontextualize his political vision from the past in making it relevant for today's times. The lyrics below appeal to the syncretic nature of their Asian-inspired dub-Rap music in making available new kinds of identities that transgress and contest ethnocentric forms of cultural containment. In similar fashion to Nazrul's original poem, the track imagines a new transracial utopia.

> A radical fusion
> Strange alliance
> The siren and the flute in unison
> 'Cos it's part of my mission
> To break down division
> Mental compartments
> Psychological prisons
> I'll be sowing seeds of community

Accommodating every colour
every need
So listen to my message
And heed my warning
I'm telling you now
how a new age is dawning

(ADF, 'Rebel Warrior')

The power of 'Rebel Warrior' lies in its reclaiming of an anti-colonial Asian poet to a contemporary anti-racist situation. In doing so, it performs the necessary ideological work of politicizing the category 'Asian' by redefining and reconnecting it with both an anti-colonial history and contemporary struggle. ADFs lyrical messages recognize that a crude incantation of the identificatory category 'Asian' cannot secure its (anti-racist) political expediency. This pedagogic intent is promoted by many post-Bhangra rappers, especially, as we shall discover, in the music of Fun^Da^Mental.

Fun^Da^Mental: merchants of chaos

In common with other post-Bhangra acts, the music of Fun^Da^Mental is far from limited to the sampling of Bhangra rhythms. It includes a vast mix of Indian classical and popular film music, Moroccan/Eastern drum beats, Qawwali sounds, Islamic chants, and the ingenious interweaving of dialogue from famous Hindi movies. A multiracial band, Fun^Da^Mental clearly calls for unity between Asians and Afro-Caribbeans in the fight against racism – most forcefully expressed in the lyrics of 'Dog-Tribe': 'There comes a time when enough is enough Afro-Caribbeans, Asians together is tuff.' (This is also reflected in the group's changing membership, with two Afro-Caribbean members joining, and Blacka-D as one of lead rappers.) But the group's identity politics are far more complex and contradictory than a simple anti-racist unity under the label 'Black'.

Fun^Da^Mental potently samples voices and rallying cries of political leaders from the past, such as Gandhi, Malcolm X and the Black Panthers, as well as in the present, particularly the controversial Nation of Islam leader Louis Farrakhan. The group is clearly inspired by the American Black Power movements of the late 1960s. As Decker (1992) notes, as 'organic cultural intellectuals' many rappers have attempted to reclaim and recontextualize the black militancy of the 1960s, making it meaning-ful for the 1990s. The Black Panthers' slogan 'seize the time' is the name adopted for the group's first album (and constantly flashes before our eyes in the video of 'Dog-Tribe' – see Chapter 7). More specifically, Fun^Da^Mental articulates eclectically a kind of militant Islamic-influenced, pro-Black anti-racist identity politics. Fun^Da^Mental's Islamic-inspired militancy appears to be drawn more from the Nation of Islam than from Middle Eastern or North African Islamist movements. In the track 'President Propaganda', the notorious rhetoric of the Nation of Islam is adopted to assert a resistive anti-Western/white position predicated on a politicized Black, pan-Islamic identity.

> I'm the soldier in the name of Allah
> So put down the cross and pick up the 'X'
> Do you know where you're goin' to
> Do you know where you're comin' from
> You're scared of the sun, I live in the sun
> 1995, Elijah is alive
> Louis Farrakhan, the Nation of Islam
> That's where I got my degree from
> So watch out now I'm comin' at ya!
> ...Back in the days of slave ships
> You had us whipped, raped and lynched
> Took away the Quran, you gave us the bible
> Now we're livin' a nightmare
> Where black is bad and white is supreme
> Fuck that shit, I'm comin' at ya!
>
> (Fun^Da^Mental, 'President Propaganda', Nation Records,
> 1994. Published by QFM Publishing/Warner
> Chappell Music Ltd.)

Fun^Da^Mental to some degree also reproduces the masculinist politics that was common to the 1960s Black Power movement, and still remains present in today's anti-racist movements. In another of the group's tracks, 'Mother India', the lyrics do attempt to portray various heroic past and present South Asian female figures as active agents making history.[9] But there is an inclination to objectify (Asian) women in the sign 'Mother India' that also occurs in other Black-consciousness Rap tracks in the sign 'Mother Africa' (Decker 1992). The confrontational anti-racist politics of direct action articulated in a few of Fun^Da^Mental's songs e.g. 'Dog-Tribe' and 'Bullet Solution?' (and in the Hustlers HC track 'Vigilante' or the Kaliphz's 'Hang 'Em High'), remains problematic in relation to the issues of gender and female agency. It should be pointed out that many militant Left groups in Britain today, particularly those with a confrontational style of anti-racism, have tendencies to reproduce this type of masculine-orientated activism.

It would be unjust to place the burden of Black representation on the few bands that I have mentioned alone, as they are only one group of many Black cultural workers in Britain. But post-Bhangra Rappers (like most consciousness Rappers) are challenged by the need to develop a self-reflexivity in their cultural politics by intervening against excessive male posturings, and against some of the more conservative trajectories found in their lyrics.[10] Whilst Fun^Da^Mental is selective in what it strategically appropriates from the political philosophy of the Nation of Islam, this should not discourage Black cultural activists and fans from challenging critically the symbolic championing of Farrakhan. There is no easy reconciliation between the eclectic ideological positions and political influences embraced in Fun^Da^Mental's music. The contemporary American black Islamic cultural nationalism of Farrakhan, the politics of Malcolm X, the Marxist–Maoist revolutionary vanguardism of the Black Panthers and leftist British anti-racism have no simple political commonalties. The tensions between these differing and contradictory ideological positions may sometimes result in Fun^Da^Mental's desire for a coalition-based politics or a transracial utopia (as promoted in the track 'New World Order') being subsumed under a masculinist-and/or separatist-inclined politics.

Nevertheless, it is perhaps in Fun^Da^Mental's musical performance that most readily 'identity is fleetingly experienced in the most intensive of ways' (Gilroy 1993a: 78). (In this respect we should resist making prematurely, crude-textualist final judgements over the kinds of cultural politics this group may engender.) Their stage performances are highly energetic, a riotous spectacle of agitation, frustration and anarchic political dissent. Whilst their musical content differs considerably from that of Public Enemy, Fun^Da^Mental similarly display a phenomenal musical density for Hip-Hop (see Frith 1990). They use coarsely produced music samples and harshly juxtapose a range of provocative sounds: air-raid sirens, explosive beats, rallying cries, and hypnotic looping Islamic chanting. Their music's incessant rhythm patterns and multilayered intertextuality generates a sense of claustrophobia, confusion and panic. And alongside the output of other contentious Rap groups such as Public Enemy or Ice Cube, the political and aesthetic appeal of Fun^Da^Mental's music lies in the everyday urgency it invokes (see Decker 1992). The group might also be described as 'chaos theoreticians', providing 'handrails in the hour of chaos, a way of mapping the confusion of the contemporary political landscape and forcing it to make "sense"'(Frith 1990: 160).

I admit a difficulty in reading Fun^Da^Mental's political–musical pedagogy. If we are to believe that we reside in an age of intellectual crisis, political and moral uncertainty and ambiguity, then the forwarding of a politics in advance is a risky business. As Hall has argued pertinently, '[t]here is no guarantee, in reaching for an essentialized racial identity of which we think we can be certain, that it will always turn out to be mutually liberating and progressive on all the other dimensions' (1992: 31–2). In various tracks, Fun^Da^Mental advocate inchoately their own utopian visions of society, and they do revel in a Gangsta Rap dystopia of the white world (as found in the tracks 'Seize the Time' or 'Mr Bubbleman'). But they often do not articulate realist linear narratives or end on simplistic ideological closures in their songs. Fun^Da^Mental's musical output is concerned primarily with overcoming white racial terror, neo-colonialism/imperialism and global racial subjugation 'by any means necessary'. This does not necessarily lead to a coherent political strategy and, in particular, is radically disruptive and transgressive of any sense of a unitary or stable (Asian) identity politics.

TIME TO FLIP THE SCRIPT?

The journey traversed in this chapter leaves us with certain limitations in understanding both Bhangra and post-Bhangra dance musics solely in relation to the articulation of an Asian identity politics. The concomitant affirmation and de-centring of Asian identity that occurs in these musical sites is suggestive of more complex discursive identity productions, beyond that imagined in the framing of this work in progress. Similarly, Gilroy's (1993a) observation that music is sometimes overburdened with the quest for liberation politics should restrain us from innocently constructing our own meta-narratives about Asian musical cultural production and its relationship to political and cultural fields of social transformation. Nevertheless, from the outset, the limited purpose has been to read Bhangra/post-Bhangra music *strategically* in order to redefine and reclaim the category 'Asian' against hegemonic notions and movements that prematurely close down alternative points of identification and ways of being. It is to be hoped that this counter-hegemonic intention has matched the efficacious pedagogy of the musics explored. It should be reiterated that the sutured term 'Asian' is a temporary positionality which can be used in contemporary anti-racist struggles, but it would not necessarily be lamentable if it becomes politically redundant when in future struggles and alternative conditions of racial subjugation we discard its possibly exhausted use-value in favour of other alliances.

An attempt to rethink these dance musics and move beyond customary identity-speak, needs to engage with the wider issue of how cultural difference is being articulated in a capitalist social formation that controls and neutralizes counter-cultural movements. One place to begin is to extend our understanding of the significance of interstitial identity productions found in the musical modalities of Bhangra/post-Bhangra. That is, how the musical fusions of different cultural predilections can be productive of new and transgressive ways of being in what may identified as the 'third space' (Bhabha 1990; 1994). Bhabha contends that the articulation of cultures is possible because they are a 'signifying or symbol forming activity' lived out through forms of representation that can never be complete in themselves.

> [C]ultures are only constituted in relation to that otherness internal to their own symbol-forming activity which makes them de-centred structures — through that displacement ... opens up the possibility of articulating different, even incommensurable cultural practices and priorities (1990: 211).

Bhabha points usefully to the process of the hybridity of culture, in which a 'third space' exists which opens up possibilities for new structures of authority and political initiatives, and which may not fit into our conventional (political and ethical) frames of reference or rules of interpretation.[11] It is precisely at the boundaries where cultural practices meet that the hyper-syncretic music of Bhangra/post-Bhangra most imaginatively and seductively operates. It is at these liminal sites that new modes of cultural authority can be produced, new meanings and practices are formed which open up the possibility of different ways of knowing and nodes of identification. However, once we move beyond the security of normative subject positions induced by identity politics and pre-given structures of cultural authority, we enter into the arena of 'risk and possibility' where alternative political priorities and meanings are engendered. This does not suggest the relativist pluralism of a status quo multiculturalist politics. Rather, as Grossberg (1994: 20) maintains, 'we must collectively articulate a common affective vision of a shared political future based on a politics of practice (what people do, what they invest in, where they belong)'. It may be that the Asian dance musics are one set of new cultural spaces in which this kind of politics of practice is a happening thing.

NOTES

Shout outs to: all those involved in making this article happen, including the RG posse (especially John, Bobby and Shirin), the old crew (Paul B. and Anunay), Esther at Nation Records, and Prita for being there. A big 'Yo' to Ash for the endless phone chat and inspiration.

1. It is worth reiterating that Back presents an interesting theoretical analysis of post-Bhangra Apache Indian, but Back's ethnography remains highly dubious. Also, it is not clear whether Bhangra necessarily engenders similar intermezzo subjectivities, but my main point here concerns Back's reductive characterization of Bhangra.

2. It may be the case, as Neiyyar (1988: 6) suggests, that the 'suspect contents of the songs is overlooked as homage is paid to the beat'. But the affirmation of a gendered Asian identity for female listeners in the performance of Bhangra would be in constant negotiation and contestation with the patriarchal expressions present in the music. Also see Chapter 9 for the subversive pleasures of the female-centred Bhangra dance of Giddha.

3. I do not have the space here to fully rehearse the sophisticated arguments that Sayyid (forthcoming) and Žižek (1989) use in making their claims.

4. My own politicization took place during the 1980s, which makes me still very sympathetic to the *political* notion of 'Black'. However, for all its limitations, it is regrettable that this anti-racist moment appears to be passing – it is more common to find the culturalist terms 'Black' and 'Asian' being deployed.

5. In particular, Modood fails to distinguish between the hegemonic practices of Black as found in state (local-authority) discourses compared with grassroots anti-racist Black politics. In these anti-racist struggles the political identification of Black was always contested and forged 'in struggle', and never simply imposed on to a unitary Asian identity. For more passing critiques of Modood's work, see Brah (1992) and Yuval-Davis (1992). For what remains a good critique of the 'ethnicity paradigm', see Omni and Winant (1986).

6. These Rap groups embody many trajectories and projects, only some of which are concerned with articulating an Asian identity politics. For instance, the Kaliphz musical content does address issues of Asian identity and racism in Britain, but they are equally, if not more concerned with being recognized as genuine Hip-Hop artists first and foremost. The inevitable comparisons made with other Rap groups such as Cypress Hill or Onyx (*Represent* June/July 1995), may detract from Kaliphz's 'Old Skool' originality and talent, but do indicate the group's acceptance into the wider international Hip-Hop community.

7. I am focusing here on the limits of an identity politics predicated upon an essentialized Asian ethnic identity. However, it is important to understand that the practice of politics invariably generates political identifications based on the formation of social collectivities and subject positions. For example, a trade unionist or a member of the Conservative Party both express forms of identity politics. (Thanks to Bobby for pointing this out).

8. Nevertheless, contrary to Gilroy's (1993a) misplaced critique of textualism, I do not wish to valorize *performance* as the only possible mode of subject

SANJAY SHARMA 57

production in music. Although the 'total experience' of music is neatly captured by this notion.

9. The song title 'Mother India' also refers to a classic popular Hindi film of the same name, in which the heroine is a struggling, poverty-stricken rural female, symbolizing the project of nation-building for post-Independence India.

10. It is interesting to note that both Fun^Da^Mental and Hustlers HC (for their song 'Runaway') have approached the radical anti-racist feminist organization, Southall Black Sisters.

11. Bhabha's use of the term 'hybridity' does not assume that pure cultural entities pre-exist which are transformed when fused. For Bhabha (1990: 211), cultures 'can never be said to have a totalized prior moment of being or meaning – an essence'. Nevertheless, much of the academic discourse of hybridity concerns itself with only those groups residing at the 'margins', often leaving 'whiteness' intact and naturalized.

PART TWO

EXPRESSIVE STYLES

3

ASIAN KOOL?

BHANGRA AND BEYOND

Rupa Huq

British Bhangra music – Punjabi folk and western pop shoved in the rock'n'roll blender at high speed – provides heaven-sent fodder for cultural critics of both the popular and academic spheres. In its recorded and live forms, it is cross-cultural musical expression, a subculture hailing from the twin sites of turn-of-the-century urban Britain and the sub-continent inextricably bound up with the identities of 1990s UK Asian youth. This chapter will attempt to peel away some of the issues asso-ciated with the scene and look beyond Bhangra at the music and movement(s) that it has spawned, in particular the so-called 'new Asian Kool'.

BHANGRA AND BEYOND

A World Wide Web Bhangra page (url: http://www.yucc.yorku.ca/~sanraj/bhangra.html) defines its subject and derivations at length: 'Bhangra is a dance style which originates from the region of Punjab ... performed when celebrating important occasions such as the harvest, weddings etc. Nowadays the word Bhangra is more associated with the style of music which has singing and the beat of the dhol drum... Bhangra has always been popular amongst Punjabi people all over the world but it has enjoyed a resurgence over the last ten years or so. Its raw traditional sound is often supplemented with contemporary musical styles. Most of these trends come from the UK.' The global claim of the Web, with its reach estimated by 1995 to be at 40 million and rapidly expanding, provides a fitting international medium for Bhangra's message – yet access to the Web is uneven, marked across the international division of labour and resources. Despite its global circulation, Bhangra music has failed as yet to make major inroads into the mainstream, even in a now 'webbed-up' UK. Three main reasons can be isolated: musicological, cultural and economic.

Academic work on Bhangra has not, to date, been plentiful. The subject of ethnicity and musical cultures has never been a particular favourite for subculture theorists, with a (very) few exceptions (Hebdige 1979; and Jones 1988). Ethnicity, it seems, can be added to the list of omissions of the 'new subcultural theory' of Birmingham University's Centre for Contemporary Cultural Studies (CCCS) that has been the prevailing paridigm in the study of youth culture since the 1970s, an omission alongside gender and feminity, conformity and middle-class youth. Moreover, South Asians as a whole have in many ways remained an invisible community in the eyes of academia. Stretching the applicability of theories of 'black' music (the next best thing) to fit Bhangra can be problematic. Oliver (1990) grapples with this difficulty, suggesting the compromise term 'Afro-Asian' whilst acknowledging himself that this is a clumsy compromise. 'Black music' after all could potentially encompass a very broad spectrum of musical forms for which it would be inappropriate to formulate an artificial all-embracing theory. As the CCCS has faded from prominence in the 1990s, American accounts of black musics (such as Lipsitz 1994; Rose 1994) provide the most interesting work in this area, having a two-fold use: offering points of comparison and also reinforcing the tremendous impact that black musics have had on British youth culture, including Asian dance music.[1]

A number of reasons can be advanced as to why it has taken Asian musics so long to arrive. The *Independent* points out: 'George Harrison has a lot to answer for. All those tedious sitar passages you skip over on the Beatles albums are not designed to dispose an audience favourably towards Asian sounds. And the muzak played in Indian restaurants doesn't help either' (25 September 1992). Bhangra's slow crossover into UK mainstream music can be partially explained by the fact that, to the Western ear, in its purest form Indian music is quite simply 'uneasy listening'. The timings are different, with a different system of counting and rhythm, unlike the Western equal bar patterns. Combinations with other musical forms are certainly going some way to overcome this difficulty; to date Bhangra has demonstrated an appetite for the adaptation and incorporation of other styles: at the time of writing in particular with Jungle or drum'n'bass. The language factor could also prove to be something of a barrier. The UK charts have never proved particularly amenable to foreign-language hits. Yet Bhangra itself is at least as quintessentially 'British' as it is 'Asian'. The point has also been made in Gurinder Chudha's aptly titled film *I'm British But...*[2] although Bhangra's influence stretches beyond the UK to Canada and the USA – and to other areas of Asian settlement, and of course the music has been re-exported back to South Asia.[3] Despite attempts to make it fit (Awan 1994), Bhangra does not fall easily into the category of World Music, at least in the strictest sense of the word (Hardy and Laing, 1995: 3) because in many ways it is too British. Its impact can be felt, however, on contemporary UK popular culture.

UN-KOOL ASIANS

Despite a short-lived selective flirtation with, and exoticization of, the Indian subcontinent's supposedly mystical side in the 1960s, Asians have simply never assumed a principal place in *Top of the Pops*/MTV youth culture mythology; instead they have perennially been considered unhip. Western popular culture has long been over-endowed with stereotypical images of Asians as submissive, hard-working, passive and conformist. These deep-seated media representations spanning three decades of mass migration are still crucially important in shaping perceptions of contemporary Asian club culture. Black iconography in popular culture contrastingly has always been seen as cool and hard by youth culture at large: something to aspire to. Hewitt (1986) has shown how this even applies to the ways in which young people use the English language: words from the West Indian vernacular such as 'hard' and 'dread', for example, have entered everyday youth-culture-speak. When Apache Indian duetted with Maxi Priest, the former delivering his lines in patois and the latter in Punjabi, it was seen by Gilroy as an important gesture of mutual cultural respect.[4] Lou Reed memorably sang 'I Wanna Be Black'. Rick Astley, Jamiroqai and Mick Hucknall arguably made careers out of the same wish, but no one at any time expressed desires along the lines of 'I Wanna Be a Paki'.

Much of both the academic and popular discourse on Bhangra seems to paint it in a 'happy families' way, often seeing it as expressing a coming together of the tribes'. Gillespie claims 'it has become a focal point for the public emergence of a British youth culture which transcends traditional divisions and aspires to a sense of ethnic unity.... It is a form and style that British Asian youth can claim as their own and be proud of: neither gori (white) nor kala (black) it has made Asian youth both audible and visible for the first time' (Gillespie 1995: 45–6). Gillespie's project concentrates on television viewing patterns –

observations of Southall youth observing the Australian soap opera *Neighbours* – so Bhangra is only fleetingly skated over. This mythology has also been perpetuated in popular discourse. ID magazine enthused thus: 'Of course, it's no revolution to the kids who listen to this stuff day and night. To them like all urban musics it's a soundtrack for life.... It's the sound of Bhangra, the Asian music where the language is Punjabi but the following crosses cultural and religious borders' (April 1993). This is something of a generalization – only true up to a point. The term 'Asian' is dangerously catch-all; any uses of its connotations are potentially loaded.

Bhangra is a music of very specific derivations, namely Punjabi folk dance, which by definition cannot carry equal appeal to the inhabitants of an entire subcontinent. The group Joi Bangla, of Bangladeshi descent and based in East London, for example, have expressed reservations about Bhangra's narrow Punjabi focus and instead use Bengali lyrics, as have Asian Dub Foundation. It is something of an over-simplification to see Bhangra as the one force uniting the disparate members of Britain's Asian youth. Indeed, an effort to maintain a distance from (old-style) Bhangra is one of the defining features of those associated with Asian Kool.

PRESS TO PLAY: REPRESENTATIONS OF BHANGRA

Banerji and Baumann meditate on the economics of Bhangra in a piece that already comes across, as many tracts on youth culture inevitably do, as somewhat dated. Their argument, which is that most frequently advanced for Bhangra's absence from the pop charts, is that the alternative economic structures upon which it relies operate as an obstacle to breaking out of an insular 'ghetto' culture. Of its many resources the scene has developed its own production and distribution conventions as well as genre styles. There is a curious 'parallel universe' space that Bhangra sales seem to occupy in this particular explanation: selling copious amounts in Indian cassette shops yet making no impact on the mainstream top forty album and single lists.

Bhangra has not received much attention from academia but its existence can be detected from popular reports. The musicological, cultural and economic reasons for Bhangra's lack of progress all are apparent in its British press coverage, throwing up some interesting questions of representation and the ways in which Asian youth in the UK are viewed by the respectable media. By 1993, the *Face* (August

1993) was calling Bhangra 'a scene that parallels the dancefloor revolution of acid house' but it took the British media until 1986 to discover it (Banerji and Baumann 1990). In March of that year the *Face*
itself featured a daytime event, termed by Baumann 'the classic public
event for Bhangra music'. However Baumann despaired of traits in the
early reporting of Bhangra: 'Not all of this publicity was welcome for
apart from its often patronizing tone, its pictures of a new generation
of Asian youth regularly bunking off school to attend live shows created images that did justice to neither parents' attitudes nor to youngsters' aspirations' (Baumann 1990: 146). These tabloid attitudes are still
prevalent in many descriptions of Bhangra today.

The media focused on the repressed-Asian-youth angle. A *Guardian*
article of 1990 was entitled 'Rave of the secret rebels: the clandestine
clubbers who do their kicking against cultural restraints on the dance
floor'. We are told: 'Normally the girls here would not be allowed near
a club; their culture and parents forbid it. Now they had five hours to
release their frustration and rebel.... Asian girls have to be protected
from "Western depravity". They are kept at home.' It is a cautionary
tale including adventure and deception: 'Nazreen quickly dismissed the
insane urge to blab all to her parents, the next afternoon was only a
month away.' This tone spread to television as well as the press. Benjamin Zephaniah in a BBC documentary in 1993 told the camera at Le
Palais nightclub, Hammersmith: 'Raving from eleven a.m. is quite
normal in the Asian community. This is a real cultural melting pot and
most Asian parents think that daytime raving is safe.'

Interestingly, the *Independent*'s 1994 commentary on Bombay Jungle,
a weekly night-time Bhangra rave at the fashionable Wag club in central
London, contrasts with the Guardian's report of four years before. In
1990 we were told, 'Hardly anyone smoked, no-one drank, knowing
that if the secret was to be maintained they had to arrive home as
spotlessly as they had left.' Those attending night-time events it seems
are not subject to the same code of conduct. By 1994 the *Independent*
notes, 'Couples don't restrain from physical contact and both sexes
smoke and drink freely' (24 May 1994). As with other youth culture,
Bhangra has attracted lay speculative theories. A raver quoted in the
Independent explains: 'For once Asians can conduct themselves in a way
they would never dream of doing in front of their parents. Coming to
the Wag reassures me that I'm not the only one suffering an identity
crisis.' This quote in particular reinforces dominant representations of
Asians – caught between two cultures, desultory, directionless, confused. It is, however, rather reductive to see Asian youth as perpetual

victims of the system when the reality of dual or indeed multiple identities is much more complex.

The Bhangra gig is here being celebrated as an event rather than for the musical content of the records being spun. Guardian rock critic Caroline Sullivan wrote: 'One day in late January I attended a Bengali rave. "Day" means literally that. The action kicked off at three in the afternoon and finished at nine. This is the standard at Asian raves; it appeases parents and enables girls to attend' (13 September 1993). The *Independent*'s Bombay Jungle correspondent (Dhingra), surmises: 'The absence of parents, relatives and older members of the community adds an element of spice that most other Asian social events lack.' The Bhangra disco is then fulfilling a need amongst Asian youth: 'Weddings and other religious occasions are still largely the only events where [Asians] can gather to meet other members of the community and tend to include members of the same religion or caste.' As a result of press coverage, the creation and dissemination of stereotypical images of Asian youth follows. Such images become received opinion, particularly when the harbingers are the so-called 'quality' press, themselves seen as mechanisms of serious professional scrutiny.

By 1993, Bhangra music had impinged on the national consciousness to the extent that its derivatives could be discussed in the music columns of the national press without requiring its definition and in relation to other musics: most importantly the emergence of a new paradigm. In place of the 'old school' Bhangra discussed by Gillespie (1995) and Banerji and Baumann (1990), or more accurately coexisting alongside it, other new mutant musical forms were emerging on the musical landscape. Bands such as the Kaliphz, Fun^Da^Mental and Cornershop were making themselves known, as were some of the more big-league players Apache Indian and Bally Sagoo: none could strictly be labelled Bhangra. Writing about this music differs in many ways from the straightforward observation-infused press descriptions of Bhangra discos. Reworking Asian clichés is common, such as *ID*'s recommendation of Bally Sagoo's 'Bollywood Mix' album: 'tastier than a midnight balti'. Dave Gelly of the *Observer* (23 March 1994) calls Nitin Sawney's music 'A melting pot: an acclaimed mix of jazz and classical Indian rhythms with added spice.' The most familiar observation that consistently recurs of Bhangra music is that it has spawned a welcome if unusual and unfathomable sonic combination; thus Robin Denselow in the *Guardian* (20 August 1992) writes of a 'global mix up' and the *Independent on Sunday* writes of 'a weird and compelling hybrid', both on Bally Sagoo.

The chronicling of 'beyond Bhangra pop' exemplifies the trend of journalism supplanting cultural studies. The two are fast becoming inseparable, as can be seen from sociologist Les Back's coverage for the *Guardian* (19 October 1993) of Apache Indian's anti-BNP single 'Movin' On' released following the neo-fascist British National Party's local election victory in Tower Hamlets, east London (sample quote: 'Fascist cultures have always espoused cultural purity. It ['Movin' On'] is a celebration of cultural fusion'). The popular quasi-cultural-studies author Simon Reynolds (1990 and 1995) labelled Bally Sagoo in the *Wire* as 'joyous intoxicating polyglot pop, although as pan-cultural hybrids go, Western dancefloor requirements dominate'. Press representations of Bhangra rehearse Cohen's 'specialized modes of amplification' theory of youth cultures and deviance (Cohen 1980). Demand-led and dependent on a story's 'sexiness' factor, Cohen pointed out, 'The mass media operate with certain definitions of what is newsworthy.' Notions of 'clandestine clubbers' defying parental authority and shaking the shackles off their traditional Asian upbringing satisfies this requirement, buttressing existing preconceptions and misconceptions of Asian youth.

NO SELL-OUT: THE BURDEN OF REPRESENTATION

Much expectation is vested in the executants of the new Asian pop: much more than in their white counterparts, who are not subjected to the same continual pressure to supply self-justifications. All those involved are immediately seen as spokespersons for the 'community' and 'their generation', even if their music is not particularly Asian. This has been termed 'the burden of representation' (Mercer 1994: 233–58; Gilroy 1988). The burden of representation is intrinsically bound up with media representation because of the mass media's role in legitimation of cultural production. Many are aware of the restricted frameworks in which they are forced to operate. Gurinder Chudha has said (*Guardian*, 7 August 1992): 'This burden is very much a noose around the neck, but it also keeps us in check.' Playwright Hanif Kureishi has also met with a critical response from some sections of the Asian community as did Chudha's feature *Bhaji on the Beach*.[5] Kureshi has rejoindered: 'The Asian community is so diverse, so broad in terms of class, age and outlook that it doesn't make any sense to talk of the so-called Asian community' (*Guardian*, 7 August 1992). This shows a self-awareness on the part of artists regarding their positions in Asian cultural production. Cornershop's Tejinder Singh has commented (*Asian Age*, April 1994): 'Other bands are just there. We're not easy to categorise like Transglobal Underground or Apache Indian. We've had to justify ourselves a lot more than anybody else.' The burden is closely interwined with stereotypes and operates on two levels: within the artist's own 'community' itself and outside. In commonsense terms it can be described as 'not letting the side down'.

Many Asians are constantly described in terms of other (invariably non-Asian) acts that have gone before. As a guitar band, Cornershop are challenging the 'Asians can't rock' orthodoxy, but in journalistic shorthand are 'the Asian Jesus and Mary Chain'. Bally Sagoo's press release describes him as 'the Asian equivalent of Jam and Lewis or Jazzie B'. Fun^Da^Mental's fusion of samples, Rap and Islam has earned them the epithet 'Asian Public Enemy'. I asked rapper Blacka-D (real name Dave Watts) if he minded:

> D: A lot of people use that tag because it's convenient and also lazy. You could see Public Enemy as militant, aggressive and anti-white or pro-black and humanitarian.

Singer Aki Nawaz agreed:

> A: Politically there are connections. Musically we are miles and miles apart. Basically, this is us, we have our own identity, culture but we're not scared of anyone else's...

Asian Dub Foundation's Annirudha Das, who describes the group's mission as 'demystifying the role of Asians in making music', also raises the question of politics and the expectations of the white media with reference to what Asians are or aren't supposed to do.

> RH: What are you trying to represent?
>
> *Annirudha*:   The politics of culture, to us as Asian people in this society. How we're expected to have a certain type of sound. First we're not expected to make music at all then people expect to hear sitars and tablas. We're still using those sounds but we're trying to invert it into a much more militant, aggressive context.
>
> RH: Do you see yourselves as spokespersons for a generation?
>
> *Annirudha*:   Asian youth are just people. They've all got a lot of opinions but we've got a lot in common. Asian music is very much part of the World Music scene, but we make music – the music we hear every day. It provides us with a medium to talk to people, to get social and political ideas across, to get the attention of youth.

SMASHING STEREOTYPES I:
ASIANS WITH ATTITUDE

'Belligerent Paki-fists', the Observer stormed (3 November 1993) about Asian rappers Fun^Da^Mental. The well-worn path straddling politics and pop has been documented among others by Denselow (1989) and Frith (1978), but although the purchase of pop as a radicalizing force seemed to be spent by the 1990s, it is interesting to note that at a time when mainstream pop music continued to disengage with the political, many of the new wave of Asian pop groups were addressing two campaigns in particular: the Criminal Justice Bill issue and anti-racism. Tactics for both drew heavily on the Rock Against Racism tradition of the late 1970s (see Chapter 6). At open-air awareness/fundraising gigs for both causes, Cornershop, Asian Dub Foundation and most prominently Fun^Da^Mental (see Chapter 7) were appearing regularly on the bill.

I spoke to the group's Aki Nawaz on the subject:

RH: Are you in danger of devaluing the art by turning into a 'rent-a-cause' vehicle on a multicultural crusade?

Aki: We've got a lot of energy. Everybody sees us as controversial – all that stuff. I think it's again laziness, the usual things a lot of white people will put against you because they're not used to you speaking out.

RH: How would you, in a nutshell, summarize your politics?

Aki: We're humanists, that's all we are. It's all human rights. We're all equal.

RH: Aren't you just seen as a single-issue band? The issue being anti-racism?

Aki: It does go beyond racism, to global issues – politics, religion, tradition, culture, roots. You know, I think that we could easily be a thorn in the backside of a lot of liberal people, or people that think that they're liberal. I think as Asian people we're kind of throwing back at them. They'll come up with their terms, what they've thought up, but it's all bullshit.

Asian Dub Foundation similarly have played benefits for different factions of the anti-racist campaign. DJ John Pandit, the band's 'political strategist', is a youth worker for a civil rights advice and support group in Tower Hamlets, east London – a major area of Asian concentration and troubled by racist violence in recent years. I put the same question to him:

John: We find it difficult to be just entertainment. A lot of groups will have a radical sound and attach themselves to these campaigns because it's flavour of the month, not having been involved in these campaigns. We've done all this, we've been through this, seen it all, Ani from his educational point as a tutor and me being involved in anti-racist work for 10 years now. There's no problem working with all of these people but they need education as well. They're front groups, sure, but then all groups are a front for something.

Meanwhile 2Phaan of the Kaliphz in an interview in October 1995 recognized the potential for political tracks having a limited appeal and questioned the relationship between black performance and white pleasure:

> *2Phaan:* 'Yeah, there is a danger of it falling on deaf ears. It's just for the white kids, to ease their consciences so they can spin a record, put it to the back of the pile and then say 'That's it. I've done my bit for the Pakis for the day.'

Cornershop's lead singer Tejinder Singh, a former student union activist in the Midlands, has delivered lectures at conferences at both Cambridge and London universities on the role of politics and pop. Speaking on the subject of youth and cultures of resistance at the School of African and Oriental Studies in March 1994 he told delegates of the Socialist Forum Youth conference:

> Music is very accessible and is a simple language which can travel nationally and internationally, which can't really be said of other mediums. Over the centuries music has been a vehicle for the expression of political ideas. People, especially young people, tend to look towards music to help define themselves, organise themselves into groups or to create their identities. I would say that music certainly can provoke youth to get into politics, which in turn may create cultures of resistance. However when you are given the sort of rubbish, bullshit music we have got today, and there is a tendency of politics changing from week to week, then at the end of the day 'no real true politics' is not going to give music the full potential to create an opportunity to create cultures of resistance.

The 'political' side of the new wave of Asian-produced second-generation pop can further be seen from some of its lyrical content, some of whose themes certainly have at least political undertones, tackling old taboos. After all, according to its Web page definition, 'Lyrical content of Bhangra songs relates to celebration, or love, or patriotism or current social issues.' Tracks such as 'Runaway Child' and 'Big Trouble in Little Asia' from Nation Records signings Hustlers HC serve as examples, as do the Voodoo Queens' feminist leanings. Hustlers HC's DJ Paul told Hip-Hop fanzine *Represent* (October/November 1994):

> We always try to do a release with one side political and one track non-political because that's how Hustlers are. Like if you see us on stage, we'll

start off with all the political tracks, then we'll take it to just pure hip hop, rappin', flexin' our styles just creating a really good vibe 'cos you don't want people leaving your show thinking 'ah man life is really fucked.

Of course not all Asian pop can be filed under Political. Producer Bally Sagoo's trademark is revamping and revitalizing old Asian film-score classics by interweaving thumping Western bass lines amongst the string-draped sitar and tabla tunes. It is worth emphasizing here the complex intertextuality and array of musical reference points available to Asian youth. (Aki of Fun^Da^Mental, for example, cut his musical teeth in the early 1980s punk outfit Southern Death Cult). The willing-ness to subvert convention and tweak about with accepted musical forms is reflected elsewhere. Media analyses of Asian pop always look at it in terms of the 'Other'. However Asian pop has not been afraid to laugh at itself and be more 'playful' than simple po-faced political posturing. The politically conscious name of the group KK Kings recalls both Guru Nanak's prescribed five Ks of Sikh conduct and the Ku Klux Klan. Their single 'Holidays in Asia' is a bastardization of Cliff Richard's 'Summer Holiday' and the Sex Pistols' 'Holidays in the Sun'. Other Bhangra titles recall earlier moments of rock history, such as the 1992 album titles *Never Mind the Dolaks* and *Bomb the Tumbi* from Satrang and Safri Boys respectively, playing on the Sex Pistols *Never Mind the Bollocks* album and on the name of chart dance-outfit Bomb the Bass by substituting the names of two Indian music instruments. This dem-onstrates conversely the way in which Asian pop can be seen assuming its place at the heart of pop music in Britain rather than at the periphery only to be 'othered' by the media. The cultural producers and receivers of Asian pop do not operate in a vacuum.

SMASHING STEREOTYPES 2: SISTAS ARE DOING IT FOR THEMSELVES

If Asians have long been the 'invisible community' in British academic and popular discourse, an important invisible sub-community is Asian women. The several Asian women DJs, band members and singers – and, of course, audience members – have been largely ignored despite a slew of journalistic accounts of 'women in rock' published in 1995 (Raphael, K. O'Brien, L. O'Brien and Evans).[6] Unsurprisingly gender has not been uppermost in the few analyses of Bhangra that exist, although, perhaps surprisingly, many of those centrally involved in the scene have been women. Outside Bhangra, artists such as Sonya Aurora-

Madan of Echobelly and Anjali Bhatia of the Voodoo Queens have been outspoken on the subject of Asian women in rock.

As well as Radical Sista (see Chapter 4), a prominent figure on the London club scene is DJ Ritu, who also broadcasts on radio on the London station Kiss FM and the BBC World Service. In an interview with her, it became clear that Asianness is not her only component. For female Asians, there is the added expectation of traditional role play.

> *RH*:   Does it make it worse that you're something of a pioneer, voyaging into uncharted waters?
>
> *Ritu*:   I think some people expect a lot of you, other people just appreciate what you do. I think it's hard being the first one, or one of the first ones because I think you can end up taking that much more shit. The amount of shit I've had from men Asian DJs or Asian male promoters.... I couldn't begin to go into it because it's not very pleasant. It's really hard to actually keep motivating yourself that you're even any good at what you do when people are constantly telling you that you're not or not booking you ... me being me I assume it's because I'm crap. The other disadvantage of being a pioneer is I suppose there are people who will pick up on you in terms of the novelty aspect so it kind of balances out in the end but yeah it certainly has its frustrating moments.
>
> *RH*:   How representative are you then of Asian women?
>
> *Ritu*:   I think change is very slow. It's not as we would like it to be. It's certainly not as fast as I would like it to be and I'm fully agreed that there are too many women that have very few choices in terms of their personal freedom, in terms of their professional freedom, in terms of any kind of freedom. I think 'what a waste' because there's so many Asian women out there that must be talented or skilled at this, that and the other. Their contribution to society is basically ruled out because they're at home giving birth to the children. That has started to change and there are more and more Asian women starting to come through. For those of us who are already emancipated and can be kind of out at two o'clock in the morning out at a club night and in my case and your case working at it, I think it's important that we recognize what power I suppose we have and use it to its best effect. If we can enable other people, even if it means appearing on a radio programme or a TV programme or whatever, just by the virtue of being there as a role model, that in itself is something.

Anjali Bhatia is the lead singer with the all-girl punk band the Voodoo Queens, an outfit that musically has more in common with 1970s punks X-Ray Specs than Apache Indian, and was initially labelled as part of the short-lived, US-imported, riot grrrl trend, based on abrasive female guitar rock. She too accepts the notion of a burden of representation, and claims that this is accentuated by being an Asian female via the cliché of east-meets-west 'exoticness'.

VOODOO QUEENS

RH: How would you describe the Voodoo Queens?

Anjali: When we first started out we were very pigeonholed. Talking about the press is I think wasting time but I think it has to be said, if you're asking a question like that, that they took up on the fact that 'hey they're Asians, women as well, what a brilliant press angle' so they just hyped us up to that, one as being Asians and one as being riot grrrls. I think it's detrimental to be pigeonholed and I think the press is very racist and sexist as well.

RH: So there's a difference between what you are and how you've been portrayed?

Anjali: I find it sort of an insult, to be a fad. To be Asian is a sort of fashionable thing now whereas when I was growing up it wasn't fashionable to be Asian. I was being called Paki every day. You should know. You get abused for being Asian and suddenly, like, Asian women are the new thing. Even modelling agencies are looking for Asian women as the new cool. I just find that an absolute insult. We've been around for a long time and now they've just discovered that Asian people are cool.

RH: Do you think that the Voodoo Queens could turn into role models for people growing up now?

Anjali: I'm not really into role models myself. I think everyone should aspire to be no one but themself, but no we have had a lot of fan letters and things from young Asian girls. Before, putting on a guitar was totally alien to them. It's great.

RH: Isn't your audience all made up of white indie kids though?

Anjali: Erm, most of it is, yeah. I mean, of course, there's always a few Asians in there but its always like 'spot the Asian,', you know 'token Asian'. There's a few more than before. I think people tend to think that if you're Asian you only like Bhangra which is again a real pain because once again that's pigeonholing people too.

Perhaps the female Asian performer most eager to distance herself from the common associations with Bhangra was Echobelly's lead singer, Sonya Aurora-Madan, who described the intense media pressure of living up to the media hype:

Sonya: Everyone expects me to be this Asian-female-escaped-from-an-arranged-marriage freak.

RH: What do you reckon of Bhangra?

Sonya: I grew up listening to Blondie and the Jam. I've never been into Bhangra in my life.

Since this interview, Echobelly's straightforward drums/bass/guitar pop has catapulted them into the public eye on *Top of the Pops*. Aurora-Madan has since stopped doing interviews with the Asian press on principle, signalling a desire to be evaluated in purely musical terms rather than for ethnicity.

CONSCIOUS KOOL: THIS IS WHERE IT'S AT

Claims that the beginning of the end is nigh for Bhangra events were being made as early as the first academic article that the subject merited in the UK. Citing the four coinciding and consequently poorly attended Bhangra shows staged in central London at Christmas 1987, Baumann wrote of 'an acute sense of crisis... shared by the most astute observers of the Bhangra scene' (Baumann 1990: 146–7). Shows such as February 1994's 'Valentines Bhang (*sic*) all-nighter' in Ilford, east London were promising much: live bands, DJs, spectacular fashion show; but they often fell short at the delivery stakes with shows half full as the optimist would put it, or more pessimistically half empty. The specialist press and mainstream media had additionally reported the incidence of violence at concerts.

Media attention switched focus with the advent of so-called Asian Kool. In November 1994 a 'special issue' of *Time* magazine addressing, fittingly enough, 'the state of the planet' featured Bally Sagoo. 'Sagoo's records and tapes', readers were informed 'are a fixture of the "New Asian Kool" – the name for the hip Anglo-Asian club scene.' *Time* is not renowned for its youth culture commentary but here, as in earlier cases, it was fulfilling the classic function of media-as-gatekeeper. By mid-1995 a number of Asian clubs were emerging in London, setting themselves up as noticeably and deliberately fashionable. They were almost elitist establishments, making an explicit effort to distance and indeed disassociate themselves from the perceived 'naff' Bhangra nights that had taken place before them. After the first wave of 1980s all-dayers and the later large-scale Bhangra nights of the early 1990s (Bombay Jungle etc.), these clubs can be seen as a further mutation of South Asian popular culture. Mohabhat at the Watermans arts centre in west London, for example, set itself up as a club to appeal to the 'older crowd'. Outcaste, lauched in June 1995, was both a club for style-conscious Asian youth and a record label of the same name specializing in the types of music exemplified by the 'beyond Bhangra' sound. This club was in the smart West End rather than tucked away in east London Asian ghettos. 'Forget Brick Lane curries, trust-fund hippies and sitar players thwacking away through the East End night; London's Asian scene is about to take a sharp left turn,' the *Independent* had promised. Outcaste's aim was to be a 'trendy' Asian club. The Independent claimed that Outcaste 'hopes to give Asian bright young things the kind of profile currently reserved for Black music culture'. Listings magazine *Time Out* rated it the evening's essential event.

Many of those I interviewed on the night reiterated the claim of not being particularly fond of Bhangra. They included the principal organizer, 26-year-old Vikas:

RH: What's your function in all of this?

Vikas: I'm just running the club basically. I organized the club for Outcaste. Outcaste is this new label. You can see [motions to packed dancefloor], you can hear for yourself what the label is. You can feel the vibe. You can see the vibe: Asian, white, black, straight, gay, everyone's here. This is new stuff. This is where it's at basically.

RH: Were you there from the Bhangra days?

Vikas: No. I was never. I've never been into Bhangra. I've never understood it.

RH: What about this term, the new Asian Kool?

Vikas: I haven't heard it.

The club represented a departure from old-style Bhangra: the venue's lay-out – tables and chairs around a dancing area, lower-level sofas and Eastern fabrics adorning the walls – created a 'civilized' impression. Those present included the Asian glitterati out in force.

Parallels were drawn with Acid Jazz (*Guardian*, 30 August 1995), the label that spawned a genre: 'The feeling of pioneering enthusiasm around the collective convinces that Outcaste can make the same kind of cultural and musical impact for this marginalized section of British creativity': once again, Asian initiatives were described in terms of white antecedents. The organizers, however, emphatically rejected Bhangra comparisons. Its timing, in the same Tuesday-night slot as the Wag club's Hot 'n Spicy night, demonstrated the unwillingness of large West End club owners to surrender prime time (Friday, Saturday night) to what was seen as marginal tastes. Ritu told the *Guardian* (30 August 1995): 'the crowd here is considerably different [to Hot 'n Spicy/ Bombay Jungle]. We don't get requests for Bhangra in here. It's about hybrid fusion, mixing Asian elements with hip-hop and jungle beats. The club and label are really innovative.' Both Vikas and DJ Ritu confirmed Outcaste's remit:

RH: Was there a conscious effort to move away from the traditional Bhangra do?

Vikas: Totally, of course.

RH: Isn't a lot of it just the appropriation of black models of popular culture, though?

Ritu: One of the reasons why we set up Outcaste, the record label, was very much for that reason. One of the reasons was we could see that it was cool for Asians, Cypriots and white kids to be down with the black, be down with Afro-Caribbean culture in terms of music, language, dress style, everything, and one of the things I said to Shabs before we started the label was 'wouldn't it be nice to see a day where it'd be cool to be down with the Asian?' I think the music has an awful lot to do with it. It's broken down barriers. It's given us predominant street style, credibility. I would hope that with our label we could push the music out to different markets, bigger markets, and create new forms and styles of music that encompass being Asian and being British and maybe it will be cool one day to be down with the Asians too.

CONCLUSION

It is a mistake automatically to assume that all Asian youth will somehow be adherents of Bhangra, be it of Punjabi folk-dance tunes or their nineties legacy. As Annirudha Das of Asian Dub Foundation told the pop weekly newssheet *Melody Maker*, 'Just because of our skin colour it doesn't mean we have to be into Bhangra' (22 April 1995). Similarly the audience of a Cornershop or Voodoo Queens gig will be largely white. Within the category of 'Asian Kool', a number of noticeable changes can be determined. The more recent wave of clubs including Outcaste, can be described as 'conscious kool', established to destroy old stereotypes of Asians shipwrecked on 'uncool island'. Such negative stereotypes will not evaporate overnight, but 'Asian Kool' should go some way to erode them as long as the new groups' readiness to distance themselves from Bhangra does not blind them to their audiences and to their own stated intentions. It must be borne in mind that Bhangra takes on a number of forms – un-kool Bhangra being just one of those.

Bhangra music and all its derivatives have demonstrated a longevity in British pop music; it has outlived many of its Western counterparts since its initial emergence in the mid-1980s. Possibilities of mainstream market penetration present further avenues for commercial opportunism. The argument that all youth culture ultimately submits to the processes of capitalism and market forces has been made throughout its post-1945 history. Much attention has been focused on the alternative economic systems that support the manufacture and distribution of Bhangra cassettes (e.g. Baumann 1990). However by the mid-1990s more concerted efforts at a mainstream crossover were noticeable. First, Apache Indian was signed to Island Records, then Bally Sagoo went to Columbia in a widely reported £1.2 million deal (*Observer*, 7 August 1994). Meanwhile Multitone, one of the leading labels in the field, had been licensed to RCA Records, part of the multinational BMG group. Asian Dub Foundation's John Pandit told me:

> The music industry is so important for British capitalism that they need to compartmentalize everything. They have their own markets like the gay market, the pink pound. Now there's the rupee pound, a new Asian audience. It's the history of Western imperialism: Let's talk about exotic Asians.

i-D Magazine also made the point: 'Of late, [Bhangra] has begun to seep into the mainstream pop world, where it's a new wrinkle to a business forever seeking something different, devouring 'exotic genres' like a starving dog in a butcher's shop.' Was this, then, another great rock'n'roll swindle in the making? Despite efforts to mine this untapped source, as yet (1996) Bhangra still does not appear to have set the charts alight. Perhaps part of the problem is that Asian music buyers prefer spending £2 on a tape locally to taking a trip into town to a megastore to part with £15 for a CD.

Writing on the World Wide Web Bhangra page (1995), Cynthia Rose declared, 'What began as a flourishing tape culture has now exploded.' Indeed, Bhangra goes far beyond simply recorded music to be played in the home. By 1995 there were at least ten different UK radio shows exclusively devoted to playing it, ranging from 'Ghetto-blasting' on BBC Scotland to 'Bhangra in Beds' on BBC Three Counties serving the southern England shires. These programmes, interlopers on the mainstream radio stations, are only part of the story; coexisting alongside them are the 'franchised' Asian community radio stations made possible by the deregulatory 1991 Broadcasting Act.[7] More broadcasting space was opened up to settlers from the Indian subcontinent with the launch of cable and satellite services such as Zee TV.

Just as the study of youth is often framed in problem-solving terms, Asian youth are forever examined through the prism of race and racism – the recipients for example of 'Paki-bashing' (Mungham and Pearson 1976) – constantly caught between two cultures or suffering multiple identity crises. Asian identity is now, however, more acceptable and more recognized than ever before. Young Asians are in a stronger position to assert themselves positively in ways previously unavailable. Awan (1994) claims that 'young Asians are much more interested these days in breaking into the mainstream market by producing a sound that appeals outside the Asian community without altogether abandoning their Asian identity'. Perhaps the most critical lesson to be drawn from the burgeoning new Asian forms is that they collectively demonstrate that Asian youth are staking out new territories on the (sub)cultural landscape of 1990s Britain and claiming them as their own – devoid of the baggage of cross-cultural crisis. The fiction of the 'passive Asian' stereotype, an extension of the largely middle-class phenomenon of the 'academically achieving Asian', was further undermined in the public eye in June 1995 when young Asians 'rioted' on the streets of Bradford, Yorkshire (a subsequent review showed that the disturbances were provoked by police, though no disciplinary action was taken beyond 're-education' of one officer – *Guardian*, 11 April 1996). Perceptively reflecting on media marketing, ADF's John Pandit told me at the time, 'There is no Asian kool. The only new Asian kool that's happening is in Manningham, Bradford [district of the disturbances]'.

Until Apache Indian's success of 1993, the nearest to an Asian presence in the charts was Monsoon's quasi-Indian-flavoured novelty hit of 1982 'Ever So Lonely'. By 1996 an Asian had been number one.[8] In many respects Bhangra has moved on, but then again this is hardly surprising. Some elements of current Asian club culture may represent something of an elite – the 'I've never liked Bhangra' chorus of conscious kool – but in the meantime other musical developments have occurred such as the rise of non-Bhangra pop. These two strands can be twinned together in a new phase of pop that is 'beyond Bhangra'. Yet, for sure, Bhangra will remain one of the fragments, one of the many, many (di)versions, through which youth culture manifests itself in the current period.

In the late twentieth century, ethnicity was being used as never before in popular culture. Multicultural babies were being used to sell multi-coloured co-ordinates (United Colours of Benetton) while Michael Jackson assured the world that 'it doesn't matter if you're black or white.' At a time when the mainstream charts were dominated by the Britpop trend, reheating old sixties/seventies leftovers with its whiter-than-white selective amnesia view of pop history, Bhangra and its spin-offs, involving Rap, Ragga and Jungle, reflect the diversities that Blur, Oasis and Pulp deny. *The Times*'s David Toop mused of Bhangramuffin, 'few could have imagined the latest of these unlikely collisions since it seems to cut right across the tight racial divides of inner-city Britain' (15 January 1993). Britpop bleaches away all traces of black influences in music in a mythical imagined past of olde England as it never was, whereas Beyond Bhangra and Jungle are rooted in the urban reality of today's Britain. It's village green versus concrete jungle and we know where we'd rather be.

NOTES

1. Examples include Bhangramuffin, combining Bhangra with reggae-derived ragga music (see 'Birthrights: Crossing the Tracks', BBC2, 2 August 1993; *i-D Magazine*, April 1993). Angela McRobbie calls Ragga 'The fiercest reference point in contemporary youth subcultures. It conveys an uncompromising sense of blackness.... This moral panic has made ragga all the more attractive to young

people, and it has also been taken up by young Asians (raggastanis or Bhangramuffins) and also by white girls.' More recently this has been superseded by what Cynthia Rose has called 'bhangle' (World Wide Web Bhangra page): 'Asian music has a whole new focus: marrying the jungalist theme (cutting percussive beats and break-beats so fast they trip each other) to Hindi, Punjabi and ragga rhythms' (McRobbie 1994: 183).

2. The film opens with the memorable spectacle of the director dressed in salwaar kameez and a leather jacket walking a bulldog (a breed with particular associations as the epitome of ultra-right-wing notions of Britishness) down Southall Broadway.

3. Apache Indian, for example, managed to turn his treatment as quasi-royalty in the Indian subcontinent into a UK television series.

4. 'I think it's an intervention in the way culture is breaking up because I think it says "it's legitimate to do this", legitimate to mix and match, to cut and blend things. More than that it shows that's what the future of this country has to be. It's not a matter of debating whether or not we should allow this' (Paul Gilroy, 'Birthrights').

5. Following the video release of Chadha's feature film *Bhaji on the Beach*, several Asian video stores refused to stock the title which was accused of depicting British Asians in a poor light. There were also protests outside cinemas by some conservative elements and the Indian High Commission received a number of complaints. Kureshi's television adaptation of *The Buddha of Suburbia* elicited a large number of complaints to the BBC for supposedly gratuitous sex scenes.

6. Sonya Aurora-Madan was interviewed in both Raphael and Evans. Kate O'Brien included an interview with Sheila Chandra.

7. Such as Sunrise Radio and Spectrum Radio in Greater London.

8. January 1996 saw Britain's first Asian at number one in Babylon Zoo's 'Spaceman'. Lead singer Jas Mann's Asian background gave rise to tabloid headlines such as 'Sari girls, he's still a virgin'. Formerly he played in the Midlands indie band Sandkings. The *Guardian* commented (2 February 1996): 'Early eighties fusion outfit Monsoon, fronted by Sheila Chandra, and Bhangramuffin hitman Apache Indian were both restricted in mainstream terms because others were unable to separate their ethnicity from their artistry. Mann's good fortune is that he 'happened' before that constriction could be applied.' Not long after, the Kaliphz offered a duet with Yorkshire Asian boxer Prince Naseem Hamed which charted, resulting in their memorable *Top of the Pops* appearance with this boxing-for-Britain new hero/curio for a new generation.

4

RE-MIXING IDENTITIES:

'OFF' THE TURN-TABLE

Shirin Housee and Mukhtar Dar talk to Bally Sagoo and Radical Sista

Much talk about the hybridity of cultures and transnational cultural exchanges has occupied cultural commentators in the 1990s. In a discussion conducted in August 1995, Shirin Housee and Mukhtar Dar talked to Asian dance music producer Bally Sagoo, recently signed to Columbia Records, and Radical Sista (Ranjit Kaur), one of the more successful Asian female DJs in the country. Together, they explored some of the issues of how the crossing of boundaries and constant re-making of identities takes place on the dancefloor within the context of contemporary multi-racist Britain. In particular, the interview also examined the practices of the music industry and issues of entry into the mainstream, and looked towards future developments in Asian dance music inside Britain, and more widely.

Shirin Let's start with a conventional but very important question, which is about how you choose to locate your 'origins', since this is a significant issue when we begin to think through questions of identity, belonging and artistic production. What do you think led you to the position you are in now? Your background and the role of music in your life and the ways you think your family background has informed you musically?

Bally I've been brought up here in this town [Birmingham] even though I was actually born in India, in Delhi. We emigrated in 1964 ... and we were one of the first Asian families to set up in Birmingham. My father was in one of the first ever Indian bands in this country, way back in the early sixties. What they used to do was film tunes, and they were like the Shadows, there were four guys with these black suits and black ties. Obviously that was the era they were in, it was the way they were thinking and the way they were dressing. There's a record sleeve that's worth seeing, they looked like the Beatles – they were called the Musafirs. Some people will know about their tunes, like your parents, those kind of people, and they'd do famous film tunes on accordions and things, so music has always been in my family really.

My mother is a priest in the temple, she's doing shabads and gurbani all the time. She's very religious. She plays the harmonium all day long, so knocking about around the house all the time is the keyboard, which excited me when I was a kid. I used to play the harmonium, and copy people; if I used to see people playing a tune I could pick it up very quick and then I'd start playing it. In our house there was always Hindi and Punjabi music, all this was the background that has influenced me today.

Mukhtar Ranjit, Can you tell us a little to start off with about your background, where your parents came from, whether you were born here or born back in the subcontinent; what kind of things were happening at the time? Was there a strong influence of music in your background too?

Ranjit Well, I was born in 1969 in Huddersfield, a town in the North of England, and my parents are both from the Punjab in India. When I was young I spent most of my life, literally every day of the week, listening to pop music, you know stuff like that. I used to watch my dad with a group of guys do dancing and stuff. That was my first real taste of Bhangra, as it were, but I wasn't really into it then. I liked the dancing but I didn't like the Asian music.

Shirin Why do you think you didn't like it?

Ranjit it was really old and staid for me. It was really old-style Bhangra and you know we didn't relate to it 'cos it wasn't ours, do you know what I mean? It clashed with the influences I had in my teen years when I was listening to Punk and Disco, and stuff from the era of Gloria Gaynor. I really loved that and I never listened to Asian music much at all, until I was about fifteen.

Mukhtar What do you feel changed?

Ranjit I started listening to Lata Mangeshka at home and I thought, 'this is quite funky, this is all right', and developed a real taste for it. That was 1986, that was when the daytime dos started as well. I liked daytime gigs and stuff but they weren't Bhangra then, they were like folk parties. So I used to go to them and to college gigs and stuff. We didn't have Bhangra then, no one used to play it, so I used to dance to Funk and Hip-Hop and Breakdance. Breakdance was the thing that came out and really changed my life, I loved it. Then Bhangra slowly started coming in and some DJs started playing that at gigs.

Bally   I used to go to Handsworth College in Birmingham and I was hanging around with a very heavy Reggae crowd, as well as an Electro crowd, 'cos back in the early eighties really Electro was so big. It played a very important part in the way I was brought up. Break-dancing and all this was around and so I was really heavily into that, completely forgetting about the Asian roots and culture.

Shirin   What do you mean by this? Did the Reggae scene get you interested in your 'own background'?

Bally   Well not right then; Indian music was Indian music. So I just left that side of things and I moved into the Western side of things and I was getting into English and American music. I was spending a lot of money on American imports.

I was a typical example of someone who didn't know what Asian people were about. I was too much into the Western society business. My friends were mainly black and I didn't have many Asian mates because of, talking fifteen years ago you know, we didn't have funky Asian music, you know... Asian music was the kind of gushy records that my dad plays at home, that are just crackling and you can't hear the vocals, there is no drum beat and it's always got this dramatic string drawn all over it, and I'm like, 'I can't relate to that'. I'm watching *Top of the Pops* 'cos that show is the in thing. I want that music and I want to hear those records that I'm listening to in the clubs. I wanted that kind of beat, but I was completely forgetting about Asianness. Then all of a sudden things just changed, I just got so much into it and my mates were like 'my god Bally Sagoo's doing Indian music'. They couldn't believe it, it was like the talk of the town, 'cos I was so much heavily into black music. But I'm glad I went through that stage 'cos that's why I can make my music.

Ranjit   You appreciate it, having gone through that...

Shirin   When you say 'Western side of things' what do you mean?

Bally   Back in 1980, I remember messing around with early records like the Afrika Bambata stuff and the Soul Sonic Force and those kind of tunes 'cos my record collection today is a full room of those Electro tunes. I'm glad that I was around in that era 'cos they form a great influence on my thinking my kind of production today. Hence the reason I can make a track sound very appealing to all sorts of crowds is because I've lived that era. I've had that kind of music upbringing. About six years ago, I decided to make Indian music sound funky like the kind of tunes that I was playing and listening to in clubs. And I think it was popular because everybody wanted this flavour of 'East and West' in a heavy way.

Mukhtar   So in some ways there was a vacuum when you were growing up and listening to Soul, Funk, Reggae and those kind of tunes. Asian Bhangra groups, like Heera, were only doing the wedding circuits, and then along came a massive young Asian population looking for something they could relate to, so this Bhangra scene exploded with daytime discos.

Ranjit   Right. At that time, in the mid to late 1980s, there was a large increase in Asians, especially going to college, before then they weren't encouraged – guys were, but girls weren't. Girls were encouraged to stay at home, learn how to cook and get married. It's back down to the traditions and it's slowly moving out of that and developing an Asian-Western kind of lifestyle. So there were more Asian women at college and they were going to the daytime gigs. As a natural development from that, they went to universities and these same kids were saying, 'What wicked times, but there's nothing afterwards.' Some of the promoters, the new ones, started off as students spending next term's grant money to put on a Bhangra gig on a night, and that's how it all started. There was a whole scene evolving from the mid-1980s onward. Now it's really established.

Bally   In the 1980s when Bhangra really hit off there were groups like Alaap on the circuit, the Pardesis and the Prem Naraj. The ball was mainly in London anyway and everyone was all excited about this thing all of a sudden, it was a new craze these Bhangra gigs, and there was a massive community of Asian people clubbing together all of a sudden. You were getting clubs purely for Asian gigs, which was exciting for us 'cos we'd never had that before. The bands were getting so popular and in demand that they now played day and night.

Mukhtar   Describe the scene at these places; what was going on? While we needed our own spaces, these Bhangra dos weren't always fun. There was also friction taking place, with Asian parents saying,

'Our kids are going to discos and in those discos there's a lot of tension between the guys, fighting each other and stuff.'

Bally   Obviously it did cause problems 'cos kids were wagging school and pretending they'd gone to school and instead they were clubbing and the parents were going wild. It started getting out of hand, with gang fights and drinking and things. But I think wherever there is alcohol, you will always get that kind of problem. And Asian people are famous for drinking and fighting too, you know. Bhangra then was something totally new, but now it's no big deal.

Shirin   How did *you* feel about the club scene back then, Ranjit?

Ranjit   When I went to my first Bhangra concert I had to sneak out and I think I was one of four girls in a hall of about six or seven hundred guys. Boy did I have hassle man, big time. I was really lucky 'cos I went with my cousin and he stayed with me all night and I just said, 'Don't leave me, man, whatever you do don't leave me.' I made sure he stood next to me all night. It was scary, they were all leering and I was getting hassled because I was standing near the front. One guy was singing to me and I was going 'Go away, please, creep.' So I had all these guys chasing me about because I happened to be there. It was kind of like 'Well, she must be a loose woman because she's here.' Or 'She's run away from home and that's why she's here 'cos there's no way her parents would've let her out.' Which is right, 'cos I did sneak out but, I sneaked out with my cousin, you know what I mean? It was that kind of attitude, that was 1986 and I've had to kind of fight it all the time, I did that for about four years, but wherever I went I made sure that I was always with somebody that I knew, no matter what...

Later on, because it got so popular the elders in the community got really concerned, and they were having meetings at the mosque and gurdwara talking about how they were going to stop this, blah blah blah. They'd spend a lot of time standing outside the gigs with cameras. I used to be really cheeky 'cos I'd go up and say, 'Are you all right?' and I just used to walk inside. I remember one guy, he looked at me and said 'it's all right 'cos she's a Sikh' 'cos he saw my kara and I thought, 'Right it's acceptable for Sikh women to go there 'cos it's Punjabi music that's playing, you're allowed to drink etcetera.' A lot of assumptions were being made and I thought what a cheeky thing because it doesn't matter what you are, if you want to go in you should be allowed to go in. When I started to DJ I used to make a lot of noise about it.

Bally   If you want to be involved in music, you have to be involved in the whole environment, the whole shabam that goes with it. It's like saying, 'I want to be an actor but I can't go in front of the camera.' If you're going to be involved in this kind of stuff, part of the package is – and this is most important – the audience. So you are going to get arseholes as well as good crowds, you will always get some idiots that want to spoil it. You have to accept it.

Shirin   What was the good side of Bhangra?

Ranjit   I remember the best buzz was when I was playing Bhangra music to two hundred white kids in Liverpool, they loved it, they listened to it for about two and a half hours. One of the women from *Brookside* [the TV soap serial] came in and said [puts on a Liverpudlian accent], 'Ay ay, this is brilliant, what is it?' I said, 'It's Bhangra.' She said, 'It's wicked,' and walked off. We're getting there slowly.

Shirin   Moving on from the 1980s, do you think Bhangra has lost its original impact and popularity?

Bally   Yes, definitely, the Bhangra scene has gone stale now. All of a sudden there's a massive fusion of Hindi songs coming out now and everyone is jumping onto a different bandwagon and traditional bands are struggling. Even on the wedding scene now, DJs are more popular than live bands. Both because the live bands charge a lot of money and people can't afford that kind of money. You can get a DJ to play any kind of record any time which sounds as good as the original recording.

Shirin   You'd have to say that, though, wouldn't you?! But this brings me more specifically to the point about your particular career development, Ranjit. How did you get into DJing?

Ranjit   At the daytime gigs I had a really good time and used to muck around on the decks. Not with the intention of being a DJ, but just 'cos it was fun, it was nice, and to get enough respect from my friends… I went to a conference in Leicester, came across a record shop that sold Bhangra records and came out with about £300 worth of tunes. I thought 'Shit, what am I going to do with this now?' Then I started DJing – it was purely by accident.

Shirin   How did your family take to you being a DJ? After all, this certainly breaks the conventional stereotypes, from all perspectives, of what young Asian women do.

Ranjit Well, on the family front it was kind of like, 'We've lost her now, we've lost her to the world of music. She's gone. No one's going to marry her,' all that kind of thing. Marriage ratings have gone down, extended family dismayed. But if I'd wanted to get married then I would've ten years ago, so leave me alone. Slowly they came round and slowly it got easier. But when I was in the clubs and stuff I still used to get a lot of attitude from men 'cos I was the only Asian woman, in fact I was the only woman full stop, apart from those who worked behind the bar.

When I first came home and said to my mum that I was going to start a radio show, she just looked at me and said 'OK.' She was cool about it, 'cos I wasn't out in public, all people could do was hear my voice so that was all right and kind of low-key. But when she was told I was going to go to Maestros and DJ she freaked. She chased me round the house with a rolling pin! Calling me all of kinds of stuff. Then after a week of absolute silence and the doghouse, she spoke to me and said, 'Are you going to do it?' and I said, 'Yeah, I am.' I'm very stubborn and if I want to do something... so, she wasn't happy about it, but she didn't stop me from doing it. Then, about a year later at the engagement party of one of my cousins, I was DJing while she was sitting in the audience, and when I finished she said, 'Is that all you do?' I said, 'Yes, I just play records.' She started taking bookings for me then, and telling everybody what I did. Even my Grandma found out that day.

Bally It's the same with me... It's funny how attitudes change though; all of a sudden if you start doing something and it's worth it. I've been through the hard times when my parents screamed at me for buying records and not becoming a doctor or a lawyer like my next-door neighbour. 'What are you buying double records for?' They couldn't understand it, 'Why have you got two record-players when most people have one record-player?'

But now they realize what I'm doing and now it's good, 'cos it's like: 'Do you know who my son is?' whereas before they were ashamed. I'd come out of college with no qualifications, driving down the road full blast with my music on. It's the impression you give. I don't blame my parents for saying [hushed], 'My God, there's my son', but now it's [loud] 'There's my son guys!'

Shirin Ranjit, do you think that things have changed for you too? Have the whole family accepted your career?

Ranjit   Yes, 'cos it was really working. Like my grandma was saying, 'Hey, this is really good' and she started listening to my radio show which was nice. Once I DJed at a mela in Huddersfield, it was the first mela that they'd had and family from all over the place came to see me. They were all in one corner going 'bhurra bhurra'. I looked up and all the women of the family were there cheering me on. They made a real special effort to bring other members of the family.

Shirin   Aside from the dilemmas of family life, how have other spheres of society come to terms with you as a women being involved with DJing. What do the men do? How do they react? It's not a usual thing, there's only really you and DJ Ritu out there.

Ranjit   At the beginning when I first started, it was kind of like a novelty thing, it was like, 'She's got to have a boyfriend that DJs or something and she's learnt it.' I used to get really annoyed when I was classed as 'the DJ's girlfriend' when I got to the door. The guys on the door would be like, 'Where's the DJ?' They thought I was winding them up.

Bally   I know a couple of the Indian girl singers and they always say the same thing... but I think you have to expect that because you don't get hundreds of girls on stage. We don't get hundreds of girl DJs. If you get more girls doing DJing it won't be such a big deal. I mean it might be now because we don't see an Indian girl playing records and stuff... [to Ranjit] You had to go through that struggle to put it where it is now...

Ranjit   I had to really fight with them...

Bally   ...because, like you said, no one was doing it. If you didn't do it, no one was doing it.

Ranjit   Nobody did it.

Shirin   Do you think it's easier now for women?

Ranjit   Definitely... because when I first started at Maestros I got a lot of hassle there and that was like in 1990. Now there's more girls that go to that club than guys. Today when I go to clubs I can guarantee that not one guy will hassle me. Its because they all know who I am and they also know that if they do anything the other guys in the club, whether they know me or not, will not stand for it. Because it lets down the whole community, do you know what I mean? We've been through that phase of guys fighting over girls and guys getting into drunken brawls; like: 'you're taking our Sikh girls' and 'you're taking our Muslim girls', 'you're doing this' and 'you're doing that' and the 'Shere-Punjab' and all that kind of stuff that happened years ago. We've kicked that out, we've managed to get rid of it. Hopefully it won't come back, but there's no guarantee so we have to constantly challenge any kind of attitude like that.

The promoters are better as well. When women go in and the promoters see guys hassling women or someone, the promoters jump on the guys and say 'pack it in'. I had one guy, dancing right next to me, really close, last year, and he was really winding me up, I just slapped him and he fell on the floor. When he got up he was going 'Kuthi, Kuthi, you bitch, I'm going to kill you' and I was getting really angry and I was saying, 'Not if I kill you first!' and the security guard had to drag me away from him because I was getting so angry and there were all these other girls behind me waiting to beat the shit out of him. So the girls are saying, 'We're going to come here and have a good time, we're going to come out with our sisters and we're going to have fun just like you guys. If you hassle us we're going to kill you. We ain't taking it anymore.'

That's why now, it's kind of like fifty–fifty when you go to clubs. Even at night time 'cos the student scene is so big and most of the girls that go out now are at the university and stuff... or people that have had to fight really hard to get out of the house. I had to constantly fight, even now, if I know I'm going to be away for about a month it's like 'please mum, don't give me a hard time, I have to go', stuff like that. But we have to constantly work at it. It's better for me and it's better for everybody 'cos if we develop some kind of a scene then it's easier for others to follow.

Shirin You both seem to say that the scene at clubs has certainly changed, and for the better, particularly for women. What about in terms of changes in the music itself?

Ranjit Well, most of the time I play to young kids in clubs whether it's the daytime parties or the Bhangra at night. When I play to a mostly white audience, like when I've played the Mambo in London or the Bass Clef or various places like that, I've played a lot of remixes 'cos they tend to relate to that better than they do to traditional stuff. But, in the mixed club environment, I play predominantly Asian, and I can mix both quite happily and get a good reaction.

Mukhtar   Bally, you said somewhere how one of the things you wanted to do was, in some ways, to Westernize the music. Did you feel that the kind of music being played by bands like Alaap and that, that they were very much rooted back in the subcontinent, that the lyrics were desi, and that whilst people were dancing to it, their own life experiences of growing up here weren't really reflected?

Bally   Well, yes. I'm saying to people that the reason I want to make my music sound like this is because the stuff that the traditional bands were doing was talking about their days and the way they were growing up. Every single song was always on a similar line, and based on this typical boy-meets-girl song. They've always got to have loads of '*hoi*'s in there, and so on. Like most of the Western youth, Asian kids brought up here also wanted the punchy, racy bass lines, the great drum beat and the powerful female vocals coming across. I wanted to hear, probably, more melodies than lyrics. I just wanted a good beat and a good vibe, a good song on the dancefloor. Because, obviously, that's what makes everybody get up and dance.

Shirin   Why do you think these remixes are so popular?

Bally   Because we never had that before, Asian people had Asian music or we had Western music. We could never compete with the Western market because their music was so much upfront. That's why people like myself, Indian producers, Asian producers who started making that kind of a tune, started getting Asian people back into the Asian music. Now people listen to the traditional as well as Western/Asian music. The best thing that I get is parents saying to me at least sons and daughters are listening to some Asian music, because before they didn't, etcetera, etctera. I'm the new proof of it. I listen to a lot of Indian music now and it's booming out my car and I wasn't before. Now the music is sounding the way I want it to sound.

Shirin   I think the pride issue is really important. Particularly with the youth. I remember growing up as an Asian kid in the 1970s. I'm a bit older than you, but I used to listen to Reggae and my parents couldn't understand it. I'm from Mauritius which makes it even more complicated, because we came out from India about three or four generations ago, so the only thing that I was exposed to that wasn't Western was Hindi film songs, and my parents were trying to shelter me from too much Westernization. When I was about eighteen or nineteen it was Reggae that I would listen to. I saw that as different to

English or Western music. I know if I was growing up now I'd say, 'Well there's Reggae and that's still good, but now there's something else' and I think it's important to have that pride in Asian communities. It speaks a language whether you're from Mauritius, Pakistan, India and so on.

Bally Now, music today is influenced by Western as well as the traditional Asian styles. I don't go with the people who say you shouldn't tamper with Indian music. I want to know who makes up the law about how music should sound? Why can't you have hundreds of different styles? Imagine going into HMV and having only one style of music. You want to be able to have hundreds of styles for every kind of listener, because this is the way we'll open Asian styles out into the Western market and out to the world masses – because some people don't like traditional music, some people do like traditional music and vice versa. So why not cater for all of them? This is where I stepped in and obviously hit on to something big, hence the reason why I've done so many albums and got a deal with Columbia and stuff, they want to hear something like this, the mixing of 'East and West'.

Mukhtar Why do you think they want these kind of music mixes?

Bally It's new, it's exciting, it's refreshing and people are sick of hearing the same old crap over and over again. Before you were embarrassed to blast an Asian tune in your car 'cos the people were looking, and now you want to blast that tune out and show people, say 'listen to this beat line' and 'listen to this track'. You know, I had to wind up the windows when I was blasting an Indian track a few years ago because it was, 'What's that sound?' Now it's like 'Wow, what's that sound?'

Mukhtar You were saying that most of your music originates from your life in Britain. Having grown up here you saw something lacking in the 'traditional music' and that you could produce more funky Asian music here. But there is a long history of very rich expertise in producing music in India, by people who are best placed to produce it. Often the music in Hindi films was better than the films themselves. Great music. Don't you feel that by Westernizing your music and it becoming so popular back home in India, some of our musical history is being lost at the expense of people looking towards the West and Western music? Or do you feel that you're combining the best of our traditions with the music here?

Bally That's exactly what I'm doing, I'm taking the best of both worlds and putting them together for the songs and bringing everyone together through the music. Most people probably wouldn't have ever recognized a Raj Kapoor song before and probably couldn't even relate to it. Whereas, all of a sudden, if it's sounding different, a bit of both, they might get into it. Classic example, when people first heard Churaliya on the *Bollywood Flashback* album, a lot of people didn't even know it was an old song. The youngsters who bought the song didn't know it was from a twenty-year-old movie. And so all of a sudden they were playing both versions on the radio alongside each other, and the kind of responses we were getting were amazing. Most of the youngsters were saying, 'We like the new version', a lot of the older folks liked the original version. I always liked the original version because it's my favourite – that's why I had to do a revitalized new version. Now kids are listening to the old version as well.

People are listening to it, not just our kids, I'm talking about Western kids as well. English kids, whatever, are watching Hindi movies all of a sudden, and people are asking what is 'Bollywood', the word is getting big. Of course everyone wants more exposure to their material. Every movie guy in India would dream of goras watching their movies too. I heard some people say, 'Goras shouldn't come into Indian movies.' What the hell are they talking about? They say 'Indian movies are about Indian people.' I say, 'But you want to do what goras are doing man.' I mean doesn't it give you a great boost when you see a gora speaking in Indian, it's so exciting. It's like when I see a Chinese girl speaking in an Indian language, like when we did our show in Calcutta: I was like, 'Fantastic man, this girl is Chinese.' I find it so exciting...

Shirin You seem to be saying that music is becoming more global. If so, how does the issue of language feature in this?

Bally I've done so many different languages, I don't have to under-stand the language, people don't have to understand the language. People say, 'We don't understand your songs.' I will say, 'Listen man, can you tell me half of the songs that are in the charts, what they're about?' I've done Japanese, French, Arabic, Italian; I've done Urdu and Bengali, Punjabi, Hindi, and I don't understand all those languages. It just goes to show that if I'm making a song like that and it sounds good, hopefully you can get into it as well.

The Asian scene is advancing, it's good and it's about time, and it's just because people like myself and other people who are in the business have got off their backsides and said we are not just good for making rotis, we don't just make balti chicken for a living, we can make this, we can act, we can sing, we can dress as trendy as you or anyone else in the world. Asian people are more proud now. You have to give to take as well, you know we've taken a bit of their stuff and we've given them a bit of ours. We're combining it in our own thing, and it's nice to have people like us doing something and it shows the goras as well, 'cos it's getting the non-Asians into what we are doing. My goal, my dream, is still to get an Indian song in the charts... whether it's me or not, I want to get an Indian language song in the charts and play it regularly in there and it's no big deal, but it hasn't happened yet. I think it's going to happen slowly, when regularly in the top forty we have got Indian singers, girls and boys, whatever, singing Indian songs. It's going to happen sooner or later because things are changing, major companies are picking up on what we are doing.

Shirin   Why do you think this kind of cut'n'mix hasn't happened in the past?

Bally   I think we have not been recognized because of the way our tapes get sold. We are selling more records than people in the charts, we are more than qualified to get in the charts. But in this we are being victimized, it's racism too. Everything is coming into it because Radio One and other radio stations don't want to play our songs. And as you know without major radio you're not going to chart. You need their support, you need their help. Because they're going to play your records during the day – you need more than just club play.

Mukhtar   Why is it important to get your records in the charts when they are already selling and the community is enjoying them? Isn't there a danger that commercialism will make our music bland and meaningless?

Bally   It is very important to get your record in the chart. People say it's the same for any artist, but why does any artist want to get their music in the chart? Mass exposure, nothing to do with money, it's all to do with mass exposure and obviously your cred. So that whenever you do something you'll have a big following and you'll sell a lot of music and so on... and pow – going all over the world because the chart in this country plays a very important part to people abroad.

I am now working with a major label and I'm getting treated like an artist. I'm not knocking the Asian record companies down but it's just like, what they don't know they won't miss, you see. These are the kinds of things that Asian artists have missed out on 'cos they aren't getting the treatment. Top Punjabi singers, your Malkit Singhs and your Alaaps and all these other people, they really haven't had the exposure, the treatment that they should've got being singers of that calibre on the Asian market. They've been on the Asian music scene and sold so many tapes that if they'd been on Western mainstream status they would never need to work for the rest of their lives.

Ranjit   They don't get the respect they deserve basically...

Bally   They've conquered the Asian market, they've been big and now they want to go into the Western market. They want to show everybody our music, to show their music to every colour, every kind. We want to do that with our music.

Ranjit   It's like we've had the sense of pride in the Asian community and now we want to show it all over the world. It's like 'Hey! Look at us! You can check it out too.'

Bally   Everyone wants to taste that glory of going into the mainstream. Things are slowly changing, but we haven't really done it yet and until you're sitting at number one in the UK Chart – well, then you can safely say that we have an Indian song in the UK chart!

Ranjit   It's like when I did four shows on Radio One in the evening session. The first track that I played was 'Bhabiye Bhabiye', and like over four days we had like eight hundred calls, faxes and letters and stuff from Asian kids saying 'yeah, man, this is really wicked, it's about time.'

Shirin   Did you get mail from... white folk too?

Ranjit   Quite a lot of them were English but most of them were Asian saying 'Yeah, man, we want stuff like this on One FM... we pay our license like any one else'.

Bally   I think every Asian wants a piece of their pie on a gora station. It's no big deal having it on a local Asian radio station like Sunrise, 'cos you expect it, but...

Ranjit   ...it's our own, isn't it?

Bally   I always think that if I want to make it in the West, I have to follow what is happening on the Western scene. I have to constantly keep up with all the Mix-Mags and all the magazines that are coming out to see what is big, why it's big, why is it big in Sweden, France, Germany and Italy, America and Canada and so on? England is a very limiting country anyway and so we are talking about something that's got to be worldwide. I think there's a lot of racism when it comes to music in this country. It's very difficult to chart 'foreign tunes' in this country 'cos you've got arseholes like Take That, who can't even sing, selling to teenagers that are fifteen years old. More serious music doesn't even get sold 'cos these fifteen-year-olds want to see good-looking guys on the stage prancing around... So that's why good songs go bigger in other countries like America and Canada, Germany and Italy.

Shirin   Would you say that the racism, particularly in the music scene, but generally anyway, is greater here in Britain?

Bally   There is a lot of it in this country; it's plain to see. A lot of clubs will refuse to pick up your record if it's got a slight Asian tone on it. They're appealing to Kevins and Tracys, you know, appealing to that kind of crowd. But if you go to Germany, France, Italy, Belgium, they will throw any language on a Saturday night, and people just freak out. It's good having that kind of atmosphere, because you want people to dance to your tunes. And it doesn't matter that they don't always know what they are singing about, I mean no one in the world knows what Enigma sing about, yet everybody loves it. I mean what the fuck do those people sing about? So how can people turn round and say, 'We don't understand your language so we can't play your music.' What? Is it going to offend the daytime listeners? If that isn't prejudice or racism, whatever you want to call it, I don't know what is.

Shirin   Would you agree, Ranjit?

Ranjit   Yes, I do, 'cos Yusuf D'Amour's right. The only reason his stuff charted is 'cos he did the duet with Maina, that's the only reason, and got played on the One FM 'A' list. It's for reasons like that that our stuff will never get there. The only people that play our stuff is people like John Peel or Andy Kershaw.

Bally   At 3 o'clock in the morning... There was a time when if you heard an Indian tune you had to check the radio frequency 'cos it wasn't the usual Radio One stuff – and it was Radio One! So we've obviously slowly opened the doors, but to get a record in the charts, like I keep saying, you've got to give the gora what they want to hear, but they can never ever relate one hundred per cent to a traditional anthem for the Asian people. They can't relate to it, but you have to go into their market at the end of the day.

Shirin Why do you think that's more of an issue here than in France? Because the racism, historically, and in modern times, has always been as bad if not worse?

Bally Yes, but the main issue here is, the UK is the leading trend-setter for music worldwide. Foreign countries look at the UK chart and then follow suit. So whatever is happening in the charts here, they normally like to follow suit in their chart. That's why if Indian songs were coming in the charts, you could guarantee they'll be going all over the world, big time.

It's not as bad now, you can go to HMV and buy an Indian track that's not in the corner of a dusty World Music section that nobody looks in. You want to go to that trendy dance section where all those cool, good-looking kids are hanging out. This is why we're forcing our records to be sold in those sections of the store. If you put good dance music in a corner that nobody ever looks in, it won't get sold. So it's the same with our records, we don't want them in the dusty corner with a Buddha standing there. We want our music to stand up as big as your other dance crazes, other dance styles and music scenes. But we want, not one classification, like Bhangra, we want hundreds of classifi-cations. Like Country and Rock and Soul and Hip-Hop, because what we are doing is not just Bhangra music, we all know what Bhangra music is, it's a different thing, it's a traditional thing which is done in India with dohl and Boliyaan, but we've taken it more than one step to a different league. We've taken it to the same league as what's happen-ing on the Soul league, the Ragga league. We're making the tunes as good, as fresh as those tunes, but with one major important difference and that's with our kind of a lick, with an Indian vocal and so on.

Ranjit But the best we can do is make majors more aware and say 'Hey look at us'. But we need more than that because the record companies may have the best intentions in the world and want to get an Asian artist, but if you haven't got anybody in there who knows how to market that type of music... in terms of A&R, talent scouts, marketing, people who understand the scene. We need Asian people in there, we need record companies to employ Asian people with a spe-cific aim of bringing in Asian artists and developing it.

Mukhtar The people who are buying your music are our people. You'll hear it all over India and so on. Do you not feel that the music entertainment corporations are creaming off a lot of the money? And that it's not really going back into the communities. What do you feel about things like that?

Ranjit   Like Bally, I want to see Indian stuff in the charts and I'm always looking at ways we can do that feasibly, without the money being lost from the community. The danger is that the majors are going to take a big cut and all the Asian record shops are going to lose out. They're going to go bankrupt basically.

When we set up, we set up the band and we set up the label to go with it. So, what we did as a label was that we licensed our product to the majors, saying you give us money to distribute it and promote it. When we did the promotion we did it with them, like Big Life did the promotion for the last track, and I worked at Big Life Records, and I dealt with the Asian market myself. I sent the product to the Asian record shops. I said 'Here, have product, sell it, make money.' I wasn't so worried about charting but I just wanted the exposure and all the other products were sold through HMV, Our Price and all. You have to have a parallel, you can't just expect one kind of market to sustain total sales and get you recognized on both sides, on the Asian market and on the European market. You have to do both at the same time and that's when you need your own specialist people going in there and doing it on your behalf.

I get a lot of girls writing to me and stuff about how to get started. The only mail I get from guys is 'Are you married? Do you want to get married?' Most of the girls are saying like, 'How did you get into it?' 'Cos it's really hard and they worry whether their parents will throw them out and disown them for even thinking about it...

When I DJ I go on with Asian gear on. It's really weird 'cos it really freaks people out! But, it's also great when people see you as a role model. There's a group of people now, wherever I go, a group of women and there's even like four guys that follow me all over the country. I don't even have to tell them where I am, they find out. Like one time I was at Lambeth and I just kind of stuck my head out to look and I could see these guys at the back going, 'hoi hoi', and they'd followed me from Huddersfield to London just to see me with the band, KK Kings. I was like, 'this is mad, this is really freaky'. And I've got a group of girls, about thirty women, who just follow me all over the country. One of them followed me to Vienna. She is an Asian woman and she was there – you know it's wicked, and it's not very often that you see people like that because it is a really hard environment.

Mukhtar   We live in a hostile society and you can have a club and in the evening everybody is in there having a really good time dancing away, but right outside you could have somebody being racially attacked or murdered. Now you've chosen to call yourself Radical Sista – all this shows consciousness that whilst we know how to celebrate, have a good time, at the same time we are not divorced or isolated from the reality of racial violence in the ghettos where we live. How important is that to you, to be conscious and aware of that?

Ranjit   To me, it's all-important. When I did first start out I was doing quite mainstream clubs in London and Liverpool and stuff. I got a lot of letters from the BNP [British National Party] and the NF [National Front] and stuff. I used to get death threats literally every week. It's kind of like, 'oh another death threat, put it with the others' kind of thing. It got to the stage where I was like that and I was getting religious fundamentalists trying to kidnap me and stuff in London! I'm used to it and I know it's a political thing – the very fact that as an Asian woman I am actually 'out there' for a start, and the fact that I'm wearing Asian gear just makes the point in itself in a way. Because people look and go 'What's she doing there?' You know if I was wearing Ragga shorts and a little bra top, they would hardly bat any eyelid. Asian guys would, they'd look 'phwaar, hey', but other people wouldn't really give a damn. But, seeing someone in full 'traditional dress' doing something that's like a Western concept doesn't correlate with the expected images of Asian women.

Mukhtar   We've talked about the struggles in the families and the communities to do what you want to do. But also what about other obstacles that exist, the doors that are closed to you by racism? It's present in every sphere of society, and surely there in the music industry, despite the long history of black music. The impression you get is that it's very much managed and controlled by the whites who make most of the money. And with the kinds of stereotypes that you've had to break down, you know the stuff about 'a bunch of Pakis who can't really sing, can't do more than just make vindaloos'... What about struggles against racism in this industry?

Ranjit   Well, there's a great assumption that we don't know anything about business, we know about corner shops and groceries, but when it comes to the music business they think we don't know anything. As if we're just good at making tunes in traditional Punjabi style and that's it. They don't realize that we do know about contracts, we do know about publishing, we do know about the MU [Musicians' Union], we do know about things like that. So when Sony got into the Bhangra scene artists were actually joining the MU and getting themselves more protection. Even our own companies are ripping off artists big-time [to Bally], well, they are aren't they?... They're all at it, and it's like only when our own record companies start respecting artists that the major record companies start respecting Asian artists. And the only way they're going to do that is if the artists start taking control themselves. Start saying, 'Hey hang on a minute, you can't give me £10,000 for an album and expect me to live off that and leave me to earn the rest of my living by doing live gigs four or five times a week.'

Bally Just to show how difficult it is: there are hardly any Asian people who are full-time in the music business because they've all got their own accountancy jobs, or work for British Gas. This is the top Asian singers I'm talking about. The Asian music business doesn't work the way that the English record companies work. I don't think that any top Western artist works for British Gas while they're doing gigs in the evening or they're singing songs in the charts. One main reason is because they have proper companies looking after them. They have a budget to produce a recording, they have a publishing company that does all their work for them; they are members of other unions as well. Everything is protected so when their record is played it's all logged, it's done properly. Whereas our stuff doesn't always get that kind of treatment. Even the lyrics aren't protected properly, the guy who wrote the song gets ripped off. Someone says, 'Here's £100 and you go and do the lyrics' and the poor guy is probably never going to hear the thing again. So, it doesn't work the way that the white companies work. I'm getting to know that now 'cos I've been learning a lot about what happened with me when I was with my old record company.

Shirin Now you've got this deal with Columbia, what are your concerns? Talking about the blockages by racism, are you worried that you won't have that much autonomy over your work? That you might have to compromise; are you worried about any of those things?

Bally No, not at all, 'cos I've been signed up for what I'm good at doing...

Shirin ...and you're confident that you'll be allowed to do that?

Bally ...yes, that's the most important thing; I've got a great A&R guy as well and I've got a great relationship with Columbia. I am what they call their 'touch with the East', they've seen my track record. We talked loads in detail with Columbia – they are very good for breaking black artists abroad. One important thing that I agreed with the company is that I don't want them ever to tell me that I shouldn't have Indian singing in my songs; or I shouldn't have tabla playing, or I shouldn't have an Indian sound etcetera, and they said that's the last thing they want to do because what I'm doing now obviously works.

I don't want to be limited with 'you can't do this, you can't do that'. Obviously there are parts in any contract which say you can't do this and you can't do that, within reason, but I think I've been fortunate. But the most important thing is that they said to me, 'Just do whatever you've been doing and let us do the rest.'

Ranjit   I think it's payback time basically, you know, 'cos Asian communities have lived here for thirty-odd years now, and longer than that, and they've shown some serious commitment to the country. We built it, the health service amongst other things...

Bally   Yes, you can't leave the country now without being searched by an Asian at Heathrow...

Ranjit   If all the Asians went to India, the health service would be destroyed. That's how important we are here, and in every area. It's now, 'OK, you've got our legal expertise, you've got our medical expertise, you've got every kind of expertise that you want from us. You've got engineers, our dentists, our accountants, doctors,' what I call the 'dead posse', right?... Now like what about us as artists, 'cos we have got that down too. Its like, India's the largest market in the world in terms of music. They sell billions there every year.

Bally   ...Big things are happening now for India and it's about time, that's all I can say. A lot of majors, big record companies, are going there, proper franchises of restaurants, lots of things are happening in India and at the end of the day, the best place in the world is India.

Mukhtar   You were saying before that in some ways what you are more interested in is the form: the sound and the lyrics aren't that important. Don't you think that the message is just as important?

Bally   Depends what you're listening to, though, doesn't it? I'm talking about hundreds of categories, hundreds of stars and stuff. If you're listening to a mellow song or something, you're obviously listening to the lyrics, you're not listening just to the music are you? If you're listening to a dance track that really gets you up and going on the dancefloor – 'Everybody Dance Now' – what kind of lyric is that? That's one of the biggest dance records ever and its just three words spoken. Certain songs are for certain kinds of categories. Dance music really doesn't have to have the best lyrics in the world, what carries it is the beat and the groove. Period. But if you're talking about a love song, or a song that's got meaning, like a political song or a Rap song, then yes, the lyrics are important. There's every kind of thing for every kind of listener. Lot of times, kids don't really know everything about the lyrics in a song. When it comes to Indian songs mainly 'cos a lot of kids don't understand traditional Punjabi talk. Even if you are Punjabi, even if it's a Hindi song, they still love it and buy it, mainly because of the music. They love the music. Why do goras buy our music? Can't be because of the lyrics, impossible. Obviously music is a very, very important part of it. Lyrics play an important part in a different way, at a different level…

Shirin   Ranjit, do you think about the lyrics and the choices of records you play as a DJ? Are you consciously thinking, 'Well I won't put this on because of some of the rubbish that this guy's on about'? Do you think about these issues when you're DJing?

Ranjit   Yes I do. There's one track especially that I really, really hate. It's absolutely obnoxious, that 'Patel Rap'. I banned it from the word go. When it came out I scratched it all over the vinyl… I thought, 'There's no way anyone is playing this. I don't care.'

Shirin   Tell us why.

Mukhtar   …for promoting stereotypes?

Ranjit   Yes, for promoting stereotypes, and for just killing any positive images of Asian people. If we really want to get anywhere in the music industry, in the mainstream, we've got to take ourselves seriously before we expect anybody else to do it. Tracks like 'Patel Rap' are just shit.

Bally   It would've been worse if was a gora done it; 'cos an Indian man done it…

Ranjit   …they accepted it.

Bally   Yes, if it was a gora then nobody would've put up with it, you know.

Ranjit   They'd have banned it… That kind of stuff doesn't wash with me at all. And like lots of the Bhangra songs, I used to think about the lyrics and I realized I hated those tracks. The music's nice, the voice itself is really beautiful, but the content is really winding me up. You get guys that were really pissed singing it to you. There's that kind of level of harassment.

Shirin   So they were internalizing the lyrics when they sang them to you? It probably meant something to them. Are you saying then that lyrics do matter?

Ranjit   Yes, if they're singing that crap to you, you know it's a wind-up, man. Now some Bhangra bands are jumping on the Hindi band-wagon and singing love songs and stuff which is fine, but in terms of creativity in the Punjabi lyric, there is none. A lot of it was sexist rubbish.

Bally   And it does not work. Even the public out there think that those on stage must know it's not working. But they do it 'cos every-one else is doing it.

Shirin   Finally, I want to talk about both your futures, and the developments in Asian dance music that you imagine happening.

Bally   Big things are happening for myself and what I've always wanted to do is to get my music into major mainstream audiences such as movies and it's happening now. It's only happening now simply because of the hardships I went through for so many years. It's just going to show that all that bloody frustration and all that banging down of all those doors of the major companies has finally come around, so now everybody is finally listening to our kind of music. And obviously the help of a major record company pays off, that's helping me do things, like working with Mariah Carey, that I've only dreamt about. You wouldn't have got that before. Now things are changing.

Ranjit   The stuff I do is predominantly dance. It's not often Bhangra. I've been asked to do Bhangra, and to remix Bhangra, but I'm not that interested 'cos of the lyrical content of the product. I thought, 'No, that's not me'...

Bally   So you do remixes, yeah?

Ranjit   No, I've been asked to do remixes, but I won't do them 'cos I want to do something from scratch, I want to do something com-pletely original...

Bally   To write new songs, yeah?

Ranjit   ...from bass line on and just work my way up.

Bally   Have you done new songs like that?

Ranjit   I've done dance music. That's what I do. I do dance music, with Rap, with Hindi vocals, Punjabi vocals, English vocals.

Bally   Which company is it coming out of?

Ranjit   Well I've done it through Time Recordings, Hollywood Records and Big Life, that was the last one that I did, and Sony Japan, the Jungle tracks.

Shirin   Do you have an audience in mind when you're actually doing this?

Ranjit   No, it's just something that I like doing, you know. I will get into Punjabi stuff, but that's not until I feel it's worth getting into again 'cos at the moment it's just very staid. A lot of our stuff is sold in the UK, but Italy's got a lot of our stuff, Japan as well – we've got a really large following there and Japan's a massive market. We've been featured in the major press in Japan. I'm catering for a specific market. I do dance music, and I am able to sing in three languages, and I happen to know how to write all these languages, and my musical influences come from Funk and early Techno, that's the kind of stuff I grew up on. So my influences aren't all completely different to those on the kids that are growing up now. Obviously my style's going to be a little different. It's just a natural progression for me. It'll happen slowly, getting into the charts, but someone's got to do it somewhere along the line.

Bally   I think slowly things are changing, people are going to come in, people are getting into those places now. It's early days yet still for Asian people 'cos we haven't really tasted the success of being main-stream and at the top of the charts. We've only witnessed and seen and felt the whole potential of the Asian music scene 'cos we've been there for so many years. But it's also all new and exciting and everyone wants to be a part of it and slowly but surely people will be doing proper jobs and doing things in proper companies.

Ranjit   But then it goes back to what you were saying before, Bally, about lots and lots of styles – whatever you do there'll always be a traditional circuit anyway. Mainstream success won't really kill it, it'll just kind of enhance what already exists. There'll always be people like the Alaaps and Heeras – they'll always be there because there's always a market for them.

Mukhtar   I think it's definitely positive. Like we said in the beginning, we had a vacuum, there was nobody there and we were dancing to different rhythms. At least now, Asians are making a positive space out there and doing their own thing, producing their own music, making their own dance moves. And as we've heard today, it's all related to the issue of identity in many different ways.

Bally   And now at least the kids are paying some attention to their roots and their culture, and their music, listening to the originals, as well as to what we're doing now.

Ranjit   Yes, and they take more interest as well. It's about identities at the end of the day, 'cos now, when we listen to Alaap it's like, 'Yes it's good, it's nice, it's from back home, but we can't relate to it 'cos they're only talking about life in the Punjab.' You know, I've been born and brought up here in England. I can't sing about that and feel that it's a part of me. Now we are creating our own stuff, which is relevant to British life.

Bally   We are the generation now, they were the generation in that time, so we are representing what is happening now. Maybe in twenty years' time, our kids will be saying, 'God, our folks used to listen to all that kind of stuff'… you know, way back in the 90s!' You have to go through all the stages, everybody does it. Just like how the English people have Disco and Rock and other styles going in and coming out, and then something else comes in. Our music does the same and it's doing it now… Who knows what's going to happen tomorrow.

Ranjit   Whatever happens, whether I'm behind the scenes or on the stage, or managing or something, which is what I've done before, I will always be doing something in the music industry. I'll probably still be spinning records at fifty! That's how I see it 'cos that's where I started off. It's like I'm going to be 'Radical Mother', you know! Or 'Radical Grandma', you know what I mean?

Thanks to Laura Turney for transcribing the tape of this interview

5

PSYCHE AND SOUL:

A VIEW FROM THE 'SOUTH'

Koushik Banerjea and Partha Banerjea

All I know about music is that not many people ever really hear it. And even then, on the rare occasions when something opens within, and the music enters, what we mainly hear, or hear corroborated, are personal, private, vanishing evocations. But the man who creates the music is hearing something else, is dealing with the roar rising from the void and imposing order on it as it hits the air. What is evoked in him, then, is of another order, more terrible because it has no words, and triumphant, too, for that same reason. And his triumph, when he triumphs is ours (Baldwin 1995: 47–48).

It is Saturday night and the car is loaded. There is no point in searching the airways, so the compilation tape goes in – strings, harmonization of vocals, crisp production, and it's off to zone 3/4, the land that time forgot, vicariously bounded by the burgeoning M25 belt and the Circle Line: ghost town and samosas collide. Datsuns and vamped Escorts cram the side streets and a quiet suburban street is transformed into a musical roadblock. The sounds of Arnold Blair and Oliver Cheetham bounce off the mock-leather interior of a rapidly fading Nissan and energize the baseline feeding frenzy of the car's youthful occupants. These goateed disciples of midtempo persuasion would even forgo a samosa to mentally glide the felicitous route of a post-Mizell-Brothers production. 'Trying to Get Next to You' and 'Get Down Saturday Night' were ingested like some preparatory mantra before the plush Japanese interior would be exchanged for the delights that lay beyond that other suburban façade, the front door.

Once inside, a tune, cut circa 1980 by an unknown chanteuse, slices through the sensibilities that hold early adolescent life together. An

empathetic bond, equally as mythical as the circular breathing of
Pharaoh Sanders, had been created. Yet even in the sounds of the old
there was, distinct from retrospective reference, the instinctive, almost *a
priori* knowledge of a sense of value in what was audible. A rearticulated
sense of history and identity would subsequently unfold as the semantics
of spirituality refused the limits of fashionably heroic posturing.

Created within a particular space, a momentary silence pre-empts
that bassline hook and *those* strings hinting at the promise of 'Better
Days Ahead' (Gil Scott Heron) before the start of the sweetest vocal
sermon. Smiles are being shared, the big K (knowledge) has been
delivered and the night receives its address. Philly International once
again reaches those parts other majors can only dream of. 'Don't Let It
Go to Your Head' urges our songstress, Jean Carne, with a little help
from Messrs Gamble and Huff, and the time is right for a little selective
remembrance. This is our time to tell an*other* story to those so beloved
of old wives and their 'liberal', griotic progeny.

What unfolds is an everyday tale of (post-colonial) treachery, enmity
and cultural erasure. You see, when Jean Carne dropped her vocal
science it was a case of subcontinental hands on the decks of such
'sounds' as Watergate and Phoenix Risin' in south London. More often
than not the Samuel L. Jackson clones hugging the walls at those early
dances would be revealed by the lights of familiar 4 a.m. curfews as the
real Eastern McCoy, Samir…

No apologies, then, for a personal and curiously unacknowledged
retrospective recovery of some of these 'lost' histories of Soul music
and Asians in Britain. This is hopefully 'the full shebang' from perceived farah-clad rebellion to the dangerous mimicry of charity-shop
chic and stitch-on yellow-label heaven; from the sub-post office to
subcultural formation; from zone 3 to utter (if relative) obscurity in the
seamlessly ruptured London suburbs;[1] and, importantly, from silence to
voice as stuttering 'versions' of Asianness are articulated both within
and against a colonial tongue.

A south London Soul venue stirs into action. Always too insular for
popular acceptance, too 'soft' for those needing overtly masculine
parameters to be set and too obscure for the 'fashionable' media, the
Soul movement has nevertheless endured. The adolescently lit community
hall could sound just like Prestatyn, Southport or any number of northern
venues dedicated to Soul, but this time it's south of Watford and those
involved ain't the Terrys from Ilford but the Tamsils from Hounslow.[2]

To plot the nodal points of this 'imagined' geography from bedroom
to houseparty via 'nightschool' on the airwaves is thus to reconfigure

the metropolis itself. It is to refuse simplistic centre/margin dichotomies which have been and continue to be unproblematically invoked
to mark the boundaries of Brit-Soul in general and its London variants
in particular with the currency of white supremacy. Our interest here
lies in disrupting such map-making and fact-faking which, we would
suggest, belong to the finest traditions of Mercator projection.

Just as exclusion from the 'mainstream' in part defines Asian cultural
production, so cultural theft demands improvised recovery. In contemporary terms, the 'wigger' can become as much a symbol as David
Duke of white supremacy and is frequently perceived as embodying
the limits of binarism. It follows that a certain 'version' of syncretic
musical culture may even have abjured a binary logic particular to
metropolitan Britain. However, the dialectics that actually underscored
the 'Soul patrols' of diasporic London were rarely as simple as the
warped chessboard logic of white supremacy would have it. In that
version of events the 'cool' black subject would be vicariously consumed
by the 'new' white patrons of Soul, albeit primarily through vinyl,
while Asians were consigned to shopwork, shiftwork and an intractably
sly civility.

There is nothing new in noting that such a perception of 'Soul'
within the white psyche, reliant as it is upon an essentialized 'blackness',
could only have been conceived and sustained via the mechanics of
white supremacy. Its assumption of a Manichean cultural landscape
bereft of diverse liminal possibilities does, however, have particular
significance for Asian folk denied their rightful inheritance as both consumptive and productive Soul heads. Moreover it allows us to understand how the hierarchies of reason that attempt to hide the failure of
a linear Anglo meta-narrative of British cultural history reproduce the
former imperial metropolis, London, as a centre of post-colonial reason.

Eulogized and castigated in almost equal measure, one of the more
troubling ways that 'Soul' enters the popular imagination is via the bi-
(did someone say 'multi-'?) cultural fabulizations of a nostalgic white
supremacy frequently found on the artwork of those Streetsounds
covers.[3] Cultural critic and writer Paul Gilroy, offers this useful
proposition:

> In order to appreciate the significance of the imagery of race that record
> sleeves project, it is essential to remember that we are dealing with a dis-
> possessed and economically exploited population which does not enjoy
> extensive opportunities to perceive itself or see its experiences imaginatively
> or artistically reflected in the visual culture of urban living (Gilroy 1993b).

There can be little argument over the subversive potential of record sleeves as graphic transmissions of popular cultural sensibilities. We would, however, suggest that it is ingenuous to assume a linear narrative outcome as the premise for this visual tradition. Streetsounds is a case in point, establishing an undeniably street-credible framework for an aesthetically grounded politics of binary exclusion. The irony is barely lost on a generation of Asian Soulheads as Mr Khan chooses the picture.[3] All of which begs the question: was there ever a consensus as to who exactly were 'the suckers to the side'?

Our contention is that the answer is itself contained in the artwork on those classic Streetsounds compilations. Of particular interest are the covers of the various 'Anthems' collections, knowledgeably put together and marketed as 'the official Soul-weekenders' album'. The special currency of these albums, we would suggest, lay in their mass appeal to an 'imagined community' of Soulheads bound together by their love of the music and derision for all things 'pop'. 'Soul Weekenders' extended the principle of the 'Soul All Dayer' for the duration of an entire weekend in such venues as Caister, Prestatyn and Southport, and were basically an opportunity for a 'hardcore' (hard-kaur?) Soul constituency to declare and celebrate its identity. The physical remoteness of such venues, the obscurity of the musical diet and knowledgeable hedonism of most punters simply served to underline the point: Weekenders were not for the faint-hearted. Indeed they assumed for their very legitimacy that only the most diehard aficionados of Soul would attend, exchanging disproportionate amounts of money and sweat for a slice of the 'real thing'. Their distaste for perceived middle-class 'vapidity' and attempted 'intellectualization' of the 'scene' was also legendary, and is instructive here when looking at some of the tensions being played out between the imperatives of marketing and unmediated emotional responses to both the music and the scene. Look no further for an example of this than Ian McCann's impassioned sleeve-noted plea for respect on the memorable *Anthems*, Volume 2. His strategically positioned response to what he views as abstract and unwelcome middle-class intellectualism in matters of funk clearly identifies the boundaries of the 'Soul community' along the fault lines of class:

> Do we take any notice? No chance, John. The true British Soul fraternity carries on regardless, ignoring the bull, picking up on what's really kickin' and having one hell of a good time in the process.... So if you've just been to an all-dayer and your pre-shrunk Fatback vest is three times too small after the Wet T-Shirt contest, this one is for you. If the dog swallowed your copy of 'Joy and Pain' when you were out spending the last of your cash money

on your Saturday Night at Caister Trousers, it's for you too.... And if your
weekender bag still has an intact packet of three ... when you are back home
unpacking it, these Anthems are for you too. When all your goodies are gone,
you'll still have this, the real people's music – to hear and enjoy, to love and
remember by, but most of all to dance to over and over again (Ian McCann,
'Echoes', sleeve notes, *Anthems*, vol. 2, 1987).

What is unsettling is not the text itself with its fond and familiar
recollections, but rather the images it accompanies. If we accept the
idea of the Soul Weekender as a metaphor for an archetypal 'community' then the artwork on 'the official Soul-weekenders' album' assumes
a heightened representational profile since it is presumably intended as
a visual reinscription of the spirit and composition of that community.
We can justifiably place an added premium on the absence of Asians
from such images as illustrative of a hierarchically determined cultural
binarism. Here the limits of a hybrid Soul 'fraternity' are marked by
the foregrounding of white casuals of both sexes and black youth,
gendered male. Whilst the recombinant qualities of such representations
themselves raise cogent concerns around the issue of patriarchally
ordered hybrid subculture, they also hint at ethnic invisibility as a
premise for hybrid cultural practice. 'Fusion' would then appear not to
be the freedom to 'do it any way you wanna' but rather is seen as
reliant upon particular combinations of prescribed ingredients for its
special appeal. Do it how? The implied promiscuity of the term culled
from the fusion classic by Cashmere is used ironically here, offering a
stark contrast between the promise of eclecticism and its monotone
institutional practice. Had we 'done it any way we wanna' it is unlikely
that Streetsounds' representational artwork, for instance, would have
consistently foregrounded moustachioed white casuals as a primary
symbol of the Weekender. Like Fats Wallah, we ain't misbehavin', simply
pointing out that the synergistic qualities of the music itself belie its
rearticulation as an integral aspect of a chauvinistic, ethnically treacher-
ous cultural identity throughout much of the 1980s in London.

The prevailing perception of this parochial community was that black
creativity could be usefully allied to white management as an adjunct
to this identity, performatively imagined on those Streetsounds covers.
In a worrying echo of minstrelsy, such prizing of a version of black
masculinity assumed both the legitimacy of a white colonial gaze and
the absence of 'other' versions of masculinity amongst the fraternity.
And it is here that 'the Asian' becomes exclusively imagined within a
dominant cultural framework as a definitive 'other'.

Forrest may, at first sight, have looked just like Ranjit Johal from

Leytonstone but Forrest was a Soul man and Asians 'don't do Soul', or so we were told even though the singer himself urged us down another O-Jays-inspired path. You see, Ranjit, whose voice at one time evoked comparisons with a youthful David Grant,[4] would guest on vocals for Phoenix Risin' back in the days when a trip to the New York Jazz Explosion actually meant several stops on the District Line. But Johalji never progressed any further, as jheri-curled Samir would be the first to testify, because no matter how hard he tried he could never quite forget the playground taunts of 'Paki' whenever the Forrest jibe was wheeled out. Slippin' into darkness now as the sounds of Tyrone Brunson punctuate the older domestic flavours of chicken dopiaza and newer strains of post-playground cultural reconfiguration. Let us take a midtempo journey back in time...

The dimly lit venue necessarily takes on the qualities of a dreamland – everything is possible. A kind of reverence opens up a central space around which the expectant Asian delegation would wait like the chosen tribe for a sign. Up on the musical pulpit, on twin-decks crafted by Scots, sounds are being spliced and offered up into the critical suburban night. The voracious search is on for the 'unity' toon. Our data thief plunders his promiscuous way through the Philly archives, overturning in the process many musical pebbles. And then, suddenly, a pearl as the old Eastern master, Rafi, gives way to those (relative) youngbloods the O-Jays. 'Put our heads together', doing the business 'up west' in virtually Asian-free clubs, is kicking up a storm down south too where the 'bouncer' is always somebody's cousin and the styles mock-subaltern chic.

Midtempo, mellow heaven and the night's first 'rewind'.[5] 'Chewn!' 'Aabar!' 'Shabbash!' The shouts ring out as time is frozen. Native hands rework the science and disrupt Eurocentric receptive expectations of cultural performance. Chronology, à la Benjaminian DJ, is the renegotiated historical fragment captured on vinyl, punch-phrased by Scottish needlework and rearticulated as interpellative, diasporic art. It was never enough to gratuitously present votive offerings of obscure vinyl. At such dances in the much-maligned cultural heartlands of the suburbs, respect would be given and reputations forged on the strength of the referential roots of the aesthetic delivery. When folks spoke of James Mason at a Phoenix Risin' shindig the chances were that they didn't mean the Hollywood star. Not for them the quintessential Hitchcockian badman, rather the fusion meister of 'Sweet Power, Your Embrace' fame. That was the tune that did it every time with its satisfying rarity (as a 12-inch vinyl pressing in the 1980s), hypnotic bass line and uplifting vocal mantra. Even the 'fat man' with the ever-changing hand-held widget would be moved into some kind of shuffle as Johalji's meandering vocals pierced the darkness and traced the dream.

For those that attended these monthly conventions, the days were often filled with the functional business for instance of gaining diplomas, attending shops and driving buses, demanding that the evening remain the preserve of dreams. Banality could be temporarily forsaken for an emergent mental and physical space wherein to explore latent hopes and aspirations. For a limited time, anyway, the terror of the schoolyard, the employment exchange and the debilitating self-doubt would yield to the prospect of a liminally charged identity free from the assumptions of white cultural supremacy. *Eat those yellowy sweets, talk that monkey jabber, but for fuck's sake keep it indoors.* And therein lay the crux of the problem: for diverse others and especially white folk, being Asian was essentially a matter of impersonation. Hence the post-adolescence visit to 'the Indian' and the robust statement of intent: *'Eh, Sabu! Where's mi fuckin' vindaloo!!'* The idea was that these figures of fun would humour their white aggressors and didn't even need to read Hegel to get their resilient heads around the master/slave dialectic. Divided loyalties from the 'old country' never troubled those thought of as 'brown elves' until their 'comical' bodies refused to absorb any more punishment from the boots of diverse 'others' in cities and market towns throughout the land. Absorption of plurality, it seemed, was no guarantee of 'national' integrity. Consider the fact that Jawaharlal Nehru himself never envisaged this as problematic when issues of (Indian) national unity were at hand, although the old Harrovian's wandering loins suggested his own sense of fragmented desire long before Indian partition, post-colonial migration and delayed diaspora put paid to any romantic notion of Indian 'unity'.

And it is to that diaspora that we must return to watch our story unfold. For the Asian communities forged in post-1945 Britain, migration, primarily economic in character, was built on the principle of dreaming with one's eyes open. As the harsh realities of racism and prejudice befell those who were born here, however, the disparities between the promise and the actuality of 'desh pardesh' lent themselves to bitter disappointment and even a sense of betrayal.[6] Under such conditions of betrayal it became even more imperative not to forgo the 'necessary dream' which had both inspired and become the product of subcontinental migration. It was as if the dream could not dissipate for as long as it was steeped in a creative mythology and the mores of old. Hence the sense of 'mythos over logos', of the sayings of the past informing the logic and aspirations of the present, which underscored so much of that commitment to Soul for a time during the 1980s.

One of the concrete achievements of this time was the translation of an enthusiast's passion and often encyclopaedic knowledge in the useful matter of Curtom pre-releases into the organizational principle for several small sound systems around London. Not only did these enable the public performance of intimate privatized histories, but they did so through the reconfiguration of public space itself. Whether in clubs, dance halls, community centres or straightforwardly suburban terraces, the sounds provided by the Soul 'crews' of Watergate and Phoenix Risin', for instance, became synonymous with the rearticulation of a publicly visible and youthful Asian diasporic profile in Britain. A useful comparison could be made here by considering the recent proliferation of so-called Jeep Beats in most cities in the United States. This phenomenon refers to the preference amongst many young African-Americans for astoundingly powerful car stereos nurtured on a basic musical diet of Hip-Hop. These systems, frequently as powerful in the bass frequency department as a small 'sound', are the favoured option of urban youth enabling as they do the literal 'mobilization' of the musical culture and the rearticulation of impersonal city space in terms of recognizable sound blocs. More important though than these personal lyrical signatures is their inception as a response to the deeply problematic relationship of African-Americans, particularly young men, to public space. Carceral policing and the edicts of several hundred years of brutalization have apparently obliged evasive reactive strategies for self-preservation, and nowhere is this more evident than in the relocation and privatization of the musical culture contained within the advance of Jeep Beats.

Given the upsurge in racial violence directed at British Asian folk during the 1980s, the fact that this 'alternative public sphere' prioritized the spatial prerogative of racial safety further underlined its implicitly political credentials.[7] It might not have been safe to go to school or catch the bus to work (if you were one of the lucky ones with a job) but the intangible, and quite possibly invaluable, reward for negotiating the pitfalls of an average day would be found later in the liminal spaces of London sound 'culture'. No racial fuckries at a Watergate 'session'. There, 'To Be Invisible' owed more to the falsetto spirituality of Curtis Mayfield than to the survival instinct obliged by a potentially hostile environment. Indeed, the development and incorporation of an extended 'wind down zone' at such events was wholly reliant on the assumed 'ease of presence' enjoyed by their public. Midtempo grooves and later the slower two-step selections were partially able to elicit the favourable plaudits of the Asian punters because of the psychological freedom to appreciate a detailed musical aesthetic granted such folks by the absence of fear. Simple things like the lack of 'baldheads' and ethnically singular political ideologies were integral to this spatialized catharsis.

Terry Callier spoke to those whose spirit demanded sustenance, whose Soul required a faith. Why, then, should we have been so surprised that his gospel-inflected folk-Soul provided the certainty so desperately sought within the climate of Britain's secular degeneration? When he cried: 'I don't want to see myself without you...' we were touched. Nobody had ever spoken to us like that before. It made a change from the usual: 'You're going to get your fuckin' 'ead kicked in!' or its vehicular parallel: 'You're goin' 'ome in a London ambulance!'

We grew up at a time when, notwithstanding the vagaries of trans-national capital and globalization, certain things were clearly marked as acceptably fashionable whilst others were consigned to the scrapheap of the popular imagination. In south London at least, in the early 1980s, the wordplay and associations of the term 'Asian' were with durable notions of odour, passivity, squareness, weakness and weirdness, in no particular order. (The word actually used was 'Paki' but we didn't wish to cause undue distress to our white patrons whose burden is un-doubtedly greater.) Our reasonable enough assumption was therefore that apparently being smelly, weak, square and non-violent was ample qualification to rethink our cultural identity and perspectives. We just wanted 'to be invisible' in the beautiful surrounds of Kidbrooke, south London. It paid to be invisible when the most common 'occupational status' of local people's parents was 'National Front activist'. Even here, though, there was always vague talk and some acknowledgement of 'the blacks' as 'hard' if despicable. What actually seemed to distinguish 'Afro-Caribbeans' from 'Asians' during those confusing times was the former's perceived ability to respond potently to any physical threat posed by whites and to indelibly imprint the British imagination with the strains of autonomous cultural production.

Soul, then, made its first appeal to the British children of Asian migrants, as an 'underground' cultural resource, invested with the currency of alterity and addressed with a spirit of fortitude. These appeared to be eminently marketable qualities to embattled and marginalized young Asians faced with the prospect of popular cultural extinction, and it is therefore hardly surprising that the various diasporic 'massives' quickly cottoned on.

The gravitation towards Soul signalled the desire of many Asians to begin an introspective journey to the point of reinvention. While Leroy

Hutson urged folks to get 'Closer to the Source' those distant desk-bound men with brogues and typewriters would offer us 'instruction' as to which derivatives of Soul 'should be putting the steam into our trainers and the steps into our hair' (Ian McCann, 'Echoes', sleeve notes, *Anthems*, vol. 2, 1987).

Little wonder then that most folks chose the musical path without ever looking back to see, as in some fairy tale, those modish pearls of wisdom turned into slabs of perceptively dull stone. And in moments of doubt, Chocolate Milk offered perennial clarity with their advice that 'actions speak louder than words'. For wherever we turned we could see that what was supposed to be 'happening' at the 'cutting edge' of the British Soul scene bore little relevance to its frequently contradictory organic practices. Where, for instance, was the wonderful world of Johalji, Watergate *et al.* in this stellar projection of events? Had we imagined the whole thing, down to the finest detail, such as who had been the first to discover the 'fat man's' proclivity for two-step anthems back to back with 'old-school breaks'? Or the time that Samir's hitherto unknown cousin laid down the impromptu 'live' beats when Highland craftsmanship was for once found wanting and the decks failed early on at a Phoenix Risin' All Nighter?

It was as though the 'official' version of Brit-Soul was being constructed as yet another branch of a compensatory identity politics seeking to 'comprehend' the secular narratives of post-1945 British society. If the certainties afforded by a white skin and naturalized cultural presence no longer extended to the psychic shores of Soul then necessity demanded the rearticulation of the popular cultural realm to reassure an otherwise faithless white population of their hegemonic condition. Soul, which for some time anyway had engaged white and black youth in productive, if problematic dialogue, was suddenly seized upon by the floundering cultural scribes making occasional sorties out of W10, as the desperately sought idiomatic tool for this purpose.

The purchase of Levi jeans and those cheap K-Tel compilations would later be prescribed as acceptable 'routes' into a classic, imagistically reified Soul 'bazaar' but it initially sufficed our self-appointed 'experts' to valorize a reductionist commentary on the rapidly expanding 'scene'.[8] At a time when the south of England was teeming with folk who lived and breathed a life dedicated to the underfunded pursuit of white labels, you could have believed, listening to our 'pundits', that the 'hidden' contours of Brit-Soul and its adherents were actually being shaped by their 'insights'.

The 'scene's' intrinsic hybridity, expressed by its contingent musical practices, was necessarily 'understood' as the product of a particular British urban binarism. Hence the lack of official recognition for that generation of Asians, both sides of the Watford Gap, who embarked upon a hesitant political journey and ended up on a musical mission. All those folk who set up sounds, played the music and revitalized a migrant dream by exploring and reworking the particular pleasures of Soul would this time find themselves 'conceptually' removed from the recreational shrines of their worship. Theirs was cast as a shadowy presence beyond the limits of this exclusive 'Soul Nation' – an alien constituency whose only contribution was apparently to define the boundaries of 'authentic Soul narration'.

We are necessarily reminded of the prophetic observation that opens *Culture and Truth*, anthropologist Renato Rosaldo's critical account of ethnography's spurious ethical premises:

> When someone with the authority of a teacher, say, describes the world and you are not in it, there is a moment of psychic disequilibrium, as if you looked into a mirror and saw nothing (Adrienne Rich, quoted in Rosaldo 1993: ix).

In many ways we were faced with a similar inability to recognize our world as it was being described. The discrepancy between an interpretive and an organic reality was nothing new – after all we had already been 'taught' at school about 'The Black Hole of Calcutta' and 'Africans with bones through their noses' – but the symbolic rupture it marked engaged a more developed critique of the concept of British nationhood. The idea of political safety within a love song seemed almost as absurd as those earlier 'history' lessons and flew in the face of every 'trickster' narrative passed down from Satchmo's smiling trumpet to Love Unlimited's sultry 'theme'. Indeed, the superimposed, sanitized version of events projected from a vicarious afar actually seemed more indicative of an uninterrupted interpretive hegemony than of any desire to rearticulate a positional politics.

Within this scheme of things, to acknowledge the hope of Linda Williams that we 'elevate our minds' would be tantamount to an institutional harakiri. Not only would such a gesture have endorsed a midtempo 'anthem', it would have implicitly valorized the plurality of its addressed constituency. So the gesture never came. Instead we were presented with the usual 'news' about Asians – that they were by turns thrifty, insular, academic and occasionally exotic. Oh, and before we forget, smelly, passive, 'illegal' and waiters to boot. In other words, a practical disparity of images which were infinitely recyclable as the primary definers of a mutating social politics.

If, as Salman Rushdie has suggested, we make ourselves (or are made) explicable through images, then the particularities of representational hegemony may offer a cogent explanation of the public discourses around Asianness, popular culture and Britishness that have proved so problematic. Perhaps what needs to be added is that these representations, in perversely Fanonian fashion, actually tell us more about their advocates than they do of their unfortunate subjects. Thus while an Asian cultural underground was being shaped by a generation weaned on the sounds of Pirate Radio and dusty record fairs, the 'news' update was one of pragmatic mystification.

Asians were 'understood' through their perceived 'penchant' for spicy food, illegal immigration and small businesses. Similar attachments to Horizon, JFM, Robbie Vincent and Greg Edwards unsurprisingly failed to make it onto this list.[9] When Asians made the headlines it wasn't for pre-Nusrat diasporic two-step.[10] Rather it was as a homogenized community bounded by the strictures of religion, superstition and communalism. And nowhere were these cultural formations of difference more visible than in the archetypal shopfront. If Britain was supposed to be a nation of shopkeepers then those shopkeepers were not supposed to be brown. Indeed, so many of the anxieties portrayed on those dialectical Streetsounds covers find their origins in the cultural 'exchange' first enacted around that most pervasive of icons, the 'cornershop'.

The shop never shuts: whether inside large Asian communities or juxtaposed like a satellite with the 'green and pleasant land', its lights stay on while the rest of the High Street is cloaked in darkness. In this commercial oasis everything is sold from fuses to coriander, Marlboro to milk – the all-providing mother never sleeps. It is an oasis that belies many boundaries – not solely of provision, but also of contact and indignation. Contact between a different 'native' and a new 'settler' in the urban frontier zones of an age-old crusade. And indignation that for these new 'traders' and their children potatoes simply wouldn't suffice. In a world of culturally mediated projective racism, gourd would become bitter just through its spiky incomprehensibility to the 'good island folk'. Our suggestion is that the displays of 'exotic' fruit and vegetables outside so many grocers and cornershops actually disrupted the narcissistic ignorance of that island 'race'. Their durable presence refused the arrogant logic that not just an empire but a whole way of life was proudly homegrown – that the world beyond and its citizens ungratefully benefited from the unselfish 'civilizing mission' of the West but were still held back by the savagery of their own condition. Worse still, they (the foodstuffs) were as compulsive as they were 'disgusting' to the white public, fostering disturbing feelings of attraction and curiosity as well as of incomprehending rage. Not only did these 'blacks' eat strange food and converse in impenetrable dialects but they wore colours other than blue or grey and staunchly refused to contemplate the death of 'God' in this land too. The notion that an empire had emerged out of tuber (which in any case was originally imported from South America) was becoming increasingly untenable. Indeed, as provision itself became a foundational economic principle in this recession-laden Britain, it could be argued that the cornershop increasingly epitomized a particularly British way of life.

Consider the way that Britain's manufacturing base shifted from production to service industries during this period. Rapid deindustrialization ran concurrently with a boom in the service sector whereby the notion of provision itself assumed the subtle, if obligatory, paradigms of social security payments and the cultural narcissism implicit within entrepreneurialism. Thus the apparently self-sufficient economic status of the cornershop would stand in stark contrast to the 'bankrupt stock clearances' taking place further down the High Street. And it would eventually inspire envy and loathing in the hearts of the bitter island folk. The bricks and mortar 'wet nurse' which once provided round-the-clock nourishment for the masses would now offer a constant and painful reminder to that same confused majority of the dream gone sour: a nation of shopkeepers reduced to a nation of hungry shoppers.

In one respect, however, the enduring presence of the cornershop would prove useful to the more miserly elements of an already unstable white population for it could be invoked as admissible evidence of an Asian 'separatism' conceived economically and played out culturally. Asians could be banished to the inner recesses of their 'family-run' businesses while whites and Afro-Caribbeans presumably 'went out to play'. Frail-looking Asian children would be too busy 'helping out' at the shop to enter the cultural fray. Either that or they would be precociously studying for some exam or another. And that was why they never made it down to Caister or to the front pages of Streetsounds. Instead we were treated by the 'cognoscenti' to the 'interpretive' spectacle of working-class whites and a number of blacks at an all-dayer in Essex which was fine in every respect but one: namely that this particularism would be translated into a universal paradigm for 'understanding' the hybrid contingency of youthful cultural formations. Suddenly the parameters of the emergent Brit-Soul scene had been 'set': its definitive logistics were composed of black music, white cultural affiliation and a staunchly suburban dialectic throughout Kent, Essex and the shadowy world that lay beyond zone 3. There, Leroy Hutson, Lew Kirton and Al Mason would achieve iconoclastic status with their extraordinary vinyl statements and subsequently disrupt the essentialized versions of a performative blackness so integral to the 'needs' of a white, 'counter-culture' psychopathology. Thus while such collective white idealizations of blackness were markedly external, the opposite was the case where Asians were concerned. Simplistic, reductionist logic would place a premium on versions of 'hard', black masculinity – visible, aggressive and eminently digestible. Meanwhile Asians were perceived as a hidden community lurking in the peripheral spaces of society. 'Their' women offered a glimpse of a brooding, shrouded presence, masked away behind 'the veil', and 'their' culture was derided as exclusive, alien and impenetrable, steeped in unfamiliar tradition and reworked through a by now familiar signpost: the shopfront was all that was seen. Or so 'the nation's' cultural scribes would have us believe.

Regression to the point of dialectical closure is understood, in the main, as a sort of reflex action. It is seen as a defence mechanism charged with the preservation of the body (whether individual or collective) in times of cumulative stress, for instance war. Thus a reversion to such tactics during peacetime in Britain during the Thatcher decade must be a cause for alarm or at least reflection. The idea that a British way of life was emerging with gastronomic pretensions that extended beyond Yorkshire pudding was unthinkable. That the 'immigrant' itch appeared to have outlived its seven-year celluloid lifespan was seen as symptomatic of Britain's decline, of its 'swamping' by culturally alien and threatening hordes. Indeed it was within the realm of cultural politics that the fiercest battles would be fought to determine the primacy of one .way of life over another. So goes the loveable left-leaning narrative with respect to the decade of the patterned jumper, casual sportswear, farah thing. Time, then, we reckon, for a few revisions...

Exemplary cultural formations of difference, while reliant upon a chauvinistic, parochial hegemonic structure, do not, indeed never did manage to foreclose the wider possibilities entailed by a transfigured public realm. Banishing Asians to the confines of the cornershop and Afro-Caribbeans to the heart of an imaginary urban darkness fruitfully engaged white cultural elites as the precursor to the full-time job of rewriting the history of the Brit-Soul movement. There can be little doubt as to the collective psychic anxiety of this self-appointed cultural 'vanguard' as they strove to 'discover' the 'con' in Confunk-shun and the 'Mary' in Tania Maria. Folks were advised that there was a 'promising' Soul crooner in the guise of one Frankie Beverley long after the instrumental licks of 'Twilight' were a blissful memory from the halcyon days of JFM. In these quarters there was speak too of the Mary Jane Girls though precious little was heard of Keni Burke. And the list goes on...

You see, folks for whom Curtom sounded like a house cat could hardly be relied upon to record faithfully the miasmic contours of this scene. The sons and daughters of Dartford PE teachers were as likely to speak favourably of the suburbs once they had relocated to the 'global village' of Ladbroke Grove as they were even to acknowledge the lyrical wizardry of a Ranjit Johal delivered in those 'other' suburbs. Caister, Southport, Prestatyn and Camber would be delivered intact as a sanitized package cleansed of foreign bodies and promoted as all-inclusive white excursions. Their spiritual value as 'pilgrimages' to holy British shrines of Soul and the intense passions they would arouse amongst the 'pilgrims' were conveniently sidelined as the faithless obliviously hammered out their 'truth' on ancient printing presses.

In these accounts, headed by the likes of Simon Reynolds[11] (last seen writing for 'knowledgeable' jazz-mag *The Wire*), derision for the perceived synthetic materialism and 'wannabe' tendencies of Soul, Funk and Fusion barely masks the disappointment that an instantly familiar clenched-fist, 'liberation jumpsuited' politics is absent.[12] Massa is unhappy that his natives gone learned his language and more. Why the ungrateful so-and-sos they don't even say thank you after all he's done for them. Hell, they are all turning their backs on him now. Even those bastard illiterate shopkeepers! (Professional and academic qualifications from the 'old country' had to be discounted of course. Otherwise how could you get headmasters, nurses and engineers, for example, to revert to coolie status in your factories?) Reynolds, who actually names the source of his displeasure as Junior Giscombe, renders explicit his rejection of a cultural politics conducted along the subdivisional lines of class. Perhaps, we may suggest, this is down to a perceived loss of control in spaces determined by the dynamics of 'kinetic orality'. We are thinking here of the collective antiphonic processes identified by a long tradition of black writers from Ben Sidran to Paul Gilroy as the organizing principle of syncretic musical cultures. Sidran, in particular, expounds at length on how such processes, because perceptually unfamiliar to the operational instinct of white European intellectuals, were necessarily derided as unsophisticated and illogical, being emotional. Reynolds would appear to be of this ilk. It may have been enough for most folks to holler 'Chewn!' in the hope of a rewind following a 'large' Miles Jaye bass line, but for men like Reynolds this eschewed the likelihood of a 'baadass' politics of 'otherness'. That Asians would add their voices to the collective howls of pleasure simply confirmed his worst fears. Not only had they somehow eluded the spatial segregation of the imagined cornershop but they now had the temerity to break the crude binary assumptions of the white supremacist gaze. And worse still, none of this seemed to matter to those many whites present, kitted out in Lonsdale, Pierre Cardin or their equivalents from Lewisham market.

Serious talk during such sessions would more likely revolve around the aesthetic performance of Alan Devonshire and the cerebral pulse of 'Upper Egypt'. Devonshire impressed many during the early 1980s with his 'continental' footballing skills for the east London club West Ham United. 'Upper Egypt' marked an extraordinarily complex composition of spiritual melody by former John Coltrane sideman Pharaoh Sanders. Nobody really cared that much about Robert Smith's Nietzschean pretensions or the fêted arrival of 'the global postmodern'. Less still about those meddling fanatics from the land of fashionable discourse. Our interest here is not to speculate as to the motivations behind such a poverty of perceptual imagination. Rather it is to propose a liminal politics of identity as a first step in rearticulating the cultural, political and social histories of the early 1980s Soul movement in London.

On first impressions, to be consigned to the margins of 'the nation's' cultural life would appear to be no blueprint for a productive exploration of identity. Yet the example of Asian Soulheads not only refuses such parochial logic but also calls into question the legitimacy of white cultural hegemony. The latter indicts itself with an inability to comprehend or even acknowledge the diverse cross-cultural currents of diaspora which inspired those revelatory late-night sessions with only the musical madness of Greg Edwards for company. The bleary-eyed recompense of those magical hours never seemed to inform the vacuous visions of 'the experts'. Rather, theirs was a logic split like the print into black and white. The new craniometry within the new 'Enlightenment' would suggest in classical Anglican fashion that an intellectual rewind was well under way. Black bodies would labour on the fantastically reconfigured plantations of the postmodern overseers and a whole new array of cultural products would ensue. And as for Asians, well, they'd reverted to type and a life of sly, if indentured, civility.

In a land of little recognition we are obliged to live in a world of unfulfilled dreams. Whilst the myth of self-sufficiency was fostered in a climate of increasingly antagonistic dependency,[13] for much of the 1980s in Britain there were always the possibilities of those other liminal spaces dedicated to self-determination. Johalji, Watergate, Phoenix Risin' and Samir, armed with the faith bestowed of a thousand and one imaginary journeys to the spiritual core of Caister, were always able to chase away the old supremacist jinns and put flesh on the bones of a reconfigured dream. Like their parents, many of the children of Asian settlers had been forced to embark upon their own migration. Theirs was no economic crusade, though. It was to pay homage to the sacrifices of the past so as to author the Soul of their present. When no less than Frankie Beverley told us we were 'Back in Stride' again we knew 'the man done good'. The journey had not been in vain.

So we were talking the other day about the old times, getting all dewy-eyed over Barbara Mason and West End Records, when all of a sudden there's this huge noise hurtling towards us. It's not as though there's a great space between us, the pavement and the fast-encroaching noise. Just for a moment, black hairs turned grey and calm faces ashen – before the old warrior, now shorn of his jheri-curled mane, recognized his little cousin Selim at the helm of the noise mobile. It may have been the languid pulse of G-Funk which filled the air but we would hear the pedagogic rapture of Junior Giscombe contained within its softly spoken folds. The faces, save a sage line here or a Mr Desert moustache there, had barely changed. The energetic faith was still there and the knowledge, like the tune, was waiting to break. Above all, the passage of time would temporarily be suspended as the saffron-robed Datsun sped away with its mobile, musical archive to author an uncertain text of the present tense.

NOTES

To Mum and Dad, with love and respect for making the journey, keeping the faith, and gracing the fools with their wisdom.

1. We are interested in what this assumes about critical urban cartography and its neo-imperial referents. Consider the way that suburbia inherits its primary definition from the terms 'faceless' and 'white' in spite of the presence of such 'suburban' locations as Southall, East Ham and Tooting in west, east and south London whose faces are anything but white. We would suggest that reductionist binary logic used to map an urban/suburban dichotomy is the precursor to white, cultural hegemony throughout the land. If we are to believe that suburbia is white and faceless, then it follows that Asians must be invisible. And that is precisely the point.

2. Hounslow, in west London, includes Southall, an area of predominantly Asian residential settlement. It is a good example of the contested nature of suburban definition, and the diverse cultural preferences of its heterogeneous population refuse simplistic notions (mainly of the white Left) of an unsophisticated if heroic communitarian politics. It also borders Ealing, home to famous film studios and to a 'new breed' of fêted white, British Soul musicians such as the Brand New Heavies and Jamiroquai aka Jason Kay. Once again the borders of creativity are seen to be marked by an Asian presence, that is, it is where 'the Asians' live that creativity is seen to falter.

3. Formed in the early 1980s by Asian entrepreneur Morgan Khan, the Streetsounds independent record label was, until its demise in 1989, phenomenally successful in capturing and capitalizing upon the attitudes, styles and musical proclivities of dance music 'club culture' in Britain. Khan, half Pathan, half Scot, appeared to have judged the mood of the British dance-music-buying public to perfection, and sales of Streetsounds compilation albums rocketed accordingly, becoming collectors' items following the demise of the company. While Streetsounds came to be seen increasingly as an intrinsic subcultural marker, Khan's own problematic relationship to that subculture was crystallized by his leap of faith from Soul enthusiast to archetypal Thatcherite record executive. The ambiguities surrounding Khan's involvement with 'the scene' are, however, useful in offering a way of looking at the problematic notion of 'Asianness' in relation to Soul. We are particularly interested in proposing and exploring a liminal politics of identity as a resolution to this tension as it assumes ambivalence as its point of inception and problematizes the cosy binarism that informs, either implicitly or explicitly, most theories of hybridity put forward to 'interpret' issues around cultural syncretism.

4. David Grant first came to notice in the early 1980s with the London jazz-funk/Soul duo Linx, whose 1981 hit single 'Intuition' heralded the popular 'crossover' of much Brit-Funk and such artists as Beggar & Co, Central Line, Second Image and Level 42.

5. Rewinds, taken from the original Reggae sound-system practice of lifting up the needle and 'rewinding' a 'big' tune after an introductory play, assume collective antiphony as their organizing principle. Within Soul-oriented musical scenes they also afforded an opportunity to acknowledge the crowd through a litany of 'shouts out'. This endures to the present day on many of London's pirate radio stations, particularly those playing Jungle such as Eruption, Rush and Cool FM, and offers a useful insight into the significance placed upon the crowd itself at such musical events. Such antiphonic processes would also disrupt Eurocentric notions of the disjuncture between life and art, performer and audience. Indeed the dissolution of such boundaries not only indicates the interpellative agency of such (musical) art but also its psychologically transgressive potency and appeal. We would suggest that there were at least two Asian Soulheads on whom the significance of this was not lost.

6. 'Desh pardesh' connotes the idea of 'home from home' and is employed as a vernacular correspondence to the idea of diaspora, or more particularly the British branch of the Asian diaspora.

7. The notion of an 'alternative public sphere' is borrowed from Gilroy, and

is useful to us in locating ideas around renegotiated metropolitan identities and subcultural groupings with regard to 'Asians'. It is helpful because it is premised on the recognition that the primary institutions of mainstream 'public' life and discourse assume the exclusion of the supposedly peripheral elements of British society, most dramatically constructed around febrile notions of black youth. Asians, primarily working-class Asian men, have occupied an ambiguous position within this institutionally defined hierarchy of inclusion and exclusion, as their cultural 'impact' upon British society has been interpreted as being less marked than that of their African-Caribbean contemporaries, particularly in the realms of popular culture. Once again we would advise that particularly keen attention is given to the binary logic that informs such 'understandings' of multiculture and to its interrogation by the collective antiphonic processes of an alternative public sphere. Still, in the face of violence, this sphere was always political.

8. The 'Eastern' concept of the 'bazaar' is favoured here since it offers us a way of locating the mainstream, white-determined concept of Soul as a superficially beneficial commodity, to be traded and exchanged within a neo-colonial cultural marketplace.

9. Horizon and JFM were amongst the larger London pirate stations playing 'Soul' at this time. Others included Laser, Solar, K-Jazz and Kiss, which was then still illegal. Disc jockeys Robbie Vincent and Greg Edwards, who had regular slots on Radio London and Capital Radio, were particularly popular with Soulheads as they were virtually unique in playing Soul, Jazz, Funk and Fusion on mainstream radio during the early to mid 1980s. Edwards was also one of the first black men to hold such a position and thus was even more of a rarity.

10. We are thinking of the two-step and early 1980s Soul influences on the production of Qawwali giant Nusrat Fateh Ali Khan's seminal *Magic Touch* album, and in particular the anthemic wind-down groove of 'Ali Da Malang'.

11. In his book, *Blissed Out: The Raptures of Rock*, Reynolds actually pens the following 'observations' about Soul music in its British context: 'It's quite clear that the influence of Soul music in pop has become poisonous, repressive, grey and total.... It's time to put a bullet through the head of SOUL HUMANISM and find liberation in the inhumanity of the mechanical, bestial, angelic, demonic, ghostly' (Reynolds 1990: 83). His diatribe goes on to 'lament' the 'death' of Soul and its stellar exponents such as Marvin Gaye, but he sees their demise as entirely commensurate with the 'natural' course of postmodernism, entailing as it does (at least for folks like Reynolds) the 'death' of God and of spiritual faith too.

What is interesting about Reynolds is his attempt to appoint himself as 'the good white man' in a world of evil supremacists. This is in spite of his wholly unproblematized occupation of the privileged spaces of discourse and dissemination and his woefully inept efforts at disguising his own prejudices, notably marked by the contours of class. Consider for a moment what he has to say about Brit-Funk and its adherents: 'Robbie Vincent, LWR, all the loathsome details of fake sophistication ("light those candles ... open the freezer door"). The sound is a condensation of the whole gamut of naff provincial fantasies of sophistication – vibes, Hammond organ, strings, jazzfunk ... easy listening that appeals to spivs of either political denomination' (Reynolds 1990: 89). Having hinted at his 'disappointment' with the 'everyday' imagery of this 'scene' (the savages turn out to be contrary to Massa's expectations), Reynolds then turns his irksome wrath on the music itself: 'The music is a surprisingly accurate imitation of that most toothless, spineless idiom, Britfunk ... Philly pastiches, jazz-funk ballads, Street-sounds stuff.... Its irretrievable naffness can be conveyed in only two words, Junior Giscombe' (Reynolds 1990: 90).

And to complete the effect, he finally gives away the gaff and his own middle-class, privileged pretensions to 'radical consciousness' with this admission: 'Nothing makes me more downcast than the "uplifting", nothing elevates me more than the dejected. Only music that stems from spiritual impoverishment enriches my life. Oh, like everybody else I had my summer of Soul, like a lot of white boys, thought I'd found my truest voice. But what was once a breakthrough, a crucial realignment of taste among white rock fans, has subsequently congealed into orthodoxy. In the process, Soul has been installed as something that bolsters your life, rather than knocks the ground from under your feet. The extremism I once heard in Soul has been evened out.... Speaking purely politically, in the current climate, cultural representations of failure have more resonance than fortitude-in-adversity. Give me rage and hate any day; sure, the brutal and uncaring hold the reins; sure, some people have no choice about having their lives wasted – but I celebrate the brutal and wasteful in music because I know what fascinates me' (Reynolds 1990: 90–91). Our suggestion is that Reynold's piece be looked at as indicative of a particular class-based hostility to the varied resonances of modern Soul (cf. McCann). Traces of such antagonism would appear to linger to the present day in the 'difficulty' many middle-class whites appear to have in ac-knowledging the massive Swingbeat and contemporary R'n'B scene in London. Perhaps we can speculate that Reynolds would be quite at home within such a constituency, whose major achievement to date is to have 'discovered' such labels as Puma and Adidas over a decade after the event.

12. We have borrowed the phrase 'liberation jumpsuited' from the classic 1974 Gil Scott Heron lyrical diatribe, 'The Revolution Will Not Be Televised' in which he makes clear the role he envisages white people playing come the unrest. The idea of the 'liberation jumpsuit' seems especially appropriate as it plays havoc with the notion (usually determined within a white supremacist framework of understanding) of an aesthetically marked, institutionally managed black politics of performance.

13. We are thinking here of the way in which 'Asian entrepreneurialism' premised on the traditional Conservative philosophy of economic 'self-help' goes hand in hand with an ever greater commitment to an institutionally defined 'British' way of life. Also, this marks the ambivalent relationship of economic dependency and hostility, which seems to have foregrounded so much of the 'cultural' dialogue between Asians and whites during this period and has to an extent endured to the present day.

PART THREE

ENGAGEMENTS AND
ENTANGLEMENTS

RE-SOUNDING (ANTI)RACISM, OR
CONCORDANT POLITICS?
REVOLUTIONARY ANTECEDENTS

Virinder S. Kalra, John Hutnyk
and Sanjay Sharma

The scene: a decaying Raj era hall on Lenin Sarini in Calcutta. The hall is supported by imitation Greek columns and other Victorian architectural curios, but also festooned with the red flag, hammer and sickle. Portraits of Mao comfortably fit amongst banners announcing a meeting of the Bengali section of the Communist Party of India (Marxist-Leninist).[1] Five women cadres take their place on the stage equipped with tabla and harmonium and perform a rendition of the workers' anthem the Internationale.

> Then comrades come rally
> And the last fight let us face
> The Internationale
> Unites the human race[2]

The image: five thousand miles away, but simultaneously everywhere via satellite, an MTV showing of Fun^Da^Mental's video 'Dog-Tribe' ends with the trashing of a British fascist office to the insistent refrains and Hip-Hop bass-quake frequencies of the new Asian dance music.

> What's the thing that makes a Black man insane?
> Deranged and wanna give a man pain?
> Practicalities, similarities, immoralities of what you call a racist dream.
> Skin-headed warrior fightin' for the country, killing black
> children, burning Bengalis. Enough is enough.
> Ah... people say I've gone and lost my mind 'cause I'm not
> afraid to die 'Ji'
> (Fun^Da^Mental, 'Dog-Tribe', Nation Records, 1994. Words
> by Mushtaq Uddin and Dave Watts. Published by
> QFM/Warner Chappell Music.)

Between these two moments we seek the possibility of a reconfigured politics. An explicit recognition of the historical antecedants of contemporary anti-racist movements in Britain necessitates an enlarged view, a linkage with imperialism and an understanding of the entwining of racism and imperialism. This is not a one-way story and this chapter valorizes and criticizes the efforts of anti-racist movements in Britain over the last thirty years. Failure to recognize the connection between the above two moments is in part responsible for their failure to achieve otherwise admirable anti-racist aims.

Addressing musical production in the context of organizational debates in radical anti-racist politics in Britain is difficult because much of the material for such a discussion is found only in obscure pamphlets, the Left press and in forgotten histories. The role of musical production as an organizing and historical tool in political struggle is a crucially important issue at this time, given the resurgence of racism across Europe and the difficulties that mainstream party-organized Left groupings are having in mobilizing against racism. The key to engendering new mobilizations is to combine organizational lessons learnt from Asian self-defence movements with lessons from a critique of the white anti-racist movement. The manoeuvres and critiques needed to come to this conclusion are split into three sections in this chapter. The first section attempts to reclaim the history of music and performance within organized Left Asian groupings and the Asian self-defence movements since the 1950s. A detailed history of some of the key events in the development of grassroots defence movements is explored. Music and poetry are embedded within the organizational set-up of the groups we describe. In contrast, in the second section the role of music in the anti-racist movements of the mid to late 1970s is explored in terms of debates about the significance of music to political mobilizing and, critically, the relationship between white organizers and Black musicians. This relationship parallels the organizational debates that took place between grassroots organizers and the white Left. Particularly pertinent to this is the issue of 'parachuting in' on self-defence campaigns and the use of anti-racism as a tool for recruiting to white Left organizations. 1990s Britain forms the setting for the last section where bands such as Fun^Da^Mental attempt, often with conflictual results, to bridge the gap between the anti-racist formations of the white Left and grassroots organizing by Asian defence groups. There is a lot of useful detail to be picked up in these histories, but any writing of a Black politics in the UK cannot be neatly contained, be this either in an anti-racist narrative or one about cultural production.

REVOLUTIONARY FORMATIONS:
INDIAN WORKERS AND ASIAN YOUTH

We first attempt to reclaim the lost history of music and performance within the Asian self-defence movement – beginning with the Indian Workers Association (IWA). We begin with translation of some of the songs of Asian activists in Britain that provide material to chart this history. Radical Asian politics in Britain has always used cultural performance as an organizing and mobilizing tool. Throughout the 1960s and 1970s political meetings in Birmingham and Bradford included songs and poetry which articulated the political aims, of, for example, the IWA, its anti-imperialist concerns, its anti-racist work, and its position vis-à-vis capitalist Britain.[3] The development of the Asian Youth Movements and their relationship with the white Left and the Indian Workers Association form the second part of this section. Beginning with the murder of Blair Peach and continuing through a series of public and court campaigns involving Asian youth such as the Bradford 12 and the Newham 7, the scene is set for a broader understanding of the way in which the white Left marginalized Black musicians and activists in the 1970s.

> When the Kid
> Cries in terror
> Then the leader
> On a horse
> Challenges him in the triumph of
> Supremacy
> The history of the minority
> is repeated
> again and again.
> The police reveals itself
> Pretending to be saviour of law & order
> Obeying the blind law of its ruler
> The police
> burns fires, throws bombs, destroys houses
> Showing off its power as it likes.
> Torture is everywhere
> All the time
> not knowing
> time
> country
> borders.
> The conscience of human beings is crying
> under the oppression of life

whether it is
Handsworth, Brixton, Liverpool
Delhi, Kanpur, Lebanon
You,
the cursed comrades of the minority
first identify the greater cruelty
to recognize the face of the cruel
then defend the rights of the minority
Long Live the Public!!

(Surjit Hans)

Songs and poetry are key formats for oppositional groupings. The above verses were written and performed by a member of the Indian Workers Association (GB). The IWA was one of the most active South Asian political organizations to emerge out of the presence of South Asian economic migrant labour in Britain. Its role in organizing social and cultural activities in 1950s Southall and Birmingham, working on the shop floor with Asian labourers, organizing with unions, and meeting in the back rooms of local pubs and homes, is something still obscured in the mist of languages not yet 'anthropologically' translated. Much of the history of Asian experience in Britain has been charted in Punjabi, Bengali and Urdu folk songs, and in emergent forms such as British Bhangra and today in post-Bhangra (as discussed elsewhere in this book). This musical history reflected the movement of political groupings, with the Indian Workers Association as a cultural formation with links to Indian political assemblages. The IWA was connected to the politics of the subcontinent and particularly to that of the Communist Party of India (CPI). When the CPI split in 1964, an event that saw the formation of the Communist Party of India (Marxist), a parallel occurrence took place in Britain. When the Naxalbari movement in India further split the Communist Party of India (M) and led to the formation of a Maoist party, the Communist Party of India (Marxist-Leninist), the Marxist-Leninist branch of the Indian Workers Association came into place. The cultural activities and anti-imperialist stance of the IWA reflected the mobilizing for mass support that took place in India. Every political rally would have a poetry, folk song and drama section. The songs reflected the schisms in the Indian party as well as addressing local British conditions.

I go from East Hounslow to Feltham
From my room to my work, and from my work back
to my room
This is life's journey, this life's destination.

(Ishwar Chitrakar)

Or this folk song:

> What of it if both my hands are black with grime?
> What of it if my eyes are still full of sleep?
> What of it if my hands are cracked?
> Pain has no voice.
> I eat sand and dust
> And drink the flying sparks
> And push a trolley too heavy for my strength
> We are a strange kind of tireless worker
> Who have clothed ourselves in pound notes.
> What are you saying about us?
> We work from seven to seven, seven nights of the week.
> The cold air, wrapped in snow, blows against us as we
> go on with lowered heads.
>
> (Avtar Sadique)[4]

The IWA at its peak in the mid-1970s, along with the Pakistani Workers and Kashmiri Workers Associations, could boast a following of up to 50,000 people and on many issues matched the white Left in mobilizing ability. The associations were organized along party lines with branches in most of the major cities of England, Wales and Scotland. The plight of the male industrial worker and the emergence of a radical Asian shopfloor movement is documented in such songs. Only the beginnings of a written history is available (Duffield 1987), which must be supplemented with the sort of aural story we wish to explore here. These organizations were part of an increasingly militant shopfloor movement based in factories, sustained by cultural ties through performance and aiming to combat racist and exploitative conditions common to all. These conditions, in Labour Party capitalist Britain in the mid-seventies, were sufficient to awaken attention from the organized white Left.

However the role of these Workers Associations in regard to anti-Nazi, anti-fascist movements is one marked by tension and by an autonomy which often led to conflict. The Anti-Nazi League (ANL), whose history we follow in the second part of this chapter, was largely unaware and uninterested in the forms of organization central to the Indian Workers Association and other Asian assemblages. The cultural work that brought Asians together under the IWA banner, as exemplified in the shared experiences documented in song at every IWA meeting, was beyond the comprehension of Anti-Nazi League activists, both by language and by inclination. (Translation of some of these songs begins a recovery operation and reiteration which we further identify in the work of contemporary Asian cultural activists.)

There should be no surprise that Asian musical expression addressed the difficult times of Britain in the 1970s. Enoch Powell's 1968 'rivers of blood' speech fostered the climate of race hatred in Britain, characterized by an intense hostility to the presence of Black immigrants. Immigrants were indeed seen as 'a strange kind of tireless worker' – one that Powell and racists like him targeted as to blame for Britain's economic woes. The fact that it was these workers who had the lousiest jobs and did the 'shit work' was ironic to the point of ridicule (Sivanandan 1982). Black workers became the targets of increasingly hostile police, an unsympathetic government and ever more organized fascist groupings. Facing the vicious end of this atmosphere were youth in the education system and those just entering the labour market. The policy of bussing Black children to schools far away from their homes was only one in a series of measures designed to deal with the 'problem' of too many immigrants. The more extreme version of this policy initiative was deportation. The 1974 general election saw members of the fascist party, the National Front (NF), fielding ninety candidates. Their explicit agenda of racial hatred and violent action against immigrants ensured the group the position of fourth largest national political party.

The response of the white Left to this climate is considered in the next section. Of more concern here are the grassroots responses to racial violence. The racist murders of Gurdip Chaggar in Southall in 1976 and of two Bangladeshi students in the East End·of London in 1978 saw the formation of Asian Youth Movements (AYM) up and down the country. There was an explicit recognition that if racists could come and murder people with such impunity in areas of high Asian population such as Southall and the East End, then it was time to act. The impact of the deaths was described by a member of the Bradford Asian Youth Movement:

> What I do know is that in 'seventy-six in Southall there'd been an incident where an Asian youth had been murdered, Gurdip Chaggar. And that had a big impact on us and we decided that we had to do something now ... not hang on the coat tails of, you know, the white left any more and organize our own community (quoted in Perks 1987: 67–74).

While white activists organized rock concerts to gain publicity for anti-racism, and increasingly with the Anti-Nazi League for anti-fascism, in the East End of London Asians had moved to more practical and immediate activity. An organization was formed called the Anti-Racist Committee for the Defence of Asians in East London. Its purpose was to set up self-defence patrols and gather information on racial attacks. The Bangladeshi Youth Movement formed out of this organization but failed to build on the politics of the previous committee. In 1978 the murders of Altab Ali and Ishaque Ali led to the setting up of the Action Committee against Racial Attack. The Southall Youth Movement was formed because Chaggar's death 'crystallized the political schism to responses of racism from a strategy of negotiation to one of open revolt' (Mukherjee 1988). The central task of the various youth movements emergent in England, from Southall, the East End, Bradford and Birmingham, was self-defence, but they operated on a local level with little national co-ordination. This was to change with the death of Blair Peach in Southall in 1979 and the case of the Bradford 12 in 1981. It was with these events and the organized campaigns attached to them, in different cities but united in community defence, that the assertiveness of Asian youth against the state and against reactionary tendencies within their own communities became apparent.

The setting up of the Southall Youth Movement, though predominantly male in membership, fulfilled the need for an organization that took an uncompromising position on the defence of Southall's communities against racist attack. As part of the 1979 general election campaign, the National Front stood a candidate in Southall and organized an election meeting in Southall Town Hall. The events of 23 April are well documented in *Southall 23 April 1979*,[5] but the organization of the protest against the National Front illustrates the then marginal position of the Southall Youth Movement and the Indian Workers Association with respect to each other and to the wider anti-fascist movement. Only a few months before, the Rock Against Racism (RAR) organization had pulled out of organizing an anti-racist music concert with Asian acts in Southall, so there were already underlying difficulties. When the meeting to organize the protest against the National Front in April was called by the Indian Workers Association branch in Southall, the local branches of the Anti-Nazi League and Socialist Workers Party (SWP) attended with other local community/voluntary associations. The IWA called for a closing down of shops and offices in the Southall area, as a protest against the National Front meeting. This was opposed by the other groups present who demanded a march and sit-in, which was ultimately the plan decided upon. The notable absence of the Southall Youth Movement from this meeting was due to their independent decision to have a picket on the day of the meeting outside the town hall. The intent behind this decision was that the fascist event should not be allowed to take place and to confront the racists directly. While the view that the meeting should not be allowed to take place was shared by the ANL and the SWP, there was no co-ordination between the groups. The tragic death of Blair Peach, on the day of the protest, at the hands of the police was wholly a consequence of state over-reaction to the protest and state defence of fascists. Yet, questions continue to be raised about the possibility that had there been better co-ordination between groups or had the Anti-Nazi League leadership acceded to local Indian Workers Association organizers, things might have gone differently.[6]

The events of Southall were described in the media as an attempt by strident left-wing trouble makers to cause trouble. The majority of interviews in the newspapers were with members of the Anti-Nazi League or Socialist Workers Party, giving the impression that the event had been stage-managed and inspired by these organizations. This even though the majority of those arrested were members of the Southall Youth Movement or other local organizations. Futhermore, the fact that the community had been mobilized and showed its anger was ignored by the media. Their emphasis on outside organizations para-chuting in on Southall ignored the main issue that 'the real outsiders were the National Front, who had no local branch, and the Special Police Group stationed elsewhere' (*Southall 23 April 1979*). This marginal-izing of the Asian groups was not something confined to the media but was a consistent refrain in relations between organized Black groups and the white Left. A significant example is the presence of an Indian Workers Association speaker at a Rock Against Racism/Anti-Nazi League carnival a year before. When on stage the IWA representative was greeted by incomprehension when he chose to discuss imperialism and workers' issues rather than the 'suffering' of Asians and support of anti-Nazism. The single-issue politics of groups like the Anti-Nazi League were always poor for mobilizing in communities where racism is not the only factor that binds and causes oppression. The intricate links between capitalist exploitation, racist exclusion and gendered seclusion were more fully recognized at the grassroots level than by the organized white Left. The criticism put to the ANL was that it acted as a front to attract the most advanced cadre to the Socialist Workers Party – a case supported by its disappearance with the relative decline of the National Front in the early 1980s. Racist Britain remained much the same and only a small section of the white Left continued to see anti-racism as a priority. The case of the Bradford 12, two years after Southall, illustrates the tension between those defending their own communities and both the organized white Left and the state.

Described as the 'Trial of the Decade'[7], the case of the Bradford 12 involved the arrest of twelve Asian young men who were all active members of the United Black Youth League (UBYL), an organization that had splintered from the Asian Youth Movement and took a radical approach to issues of racial attack and deportation. The police discovery of two milk crates full of petrol bombs in an area of Bradford was used to justify the arrests. But the climate in Bradford was such that racists had broadcast the fact that they were on the way to attack the Asian community. For Asian youth the petrol bombs were a justifiable means of self-defence (English common law states that self-defence is a right if the force used in defence is not in excess of what is reasonable to repel an attack). The defendants maintained that possession of the bombs was a legal act and necessary to defend the community against racist attack. As in Southall in 1979 the British state drew the line and decided to teach these 'Northern Pakis' a lesson. The Director of Public Prosecutions could have chosen to prosecute the group using the straightforward charge of 'manufacturing of explosives'. Instead the more politically divisive route of charging the twelve with conspiracy was chosen. The implication was that the Bradford 12's purpose was to undermine and destabilize the British state.

Only weeks before, Asians in Southall had burned down a pub in which skinhead fascists had organized a pop concert with the racist band Screwdriver. Three busloads of skinheads came into Southall, smashed shop windows and harassed residents. The youth of Southall, despite police protection of the fascists, organized and burnt the tavern down. The case of the Bradford 12 thus took place in the context of a widespread feeling of rage against the treatment of Black people. This song by Surjit Hans aptly describes the situation:

> Black brothers of the world
> One day you must die, so unite
> Tonight you must fight such a fight
> That tomorrow a different sun will rise
> Break the chain of slavery
> Forget the ways of non-violence
> This age of kal-yug is the black peoples' age
> Make it the age of Black power.

One year later, in June 1982, a multiracial jury acquitted all twelve accused. The exoneration of the twelve had required courts to accept that Asian communities have the right of self-defence. Wider recognition of systematic institutional racism in Britain was a direct result of the struggle for the twelve's release by the AYMs.

The importance of the events in Southall and Bradford was the approach that groups took to organizing. The AYMs built their politics on the anti-imperialist perspective of the Workers Associations. The performances of workers' poet Faiz and the singing of Ranjeeta Rani were as much part of the youth's organizing experience as they had been for the Indian Workers Associations (IWAs). But this did not mean that the youth organizations were a carbon copy of the IWAs. Tensions and areas of contest with the older guard were to bring about a radicalization of the old party structures and make the focus Britain rather than subcontinental. The primary differences were, however, tactical. Consider, by way of illustration, this tract from an IWA conference held in 1982:

> What should cultural workers do against racism?
> 1. Use all the means necessary, stories, poems, novels, folk songs, to expose the poisonous culture of racism and to document the struggles of the younger generation....
> 3. Organize all of the various organizations into a unified front: such as the Indian Youth Association (GB), trades councils. Council for Civil Liberties, some churches, IWAs (GB) and all anti-racist organizations.
>
> (Noor 1983, our translation)

One AYM member summed up what they were doing in contrast to this:

> Two things made us different; first we're proud of being Asian ... secondly was to try and oppose racism militantly, and ... if the National Front were there, to go down and make sure they don't distribute their literature. If there are cases going, ... to fight those as militantly as possible and actually do things. The main difference is we would actually do things, while they would pass policy (in Perks 1987).

This should not give the impression that these organizations did not work together or have any form of communication. Many of those in the youth movements came out of the Workers Associations, realizing that their particular need would only be met in organizations led by British Asians. The relationship was also marked by attitudes to the white Left, as one Bradford Asian Youth member said: 'Our white proletariat brothers were more likely to be attacking us and racially abusing us, we needed to organize separately from the white Left.'[8] The IWAs were also more open to forming alliances with the Anti-Nazi League and Socialist Workers Party, while the Asian Youth Movements reflected a deeper understanding of these groups vis-à-vis their approach to Black struggles and the relationships between racism and fascism. Ultimately the cultural politics embedded in the organizing of the white Left and the Black Left was such that, for the Anti-Nazi League and other anti-racist groups, the struggle against racism was the beginning of greater involvement with Black activism. The limiting factor for these white organizations was that the concerns of the shopfloor movements – strikes by Asian workers, and the constant threat of deportation – were not issues that the ANL prioritized. For Black groups these were integral to their immediate struggles.

ANTI-NAZI/ANTI-RACIST: ROCKING RACISM OR DANCING AGAINST FASCISM?

In the late 1970s Rock Against Racism (RAR) 'carnivals' were the organizational form in which the British Left, especially the Socialist Workers Party and the Anti-Nazi League, mobilized against racism. Our take on this history focuses upon the relations between organizers of RAR, who were mostly white, and Black musicians, who were often ignored. These musicians, and their politics, were subsumed within the 'anti-Nazi' focus of the ANL/SWP, or used in 'token' ways to provide credibility to the white Left. In terms of active audience, Rock Against Racism was a largely white mobilization which did not often intersect with the sorts of Asian organizations described in the previous section. Despite the musical and political possibilities that might have made such an alliance fruitful, RAR carnivalism did not result in any significant change in racist Britain. Many suggest this was a feel-good exercise for the white Left. Critiques of Rock Against Racism called for alliances between Asian defence groups and the RAR/ANL formations – these came from both the white far Left such as the Spartacist League, and from Black commentators who were suspicious of the white Left practice of parachuting in on local self-defence and anti-racist campaigns to do publicity for their rock carnivals.

Rock Against Racism was formed in September 1976. Not long before, on stage in Birmingham, befuddled rockstar Eric Clapton had announced he supported Enoch Powell and thought Britain was 'overcrowded' (*Fighting the Nazi Threat*, Anti-Nazi League educational pamphlet). In south London, punky anarcho-poseur Johnny Rotten snarled at such dinosaur rocksters to 'fuck off' and said he 'despised' the National Front, that 'no-one should have the right to tell anyone they can't live here because of the colour of their skin' (*Zigzag* 1977, no. 77: 4) and that 'England was never free. It was always a load of bullshit ... Punks and Niggers are the same thing' (quoted in Gilroy 1987: 124).

Rock Against Racism was formed as a response by concerned activists to the outrageous comments of Clapton and other musicians, and to the perception of an increasing turn towards racism and fascism within some sections of British society. Tony Parsons, writing in the music zine *Zigzag*, reported that the National Front 'intended to ban all music with black origins from the airwaves and replace the "jungle music", as they put it, with some Great British marching music' (*Zigzag* 1977 no.76: 4).[9] However absurd and lacking in even the rudiments of basic human integrity, such right-wing threats identified an enemy, for a newly politicized constituency, at the conjunction of music and politics. Two trends within popular music history are often associated at the birth of RAR in the available histories: the anti-everything anarchism of Punk and the prominence of Reggae with its anti-Babylon, anti-capitalist slacker messages. It is always difficult to assess political content and context for popular cultural forms, and never more so than for those formations that attracted the moral panic that Punk and Rastafari generated. None the less, with many Punk and Reggae bands on the bills, Rock Against Racism managed to organize almost 800 events in Britain between 1976 and 1979. The largest of these 'carnivals' in collaboration with the Anti-Nazi League attracted 80,000 people in May 1978 (Gilroy 1987: 132) and 100,000 in September 1978 (Anti-Nazi League education pack).[10]

Had it not been for Paul Gilroy we would have forgotten Rock Against Racism. David Widgery's 1986 study *Beating Time: Riot 'n Race 'n Rock 'n Roll* has been out of print for several years, histories of Punk only offer brief reminiscences, and histories of Reggae and 'Two-Tone' remain either unwritten or focus solely on the Reggae of Anglo-British bands like the Police and associated personalities. Widgery was a co-founder of Rock Against Racism and a member of the Socialist Workers Party, and though his book was described by Jon Savage in *England's Dreaming: Sex Pistols and Punk Rock* as 'full of insults for the groups who supported RAR' (Savage 1991: 484), it was the best of a small lot.

Gilroy argues that the formation of a mass anti-racist movement in Britain 'has passed largely unacknowledged' (1987: 134). It would be inappropriate to place too much emphasis on the lack of readily available histories of Rock Against Racism and the Anti-Nazi League, but the proliferation and significance of histories of the Poll Tax campaigns and of the miners' strikes (from both anarchist and socialist presses) as documentations of counter-hegemonic struggle remind us it is important to recuperate multiple versions of what goes on in anti-racism in Britain. There are various interpretations of why the Rock Against Racism/Anti-Nazi League assemblage is important. One suggests that RAR and the ANL 'gave expression to the feelings of young people who had seen the inadequacy of racist explanation [and] revealed for all to see the implicit politics of youth cultures which were defined by and often copied from Black forms and traditions' (Gilroy and Lawrence 1988: 146). The Socialist Workers Party orthodoxy is that 'Rock Against Racism aimed at promoting racial harmony through music, and was one of the first organizations to mix black and white bands at gigs' (Anti-Nazi League educational pack), and with the ANL showed the way to fight fascism. More extravagant and optimistic assessments can be arrayed alongside these orthodoxies – most famous amongst them Tariq Ali's proclamation at an early RAR event that 'Lots of people will come for Rock Against Racism today and will see that it should be Rock Against the Stock Exchange tomorrow' (*New Musical Express*, 6 May 1978[11]).

Although conjunctions of Punk and Reggae music inspired activists, it was the case that RAR remained mostly white boys' adventure rock for both organizers and performers – Buzzcocks, the Clash, Tom Robinson. With the exception of lesser known and often obscure local Reggae outfits, and perhaps Marion Elliot, aka Poly Styrene, of X-Ray Specs (Marcus 1989: 77), RAR was into a more mainstream form of crossover like UB40 and 'stars' like Elvis Costello, rather than a forum for local Black cultural productions. It is worth noting that the early British Bhangra scene was running parallel to these developments, but there was no involvement of Asian bands in RAR. Bhangra bands were playing the circuits of weddings and community events in a context largely neglected by the organizers of RAR. Politically oriented Asian musicians, for example from the Indian Workers Association, might have been invited to events, but as the imagined Other were inaccessibly beyond translation. On one occasion the RAR organizers abandoned plans to stage an event in Southall with Asian bands on the bill (Street 1986: 78–9). The potentially huge Asian audiences that might have been reached were all but ignored[12]. The diversity of the RAR crowds was often declared: 'Punks with green and pink hair mingled with skins, hippies, students, and the occasional lonely representative of the middle-aged middle classes. A lot of black kids too, though fewer Asians' (*New Musical Express*, 30 September 1978).

A key issue of interpretation in the available histories rests on the relation between the Anti-Nazi League, as organized mainly by Socialist Workers Party cadres, and the Rock Against Racism collectives working throughout the country. Though RAR was formed some time before the ANL, and organized many successful local gigs, it was when the two organizations joined forces to promote the large London marches and carnivals and a three-day 'festival' in Manchester that the movement gained widest public prominence.

A liberal view of the activities of the Socialist Workers Party in the late 1970s seems to have been quite extensive and is illustrated by Knowles in her book on the Labour Party: 'There was the carnival approach of the Anti-Nazi League, formed in 1977 to mobilize the young and unorganized in the cause of anti-racism, and providing anti-racism with an upbeat image' (Knowles 1992: 139). This 'carnival' and 'upbeat' approach characterized the ANL and SWP activity as a hip extension of real politics, and there is no doubt that many were attracted because the presentation of the ANL was more interesting than the dullard monotony of so many other political formations. Knowles continues:

> As the title of this organization conveys, though, it favoured the old official Labour Party analysis that fascism was the main problem. The Anti-Nazi League was a force for extra-parliamentary action and rapidly developed a large organizational structure capable of mobilizing thousands.... Mass action and counter-demonstration did not isolate the Anti-Nazi League from the Labour Party, though it was not officially endorsed (Knowles 1992: 131).

This parallel development with the Labour Party is very significant, suggesting a movement tailing parliamentary politics and tending towards organizational forms that were not far behind the party itself. Following Messina, Knowles reports that 'four MPs joined the steering committee' of the ANL, and 'Benn, from the cabinet, addressed Anti-Nazi League rallies' (Knowles 1992: 181; Messina 1989).

The relation between the ANL/SWP and the Labour Party is notable because it illustrates a difference of political practice that is common to the relations between the liberal Left and Black political activity. It is not without recognizing this tension that Gilroy points out that RAR had an element of anti-capitalist critique which was effectively curtailed by the anti-Nazi focus of the ANL – Gilroy writes that 'Rocking Against Racism had allowed space for youth to rant against the perceived iniquities of "Labour Party Capitalist Britain". The popular front tactics introduced by the ANL closed it down' (Gilroy 1987: 133). In contrast the SWP claims that the ANL support of Rock Against Racism was 'important in building support for anti-racism in schools, work-places and the community, as well as exposing the Nazis of the National Front', and 'Of course this did not mean that institutionalized racism ... or racial harassment was stopped' (Anti-Nazi League educational kit). In reply to Gilroy's criticisms, Alex Callinicos says, 'It is in the nature of a united front that it brings together divergent political forces which are prepared to work together around a single issue, in this case combating the Nazis', and shows that he is aware of the need to shore up criticism of this single-issue focus when he adds that 'Focusing in this way on the fascists wasn't a retreat from the more general struggle against racism' (Callinicos 1993: 64). Yet the flimsy thread running from this single-issue united front to anti-racism and then to a broader, anti-capitalist politics could be more easily tied with the sort of anti-imperialist politics of the Indian Workers Asssociations. In any case, allegations of ANL links with the Labour Party drew strength from obvious electoral opportunism within the ANL/RAR organizing committee. A stark example of this was the staging of the Manchester festival to coincide with a local by-election, in which Labour was strug-gling. In the context of the Manchester festival, Paul Morley in the NME asked: 'Has the ANL been transformed into a pure political machine?', and continued, 'Whatever, rock music is being used through the ANL, not as peoples' music, but as the supreme vehicle to reach youth. A growing deception' (NME, 22 July 1978).

Was the music peoples' music? Gilroy claims that the anti-capitalist orientation of RAR came mostly from Reggae and some aspects of Punk rebellion, although this latter with ambiguities since some punks flirted with the iconography of the National Front. A June 1977 editorial in the Punk fanzine Sniffin' Glue had characterized the National Front as 'crud', but also linked them with the 'commies, the Socialist fuckin' Workers, the head-in-the-sand brigade and the poxy Evening News' (Sniffin' Glue, 10 June 1977). Whatever the status of the Nazi symbols, it is acknowledged that Punk brought an anti-authoritarian and anti-state orientation that complemented Reggae's evocation of a Black urban militancy – Gilroy points out that the Notting Hill Carnival uprising coincided with the emergence of Punk (Gilroy 1987: 125) – and so RAR came together in a way that broke from what was considered a 'dour and self-defeating' approach, 'devoid of fun' (Gilroy 1987: 127). An organizer of RAR commented in the NME that 'for some reason or other the British left have always thought that anything electric couldn't possess any true political awareness and

that acoustic folk was the only possible music they could ally themselves with' (*NME*, 6 May 1978). There was no doubt that the ANL
and RAR were part of a moment in the political history of Britain
that, alongside tumultuous musical developments, heralded a compre-
hensive change of tempo.

In defence of fun, Gilroy suggests that the difficult crossover of Punk
and Reggae, manifest as a broad anti-capitalist anti-racism, dissolved in
the face of the organizational bureaucracy of the Anti-Nazi League. He
offers two explanations for this, both of which seem to have resonance
with general Black organization complaints about the white Left. First
of all, 'an emphasis on neo-fascism as the most dangerous embodiment
of contemporary racism inevitably pulls discussion of "race" away from
the centre of political culture and relocates it on the margins where
these groups are doomed to remain' (Gilroy 1987: 148). Second, the
neo-fascist use of the British flag and patriotism spawned an equally
suspect nationalism on the part of the ANL. 'The idea that the British
Nazis were merely sham patriots who soiled the British flag by their
use of it was a strong feature of ANL leaflets' (Gilroy 1987: 131). With
the ANL's appeal to older voters with the slogan 'Never Again', an
appeal to put Britain first and above the interests of 'foreigners' was not
far behind.

The first of Gilroy's criticisms might be questioned on the grounds
that the intention of the ANL/SWP was indeed to bring a version of
RAR anti-racism to a wider constituency, although it is conceded that
their methods and tactics were insufficient as they clumsily grasped the
symbolism of Nazism, and therefore an anti-Nazi politics, and made it
stand for anti-racism. The second criticism, of a nationalist undercurrent
within the ANL itself, is difficult to refute since in the second manifes-
tation of the ANL in the 1990s this tendency can again be found. The
way in which the SWP's Chris Bambury claims the ANL organization
and the lessons of the 1970s are 'the model of how to organize against
the Nazis' (Bambury 1992: 34) might be questioned when he even
goes so far as to recommend an ANL structure to French anti-fascists,
along with a large dose of anti-Communist sectarianism. This might
raise suspicions that there is more hype in the SWP/ANL front than
content – and especially so for those exposed to increasing racist attack
on UK streets. Support for Gilroy's analysis could be found in the
work of Bonnett who summed up: 'Unlike anti-Nazi anti-racism, the
radical anti-racist perspective is firmly committed to some form of anti-
capitalist critique' (Bonnett 1993: 120).

A common Black criticism of organized left groups like the SWP and ANL was that they arrived with leaflets and resources to impose a different agenda upon local struggles which then developed in ways sometimes at odds with the broad aims of Black groups. Writing of Black mobilizations against racism in the aftermath of the Notting Hill 'riots', Farrukh Dhondy warned that 'there are well enough anti-Nazi fronts in existence with well organized badges, posters and marching orders' (Dhondy 1978: 85). These fronts were otherwise characterized as 'a rag bag of local letterhead processors … and project hatchers' (Bengali Housing Action Group 1978: 109). Although the sincerity of many of those SWP members who did get involved in local manifestations of anti-Nazi anti-racism could not be faulted, it is clear that often the limits of this perspective caused resentment and disruption to other anti-racist concerns. Describing such worries as 'hysterical', Graham Lock summarized: 'the argument goes that the ANL is *merely* a front for the Socialist Workers Party' (*NME*, 30 September 1978, italics in original). According to *Sounds*, the 'smiling, laughing, dancing, happy' carnivalists gave 'the lie to all those cynics who try to paint the ANL as some sinister Socialist Workers Party plot' (*Sounds*, 30 September 1978). Less credibly, the ANL/RAR was also described in *Sounds* as 'a wide-ranging celebration of solidarity for freedom and against uniformity and bigotry, fired by the same spirit that fires dissidents in Russia and trade unionists in Chile' (*Sounds* 30 September 1978).

The Spartacist League's pamphlet *Militant Labour's Touching Faith in the Capitalist State*, slated 'the tradition of the ANL' popular-frontist practice of linking up with 'Anglican vicars and Labourite politicians' to confront fascism with dances. The Spartacist assessment of the ANL in the late 1970s deserves consideration: 'When the fascist National Front marched through the East End in 1978, the ANL organized an 'anti-racist' carnival *ten miles across town* [SL italics], deliberately preventing thousands of anti-fascist militants from confronting and defeating the National Front' (Spartacist League 1994: 4). Lock, in the *NME,* reported that repeated calls at the carnival for 'volunteers to defend Brick Lane elicited little response. People preferred to lie in the sun and enjoy the music.' The same writer speculated that perhaps the absence of an Asian contingent at the carnival was thus explained: 'maybe they were in Brick Lane, or maybe it is their culture tends to get overlooked on occasions like this. Where are you now Ravi Shankar?' (Lock, *NME*, 30 September 1978). Other reports suggest that the SWP leadership intentionally ignored the Asian activists (and some SWP cadre) who had assembled to confront the fascists in Brick Lane. In this scenario the SWP central committee actively worked to close out those SWP local branches with tendencies towards 'squadism' (organized militant anti-fascist squads). Subsequently many of these cadre broke with the SWP into other formations and micro-sects.[13] The Spartacist League's pamphlet pointed out that ANL equivocation was not confined to the 1970s and had continued into the 1990s – going on to record that although the large October 1993 anti-fascist rally was a significant event (known as the Welling Riot by readers of the *Guardian*), the follow-up ANL carnival at Brockwell Park was nothing more than a rehearsal of this avoidance of popular militancy (more on this later).

Gilroy, writing with Errol Lawrence, characterized as ultraleftist those criticisms of the RAR/ANL that argued it was mere 'fun music with no political connections beyond the private affiliations of the musicians'. A 'chorus of professional revolutionaries' (Gilroy and Lawrence 1988: 147) insisted that RAR had to be structured with delegates, conferences and cadre. That this 'ultraleftism' did not organize RAR and instead the SWP/ANL moved in with a popular-front anti-Nazism does not seem an important distinction at this distance. Nevertheless, the calls of the Spartacist League for 'Workers' Defence' squads as a response to the Nazis, and the calls of the Revolutionary Communist Tendency and other revolutionary communist groups, and the editorial collective of *Race Today*, for 'community defence' groups to combat racist attack, are considerably different from what the ANL offered.

In 1991 the SWP moved to re-establish the ANL in the face of renewed awareness of increasing racism in Britain and escalating racial terror in Europe. Fascists were again standing for political positions and the British National Party (BNP) was successful in gaining a council seat in one London borough. In the face of this resurgent threat, the SWP declared that Nazism was again an issue – the 'lessons of the 70s' (Bambury 1992) were to be rehearsed once again. Yet old problems remained, and the ANL was on this occasion without a national network of grassroots activists, previously provided by RAR, able to give organized Left politics a hip edge. Where previously ANL/RAR rallies had been flamboyant affairs, the 1990s versions were dominated by the mass-printed bright yellow lollipops. Seriously uncool. Nevertheless, the popular support for anti-racist expression did draw considerable numbers to ANL rallies, and the Welling demonstration in October 1993 was a success in terms of numbers mobilized, although police confrontational tactics and protection of fascists led to some disarray as we shall see.

LISTEN CONNIVING HARAMZADA:
ASIAN DANCE MUSIC IN THE 1990S

Today's new Asian dance music demands to be understood in this historical context. The reformation of the Anti-Nazi League in the 1990s amounts to a rerun of the anti-racist mobilizations of the 1970s, including carnivals, except this time we note a change in the nature of the alliances formed. Astute Asian cultural workers – and we single out for attention the new visibility of bands Fun^Da^Mental, the Kaliphz and Hustlers HC – have made attempts to bridge the gap between locally organized self-defence/Asian political groupings and the popular-front mobilizations of the white Left. Asian musicians claim a central place on the 1990s carnival platform, address their concerns to both Asian and white audiences, take speaking places at rallies organized by the white Left on other issues (especially anti-imperialist ones), and are generally more successful in countering the self-serving agendas of the Left.[14]

In the 1990s Asian musicians have drawn from the organizational practice of the Indian Workers Association and Asian Youth Movements – where politics and music were meshed in a deliberate political-cultural programme – to bring immediate self-defence concerns into a wider public sphere. In a challenge to the opportunistic approach of white Left mobilizations more interested in recruiting cadre and promoting themselves than in building broad anti-racist anti-capitalist organization, bands like Fun^Da^Mental, Kaliphz, Hustlers HC, Det-Ri-Mental and Asian Dub Foundation determined that Asian groups could not and would not continue to be ignored.

The context in which Asian musicians have brought this organizational practice to the wider anti-fascist movement has been one of general disarray. There continues to be no effective large-scale anti-racist movement in Britain. The Anti-Racist Alliance (ARA), before it collapsed in 1995, attempted to become the national umbrella organization for Black-led anti-racist groupings, and received widespread institutional support from the Left, within the Labour Party and within trade unions and trades councils. Tensions between the organized white Left (mostly Anti-Nazi League) and Black-led anti-racist organizations continued, however, and the ARA did not escape criticism from several sides. The pro-Labour stance of the ARA was a major source of contention, although this was also a charge laid before the ANL/SWP front as critics noted participation of some members of the Labour Party in the 1990s version of the ANL. This was described as opportunism as it

FUN^DA^MENTAL

appeared to some that the ANL was re-formed to capture a sudden resurgence of popular anti-racist sentiment. Both the ANL and the ARA were severely condemned for using the campaign over the racist murder of Stephen Lawrence to gain political credibility, and to claim a pseudo authenticity in their connections with the grassroots struggles of Black communities. At the hard edge of confrontational anti-racism remained those Black organizations working in the housing estate areas (rather than Westminster and the broadsheet press).

The anti-fascist Welling demonstration in 1993, led by Youth Against Racism in Europe, Anti-Fascist Action (AFA) and the ANL, gained considerable participation from semi-autonomous and grassroots-oriented Black anti-racist groups and organizations such as Newham Monitoring Project, Unity, Southall Black Sisters and Youth Connection. The demonstration took place in southeast London, an area known for its high levels of racial attacks, and it attempted to march past a building in south London known to be the organizing office of the British National Party. What marked the rally and led to arrests and the failure of the march to achieve its goal of destroying the fascist offices in Bexley was the large and aggressive police presence. Fully kitted out in riot gear, the police blocked the rally and provoked violent clashes between police and demonstrators.[15]

The Anti-Racist Alliance purposely mounted a counter-demonstration on the same day through central London. In comparison, it attracted fewer participants, and symbolized a rather outdated ARA strategy of mainstream political intervention and a belief in the parliamentary process. While the Black-led ARA marched in small numbers, many more Black activists, by far, joined the Welling demonstration. The participation of the semi-autonomous Black anti-racist groups at Welling alongside AFA and the ANL may have suggested a desire to move beyond the paralysis engendered by the warring between the ARA and the ANL. Yet even though the limitations of the institutionalized politics of the ARA were exposed, the strategic prioritising of the ANL rally by Black activists does not signify a resolution of tensions between these anti-racist groupings and the organized anti-fascist Left. One of the most immediate concerns for the grassroots anti-racist groups remains community self-defence and the countering of everyday racial violence and attacks. On the other hand it was through the tactics of forging (symbolic?) strategic alliances across the anti-racist/anti-fascist divide that the interventionism of Asian bands such as Fun^Da^Mental, Hustlers HC and Kaliphz was located.

Six months after Welling, the Anti-Racist Alliance was disintegrating and the Anti-Nazi League moved to occupy the void by organizing a music carnival reminiscent of the populist Rock Against Racism events of the 1970s. The carnival, which took place in May 1994, was huge. Yet there was little media attention. Only one television music show, the youth culture programme *Naked City*, saw fit to cover a public function that drew some 150,000 people. Few other media even picked up the story. The *Guardian* published a cynical dismissal, alleging people were only there for the free music, and then contradicted itself by pointing to politics: '...the Anti-Nazi League claim it was the biggest anti-fascist gathering ever staged ... but this crowd was never that specific. Judging from the banners along the march it was just anti. Anti-racism, anti-John Major, anti-unemployment, anti-student loans, anti-homelessness, anti-council tax.... Today's politics of protest have evolved into a kind of catch-all anti-establishmentism' (*Guardian*, 30 May 1994). It would, of course, be possible to read and publish against this conservative tone and valorize the anti-establishment spirit.

However, in an interview on *Naked City*, Asian musicians Aki Nawaz (Fun^Da^Mental) and Sonya Aurora-Madan (lead singer of Echobelly) were critical of the event on several counts. There are grounds to believe

that, to an extent, the carnival had been a feel-good publicity exercise
for the ANL/SWP, diverting attention away from more difficult
complexities surrounding racial violence and the need to mobilize against
its everyday occurrence. That the fascist BNP had not regained its London
council seat in the recent election was considered grounds for celebration, despite the fact that the most prominent BNP candidate's personal
vote had gone up from 1,400 to 2,000. Further, the BNP vote nation-
wide had increased, to some 16,000 votes, including 34 per cent of the
vote in Newham, with one other BNP candidate missing election by
just 60 votes (*Revolutionary Fighter*, 3). Mention might also be made of
the way anti-BNP sentiment was used by reformist Left groups such as
Militant to campaign in favour of the Labour Party candidate. Nawaz
complained that Fun^Da^Mental had been ignored by organizers of the
carnival and 'should have been on the bill'. At Brockwell Park there was
only one scheduled Asian band (Achanak) and they were on before the
bulk of the march even reached the park. This is not the only reported
instance of the 1990s ANL pissing off Asian musicians (the Kaliphz have
similarly had cause for dispute with the organizers of an ANL carnival
in Manchester). As it was, Fun^Da^Mental were subsequently reconciled
to their omission from the carnival with an acclaimed (by Socialist
Workers Party members) appearance at the SWP's annual conference,
Marxism 94. By July 1994, Nawaz had already been describing the
Brockwell Park carnival within the context of the wider campaign: 'I
think if 150,000 people go to a gig like that, then that's a petition. If
150,000 people are dissatisfied but can't change anything then something's wrong in our democracy. But are the Government listening? Are
they f★★★! [*Melody Maker's* asterisks]. 150,000 people and there wasn't
even one report in a daily newspaper' (*Melody Maker*, 16 July 1994).

This movement from critique to the desire to be involved actively
in organized white politics is a strategic interventionism common to
other politically motivated Asian musicians. The Kaliphz, rappers from
Rochdale,[16] most readily work in support of groups such as Anti-Fascist
Action, Red Action and the Revolutionary Communist Party to raise
political awareness amongst the community and the audiences they
attract. Their political activity extends from involvement in the
Campaign Against Militarism/No More Hiroshimas publicity, to organizing community opposition to Combat 18 in Rochdale. (Combat 18
are the declared armed wing of the British fascist movement.) The
Kaliphz have gone on record in support of the AFA's campaign to
make life hard for the Nazis wherever they appear. 'We're not scared of
Combat 18. We come from a town where Combat 18 are big and they

don't f*** with us. Yeah, Asians have a bad time here, but the way to stop that is by organizing themselves and to stop looking for sympathy' (*NME*, 10 September 1994). In the Kaliphz' own newsletter the band explain that they are not Gandhian pacifists and believe in an 'eye for an eye' (*Slingshot*), but for the *NME* journalist they explain that the 'problem with retaliation is that it has to be organized', and in response to questions about the threat to innocent civilians they say 'you have to do what AFA do: find the Nazis and sort them out. We're not talking about looking for any white person in the street' (*NME*, 10 September 1994).

The calls for direct action against racist violence are echoed in the music of many Asian bands. These musicians are doing cultural and political work drawn from Asian political formations like the Indian Workers Associations and Asian Youth Movements and putting these concerns into wider circulation through popular musical forms now accessible to more diverse audiences.

CARF, the respected journal of the Campaign Against Racism and Fascism has often been oblivious to popular cultural forms (like Rap) as a site for anti-racist struggle. In particular it has been critical of the RAR movement both for failing to mobilize people politically, and for too easy incorporation into the music industry. Nevertheless, in a recent issue, *CARF* attempted to engage with Black politicized music. It correctly noted that anti-racism in popular musical culture is increasingly being defined more by Black groups.

> The aggressive and passionate style of such music and the immediacy of its contents are things that the establishment finds problematic ... [S]uch black bands do not have a sleek, pre-packaged anti-racist politics, but speak to the immediate concerns of the community, they automatically become part of a subversive, anti-establishment counter-culture. And herein is the lesson for us anti-racists (Editorial, *CARF*, No. 22, September 1994).

CARF recognizes that the musical output of groups such as Hustlers HC, Kaliphz, Asian Dub Foundation and Fun^Da^Mental has the potential to disrupt the racial status quo.[17]

Community self-defence has a long history in Britain, and the celebrated cases of the Bradford 12 and Newham 7, and the more recent cases of the Duffield Street 4 and the Tower Hamlets 9 (*CARF*, No.17, 1993) are indicative of a continuing active resistance against racial attacks. In the light of an increased intensity of racial violence over the last few years, through their music Asian groups are urging a more widespread proactive, vigilante-style defence activism.

The articulation of the position is beyond a crude call to hunt down racist/Nazi assailants, as exemplified in the lyrics of Hustlers HC track 'Vigilante':

As the night falls it's getting scary thinking about
racist thugs that be moving about
anger in their eyes and hate in their feet
as they charge for the Paki or the Blackie in the street
I live in fear, I wanna see the next day
but on the other side of London an Asian gets beat
by a racist jerk, cos he wanted to hurt
he's a nazi skinhead treating the brown like dirt
how many more things have to wait to happen
Don't think of the Police being your protective weapon
I used to thank god for giving me a life
now I'm praying for forgiveness for carrying a knife
My mom she's worried I'm going out she's got the blues
She doesn't want to see my name headlined in the news
I'm so vexed why does it have to be
everywhere I show my head race hate is reality
we're dodging and diving to avoid the bastards
but no matter how we run they still come after us
It's like world war three or the killing season
Stephen Lawrence he died for no damn reason
Quddus Ali, he survived, but that doesn't mean nothin
he and his family went through months of sufferin
so what do I do, do I run from the country
or wait for racist Britain to scan me and hunt me down
Vigilante the peace, the silence the yin, the yang is the anger and violence
Vigilante, You live in fear of me, product of a wall of silence
conspiracy, they call me an evil thug, indiscriminate
I've seen the violence, the silence the race-hate
the beast don't care, they just do the minimal
comin after me like I'm some kinda criminal
they'll never understand what kind of man I am
I've seen mothers cry and I cry while little brothers die
but no more twenty on one, let's turn the numbers around
no more pretence, defence is from the underground
no more trying implying that I'm weak
I'm the Hindu, the Muslim, and the Sikh
The Asian youth at the end of your street.
Got to get the jackboots stomp from my hood
choose to live in peace if I could
There's a hustler in Chinatown, a 22 goes for fifty pounds
but I wonder when the time will come
when I switch from the knife and go for the gun

I'm not evil, schizo, paranoiac, but I've seen big trouble, now my anger's
    overflowing
don't stereotype me, my tactics might be,
defensive not offensive, thoughtful and pensive
patrolling the streets, I'm keeping the peace
tell me what's the point of calling the police
tell me who's going to look after the schoolkids
They are the future they need protection
My direction is anti my target is the racist coward child killer
I am the Vigilante.
Vigilante the peace, the silence the yin, the yang is the anger and violence
Vigilante the peace, the silence the yin, the yang is the anger and violence
Now I the accused won't be misused
Stand hard my brother don't take the abuse
crave to live the life of peaceful remedy
But if you mess with me I'll take the role of the Vigilante
Racists be aware I come passing through
but I ain't a thug who takes a human's life
who says a vigilante must carry a knife
it could be enough just for me to be there
the racist is a coward, easy to scare
the attacker automatically gets state defence
video cameras make prosecution sense
so playing the rule doesn't have to mean violence
huh, vigilantes move in silence
but if my cover's blown I could get beat
but it's worth it for the kids on my street
and the moms, the pops, the sisters, the brotherman,
need a barrier from the hatred of the other man
so playing this role is a must for me
so you see why we all must be – Vigilante
Vigilante – the peace, the silence the ying, the yang is the anger of
    violence
Vigilante – the peace, the silence the ying, the yang is the anger of
    violence.

> (Hustlers HC, 'Vigilante', Nation Records, 1994. Words by Paul
> Arora and Mandeep Walia, Published by QFM/Warner
> Chappell Music.)

Hustlers HC recognize the urgency of the situation right now. There
are race attacks going on; people must defend themselves; how to do
this is the question. Hustlers HC mount a scathing criticism of the
police in failing to prevent racial attacks, and, more important, of the
criminalization of Asian youth who choose to protect themselves.
Hustlers HC remain purposely ambiguous in their advocation of the
form of self-defence: 'I wonder when the time will come when I switch

from the knife and go for the gun ... don't stereotype me'. The music press – which has at least provided some sort of forum for this discussion – raised questions about the militancy of this stance which Hustlers HC were keen to clarify: 'Some reviewers have said "Hustlers have put up a good defence for violence", and we haven't. We've said vigilantism doesn't necessarily mean violence. There are various options to monitoring and controlling racial attacks. You can drive around with a video camera, you can be ready for a Rodney King' (*NME*, 15 October 1994).

Groups such as Fun^Da^Mental, Kaliphz and Hustlers HC, whilst lending their active support to the anti-fascist Left, are not easily contained by projects of anti-racism whose tendency has been to reduce Black people to the status of victims. White anti-racism has continually worked with the stereotype of the passive beaten-up Asian (youth) who must be protected, rather than the active agents of Hustlers' 'Vigilante'. The motivation behind the anti-fascist Left's limited recognition of these Asian bands has no doubt been to attempt to strengthen and authenticate the white Left's connections with Black community struggles. Nevertheless, the tensions between the white Left and the autonomous Black anti-racist groups in Britain remain apparent in the anti-fascist Left's relationship to and restricted appropriation of the cultural politics of Asian musical activism which operates beyond an anti-racist victimology.

Tracks by Hustlers HC, Kaliphz and Fun^Da^Mental challenge dominant representations of Asians (particularly males) in the media as passive racial victims – beaten bloodied faces and battered bodies is how they are come to be known. By exploiting this common-sense knowledge of racial victimology, rappers as cultural workers are able to transform it into something believed to be more progressive – organized vigilante self-defence in this case. There is no espousal of an elitist or institutionalized politics, rather, a direct attempt to express and connect with the grassroots struggles of Black communities.

These positions are at times very distant from, and in direct conflict with, the utopian 'Black and White Unite and Fight' popular anti-racist/fascist politics of Left groups in Britain such as the SWP/ANL. The identification of Fun^Da^Mental and Hustlers HC with an Asian strategic identity politics[18] is at times likely to be antithetical to the anti-racist projects of the Left, as indeed it always has been since the IWA. These bands' articulation of a de-centred 'Asianness' or an anti-imperialist Black militancy resists the containment and reappropriation of their cultural politics by the white Left.

RE-SOUNDINGS

In a decaying east London, the Hackney Empire plays host to a benefit for Quddus Ali, brutally attacked by racists and left permanently injured. On the list of performers are the Voodoo Queens, Hustlers HC, Achanak and the comedienne Meera Syal, to name only a few. The event is organized by Black-led anti-racist groups such as Newham Monitoring Project, with support from the white Left...

Making music as a means of articulating a radical politics within organized struggle against resurgent racism in Britain, and across Europe and the USA, could not be more important. This is especially so where it has become difficult for popular, or populist, party-organized Left groupings to act against racism in any meaningful way. The histories we have alluded to bear witness to a shift in radical Left anti-racist politics over the last three decades. The Indian Workers Associations and the Asian Youth Movements during the seventies were party-based organizations with anti-imperialist/anti-racist programmes. Music and other expressive cultural forms were central to their activities for mobilization, commemoration and celebration. Nevertheless, the Anti-Nazi League and Rock Against Racism were unable to foster a productive relationship with these Asian organizations. This was a result not only of the marginalization of 'race' politics by the ANL, but also of a pervasive xenophobia and nationalism in much of the white British Left during this period. In the nineties this reappeared more diffusely in the machinations of a revived ANL. A more disparate and fragmented Black anti-racist movement further problematizes the possibilities of realizing a unified anti-racist struggle in Britain.

Our contention has been that contemporary Asian-based bands such as Fun^Da^Mental, Hustlers HC and Kaliphz are doing cultural and political work drawn in part from earlier Asian political formations like the IWA and AYMs of the 1970s. Furthermore, this work is informed by experience within (and against) white anti-racist movements like the ANL and RAR, so that we see these bands putting Black concerns into wider circulation through popular musical forms, now accessible to more diverse audiences. Most significant, these bands are not connected to a specific party organization or anti-racist group, which explains their wide appeal and ability to work with the warring factions of the anti-racist Left.

It is imperative to extend the internationalist orientation of the cultural politics presented by these musicians. The first task of such an extension would be to develop a greater understanding amongst campaigners, cultural workers and subsequently their target audiences of the complex determinations of racism not only as a component of local–global capitalism, but played out in conjunction with patriarchy, the formations of nationhood and the preservation of a white European hegemony. This extension of understanding through popular cultural forms needs to occur alongside further participation in combating the immediate practical problems of contemporary racism in a way that stretches beyond the self-serving agendas of the white Left (where there are those who still behave as if anti-racism were a recruitment tool rather than part and parcel of an anti-capitalist politics). Whilst the politics forwarded by Asian-based bands resists any easy appropriation by the white Left, simply dancing to Fun^Da^Mental does not constitute a serious engagement with these bands' anti-racist/imperialist political stances, which are central to their musical productions. It remains crucial for a broad-based anti-racist coalition to emerge in Britain which recognizes the history of organizing and autonomy amongst the Black Left as well as the crucial role of cultural activism.

Our recovery of forgotten politico-musical histories is by no means the only narrative that can be told. Equally, we do not want to say that the cultural activism of Asian musicians comes without its own contradictions – particularly with regard to the politics of male-centred self-defence activism – but the point is to put these matters up for discussion. In airing these difficulties we cannot romanticize; nor do we think valorization of Asian interventions in mainstream popular or political culture is sufficient without addressing the concomitant disarticulation of such activists from their community base – but these are problems demanding several rethinks at the junction of music and politics, and they are going on. In deploying some of these problems we attempt to reconfigure and reinforce the growing alliances we identify in the resurgent Left in Britain today.

NOTES

1. A glossary of the alphabet soup of organizations we mention is included in the References section at the end of this book.

2. Our translation from the Bangla version (!).

3. In the 'texts' we use here there is a problem of distinguishing poetry and song: all poems are songs waiting to be sung and this why there is an interchange between the two. The poems and song lyrics presented in this section are translations from the original Punjabi and Urdu.

4. These three poems are presented in R. Russel and J. Shamsher, 'Punjabi Poetry in Britan', New Community 7(3), pp. 291–305.

5. See *Southall 23 April 1979: The Report of the Unofficial Committee of Enquiry*, National Council for Civil Liberties, 1980; also *Southall: The Birth of Black Community*, Campaign Against Racism and Fascism, Institute of Race Relations, 1981.

6. Whatever the case, it seemed that the ANL was dissolved soon after this event, leaving Asians to fight continued racist attack in isolation. It can be noted that the Revolutionary Communist Tendency (now Revolutionary Communist Party) made many statements critical of the SWP/ANL and in support of self-defence, as did the Spartacist League, and there was also an attempt in 1981 to reform the ANL, but this fizzled. Not that these points really matter for the crux of our argument.

7. Much of the account presented is given in greater detail in Race Today Collective, *The Struggle of Asian Workers in Britain*, 1983.

8. Tariq Mehdood, in private conversation.

9. On a very different sense of 'Jungle music' in the 1990s in Britain, see Chapter 8.

10. An SWP pamphlet claims each event attracted 100,000 (Bambury 1992: 33), *Sounds* reported an estimate by Lambeth Council of 150,000, ITV news said 60,000. Who knows?

11. We refer to music magazines of numerous stripes within the text. The *New Musical Express* is more commonly referred to as the *NME*. The *NME*'s immediate rival is *Melody Maker* (*MM*). Both these papers are weekly 'inkies', tabloid-format news and reviews papers. More glossy versions include *Spin*, *Select*, *HHC*, *Sounds*, while newsletter/fanzine-style publications include *Sniffin' Glue*, and the Kaliphz's *Sling-Shot*.

12. Doubtless this occlusion should not be overvalued since part of the expla-nation for the distance between Bhangra and 'mainstream' English music culture was an intentional and organizational separation. It is worth mentioning that this continues today in Bhangra, despite occasional major label signings.

13. The more interesting of these are Anti-Fascist Action, Red Action and the Colin Roach Centre (see the pamphlet *ANL – Critical Examination*, Colin Roach Centre 1995).

14. Much of the white Left still persists in seeing anti-racism through Trotsky's eyes as a recruitment tool rather than as part and parcel of an anti-capitalist politics.

15. There were numerous arrests which, as a consequence of the organizational confusion of the event, were not campaigned over. The subsequent jail terms for several 'rioters' picked out by the cops were passed two years later, in September 1995, with little notice.

16. Rochdale, a post-industrial mill town in the northwest of England, is a centre of BNP activity.

17. This is explicit in Fun^Da^Mental's 'Dog-Tribe' video discussed in more detail in Chapter 7.

18. See Chapter 2.

REPETITIVE BEATINGS

OR CRIMINAL JUSTICE?

John Hutnyk

Listen conniving haramzada.

> ('Dog-Tribe', Fun^Da^Mental, Nation Records 1994.
> Words by Mushtaq Uddin and Dave Watts. Published
> by QFM Publishing/Warner Chappell Music)

At the end of 1994 the Conservative government passed into law a series of measures designed to curb the 'rising criminal element' in Britain. The first arrests occurred in January 1995, many more took place over the English summer, and then into election-conscious 1996. The Criminal Justice and Public Order Act (CJA) joined US President Clinton's 'three strikes and you're out' and other 'tough on crime' legislation as part of a global crackdown best described as a 'new authoritarianism'. This new authoritarianism manifests as a wild hotch-potch of legal clauses, and corresponding media scaremongering, which should be understood in the context of racial and class politics in Britain today.[1]

To summarize very briefly, the most prominent clauses of the CJA were to ban squatting, to reduce the rights of travellers, to outlaw the activities of hunt saboteurs, and to ban raves – especially where youth gather in groups of ten or more to prepare outdoor music festivities and where the music is 'sounds wholly or predominantly characterized by the emission of a succession of repetitive beats' (this, the actual government definition, is contained in the Criminal Justice Act 58.1.b).[2]

These aspects of the Bill were debated in the alternative press, in the mainstream music press, and very occasionally in the respectable broadsheets. Throughout 1994 and into 1995, Left groups and the previously ecstasy-besotted rave scene crowd organized numerous protests and stunts to draw attention to the proposed new laws. These stunts included mass trespass on to the properties of senior government ministers, occupation of the roof of Parliament, and huge, now illegal, raves, as well as marches through the cities of London, Manchester, Leeds, Bristol etcetera. The most prominent of these marches has come to be known in tabloid sensationalized code as the 'battle of Park Lane' where the famous Monopoly site became host for a three-hour mounted police attack on protesting leftists (on my estimation, the police came off second best). Predictable media clean-up accusations of 'rogue anarcho-provocateurs' followed (including photo-kit identity pictures in the press, culled from snaps taken at Park Lane, calling on readers to shop anyone they recognized). The protests against the proposed laws included free festivals, occupations, weird propaganda pranks (including an alternative video news service, *Small World*, circulated throughout various pirate networks) and a wide range of loopy to ultra left counter-establishment gestures. Important support for the anti-CJA campaigns came from benefit performances by Asian bands Fun^Da^Mental, the Kaliphz and Asian Dub Foundation, as well as from the presence of Aki Nawaz of Fun^Da^Mental on the speakers' platform at CJA rallies.

The Act was passed through Parliament despite considerable 'alternative' opposition (100,000 at each of the big London rallies I attended, 5,000 in Madchester). The government ignored vocal public sentiment and rode the Act through on the strength of its demonization of rave fans, travellers, gypsies and squatters and other so-called anti-social elements that were considered 'criminal' in 'tolerant and democratic Britain'. Unfortunately the anti-'crusty' agenda of the Act was only a smokescreen to cover still more draconian measures to increase the state's authoritarian powers in inner cities and police control/surveillance of minority groups (not just the crusties and other anarchist music fans who like to dance stoned in remote fields, but almost all non-Conservative, unwashed, black or working-class 'rabble'). The key political initiatives in the Act can be grouped under four headings. (1) Demonstrations: assemblies (gathering of twenty or more persons) that may 'disrupt the life of the community' may be banned by a chief officer of police applying to the local council. Not only raves, but any large-scale demonstration, such as a trade union, left-wing or anti-racist 'assembly' may be banned. Although the government may argue that in practice these powers would not be used against most forms of peaceful protest, this law – in practice – relies upon unregulated police 'discretion'. (2) Trespass: a new offence of aggravated trespass has been created under the terms of which people who are trespassing will be considered to have 'aggravated' their crime if they do anything to disrupt any lawful activity (such as disrupting the hunt, the government said, but this provision could apply to all other forms of protest). A further offence has been created under which it is a crime for anyone to disobey a police officer of any rank who has directed that person to leave a particular area of land. A picket outside a workplace protesting against job losses which aims to dissuade people from entering the workplace (by talking to them and encouraging them to support the strike) could attract a charge of aggravated trespass and a prison sentence of up to three months. (3) Stop-and-search: if a police superintendent or inspector 'believes that incidents involving serious violence may take place in any locality' and it is 'expedient to do so', he can authorize powers to stop and search people and vehicles for a period of up to twenty-four hours. Even the Home Secretary noted that this was being described as a re-creation of the discredited sus laws which led to the Brixton riots in 1981. (4) Anti-terrorism: possession of items like rubber gloves, kitchen scales or fishing line may mean arrest on 'reasonable suspicion' for 'preparing for terrorist activities'. Possession of information likely to be of use to terrorists, whether or not the information is given to 'terrorists', may also attract imprisonment of up to ten years. For example, holding a list of government ministers' addresses, or those of a multinational company, might attract attention under this clause. The offence of 'going equipped for terrorism' reverses the normal burden of proof: here an offence is committed merely on the basis of 'reasonable suspicion'.

Outside Black political and communist circles, few have challenged the attacks contained in the less publicized parts of the Act. The new authoritarian turn in Britain in the wake of the end of the Cold War, the dismantling of the welfare state, and the abandonment of any other pretence of civic equity, has meant that neither of the main capitalist parties feel they are in a position to do anything but use greater repression and coercive force to maintain order and privilege. What also seems worthy of note is the strange silences of intellectuals, both academic and left-wing, in the face of this criminalization of youth, attack on political rights, expansion of the police state, and so on. Why? Most especially the absence of any discussion of the racist elements of the CJA. It seems particularly remiss that the advocates of culture – sociologists, anthropologists, cultural studies personnel, journalists – have not taken up the vanguard of campaigning against these measures. The happy opportunity of these disciplines, surely, is not to acquiesce to any role of compliant approval (for fear of further funding cuts) but to recognize that a role as apologists for state legitimacy is no longer an obligation, and that a critique of everything is (now more than ever) both a necessity and an intellectual requirement. Far worse, however, than the failure of public figures to question the Act is that a corresponding silence on race issues can be found even amongst those who did mobilize. While the inclusion of clauses to increase police powers in the inner urban areas was of special concern to Asian anti-racist organizations, these aspects were rarely addressed by white middle-class activists more concerned with the attacks on raves and parties. The most political of responses from the white Left took up the attacks on demonstrations, the anti-terrorism clauses and the abolition of the right to silence (a jury shall be directed to draw 'inferences that seem proper' from a defendant's silence if that defendant did not provide explanations when arrested), but rarely the stop-and-search powers which already in 1995 were used in Police Commissioner Paul Condon's outrageous crackdown on 'black' muggers in London – Operation Eagle Eye.

The remainder of this chapter ventures to rethink the orientations of opposition to the CJA, to reconsider the role of critics under capitalism, and to move with Asian critics of the CJA towards new configurations, practices and alliances for anti-racists. This will be attempted by way of a discussion of the Fun^Da^Mental video *Dog-Tribe* and its 'banning', and of music and political mobilizations (ANL carnival against the Nazis, anti-Criminal Justice Act raves) and of youth mobilization around anti-racism, anti-government, Parliament, police and the state. To clarify these issues I take up the (moral/ethical?) issues of defending defence squads (not the privatized police, but community mobilizations) as presented in the Fun^Da^Mental video and in the music of similar South Asian groups. More generally, the chapter points to changing configurations of identity and engagement within political struggles in the contemporary period. Examples such as the Revolutionary Internationalist League defence of the Langdale 4 and the Kaliphz involvement with Anti-Fascist Action, as well as Fun^Da^Mental's international media experience, configure new alliances and responses to the hypocrisies of the global factory in which we live and might thereby offer indications of how our predicament can be reworked, reconfigured and transformed.

In broad terms I am trying to place a specific musical work in its political and cultural context and, although peripheral and anecdotal details are not excluded, the movement of the chapter from Fun^Da^Mental to leftist self-defence activism by way of discussion of the Criminal Justice Act as it passed through Parliament is not just a contrivance – I am trying to exploit the contrapuntal effects of placing parliamentary discourses alongside rappers to illustrate Aki Nawaz's observation (at a rally against the CJA, November 1994) that anti-racist, anti-capitalist and anti-imperialist politics must be addressed together. This chapter attempts to outline some conjunctions of research on (a) music industry/televisual assemblages; (b) parliamentary and political formations that impinge here; and (c) anti-racist assemblages.

MUSIC AND POLITICS: THE DOG TRIBE

Cultural Studies approaches to political issues often seem overly eclectic and so aesthetically obsessed, or absorbed, that the issues get obscured. It seems to me that academic work in the social sciences has largely and consistently ignored or misunderstood the more interesting developments in British popular culture. Whether or not this is true may be a consequence of various discipline-shaping agendas and protocols, the vagaries of market-driven research interests (the nexus between publishers and research council), and historical–epistemological particularities. The point is, however, that Asian cultural production, and especially Asian youth cultural work, has rarely been a favoured subject, and even when it has managed to find space it has rarely been considered in any sustained political way. At best such cultural work appears as a footnote to generational, identity, or ethnicity studies, calling for further detailed ethnographic study which is rarely pursued in anything but conventional ways. In those works that do mention such matters, examples might be cited to illustrate a consistent avoidance; from the dilettante and neo-Orientalist fascination with cultural difference, exotica, aroma (spices) and ritual, to ritual acknowledgement in the couplet 'Black *and* Asian peoples of Britain' in studies about Black British cultures, it seems curious that the political force of Asian youth activity goes without scholarly attention. (Perhaps this is a good thing? Leave well enough alone – is it the role of the social sciences to do *de facto* surveillance work on the children of diaspora on behalf of the state?) Where such work has been attempted it is difficult to distinguish old-style anthropological report-backs from protestations of 'political engagement'. A recent example would be Mary Gillespie's study of ethnicity and music in Southall, London (Gillespie 1995) which, although it is conscious of power differentials between observer and observed, does not at any time break out of the formula of a reporting to the academy of the strange and exotic (see Hutnyk 1996c).

Fun^Da^Mental, Kaliphz, Punjabi MC, XLNC, Apache Indian, and a variety of emergent South Asian musicians (*not* characterized as Asian Kool – the marketing category put out by music industry press like *Select, Melody Maker, New Musical Express* inc.) suggest an intellectual, commercial, public cultural engagement that addresses contemporary issues and – within the constraints of disciplinary topicality – are still sometimes very close to the proclaimed concerns of anthropology/ sociology/cultural studies in Britain. Yet I will argue that more and more the established disciplines have been inadequate to a comprehension of sophisticated and militant social productions such as those, as a specific example, of Fun^Da^Mental, and inadequate too in comprehending the controversy around the video *Dog-Tribe*. The practitioners of the new Asian dance music are engaged in a politics of race, identity and cultural production – as well as making important interventions into campaigns against immigration laws, the Criminal Justice Act, antimilitarism, and so on – in a way that demands extended consideration. It should be noted that these bands are often characterized using various labels they might readily reject – not just Asian Kool, but 'crossover', World Music, Asian Rap, world fusion, hybrid, and so on – and much ink and air could be expended on suspect questions about the appropriateness of these terms. Racist, essentialist, head-in-sand nostalgias for authenticity and some sort of fidelity to racially inscribed audiences continue to arrive sometimes within academic forums. The point here would be to indicate the nostalgia of those who celebrate traditional forms of music and culture as unchanging, and who assume fixed notions of community and identity, and who seem to imagine that some notion of already formed 'communities' arriving off the boat as they are, and forever were, offers the only way to talk about 'ethnicity' in Britain. Bands like Fun^Da^Mental blow this kind of neo-Orientalism out of the water. The static survivalist view of the world assigns identities in a wholly modernist and discredited way, a way that must be countered by looking to organizational and cultural dynamic and flow, and identifications formed in multiple and changing socio-political contexts.

These are not easy problems and not the only ones. Writing about video in the language of a cultural forum such as this book might also be condemned – and for the same reasons the *Dog-Tribe* video condemns parliamentary processes. Writing about video sound and image is inherently fraught with difficulty. Good. This seems all the more reason to bring out contradictions in the ways academic effort has avoided confrontation in this domain – arguably a. domain within

AKI NAWAZ AKA PROPAGANDHI   Natio

which it should have significant engagement. Yet a 'banned', and so silenced, video presentation can, despite 'banning', be re-presented in certain institutionally condoned spaces (albeit an already privileged venue and audience – the not quite completely quashed liberties of bourgeois academia), and with the addition of commentaries condoned by an authority accorded in and by this re-presentative space. *Dog-Tribe* is a five-minute, roughly edited, and starkly shot black-and-white production telling the story of a race attack by young white skinheads upon a lone Asian. Its subtext charts the politicization of the Asian youth (who happens to be Aki Nawaz). The narrative begins with Nawaz painting a 'Nazis Out' slogan on a wall; he is attacked by three skinheads. They kick into him – the camera lingers too long over the violence. Three passing Asian youths intervene and chase the skinheads off. A close-up of Nawaz, bruised and bleeding, spitting teeth, after the attack is also very much in-yer-face-TV. In subsequent scenes Nawaz is observed petitioning a politician – who ignores his statistics – and attending the funeral of another victim of a race attack. The presence of a silent Asian woman mourning in front of the grave passes without comment, but the main point is that an evidently organized self-defence group, whose members are also attending the graveside, invites Nawaz to join with them – symbolized by the placing of a scarf with Islamic insignia over his face (and over his keffiyeh scarf of the Palestine Liberation Organization[3]). The lyrics emphasize the message: 'there comes a time when enough is enough … self-defence is no offence'. Both the explicit portrayal of the horrors of racial assault and several flashbacks stress the point that by joining an organized defence group the supposed passive Asian victim is no longer isolated and becomes an active agent: 'our defence is on attack'. The last scenes of the video show an anarchic and almost carnivalesque destruction and burning of materials and placards of Combat 18 and the BNP. A direct challenge to their activities is made: the signs 'we are waiting' and 'now is the time' are thrust at the camera.

> What's the thing that makes a black man insane?
> Deranged and wanna give a man pain?
> Practicalities, similarities, immoralities of what you call a
> racist dream.
> Skin-headed warrior fightin' for the country, killing black
> children, burning Bengalis. Enough is enough.
> Ah… people say I've gone and lost my mind 'cause I'm not
> afraid to die 'ji'.
> The dog-tribe seeks the skin and puts them in a pound, retaliate
> and you'll be six foot underground, pushin' up daisies,
> 'cause the devil sent you to tame me but you can't face me.
> You see I grips mikes, wrex mikes, condition my mind to
> finally come to terms,
> Anyway wake up, wake up c'c'cos I'm on a self-defence vibe,
> never down but always down with the tribe
> People wonder why I'm positioned by the window
> Ammunition close at hand though,
> looking like the man brother Malcolm
> If I can't reason, time for some action. You must hear
> me though, even though they don't know,
> don't ask for violence, just self-defence
> I'm on a Romper Stomper agenda vice versa,
> I'm the brown one, my brother Nubian,

Followin' the ways of the days of the Nazis,
Listen conniving haramzada
There comes a time when enough is enough,
Afro-Caribbeans, Asians together is tuff
our defence is on attack, minds are made up,
Bodies are fighting back. Self defence is no offence
And we're ready, ready for a collision with the opposition
It won't be a suicide mission, and one thing about me, I'm
not afraid to die 'ji'
And after me, there will always be another brother

(Fun^Da^Mental, 'Dog-Tribe')

The clip, and some performances of the band, have been discussed, if at all, in predictable ways. A focus upon their Islamic symbols has dominated attention, and the confrontational style has raised anxieties. In the magazine *CARF* (produced by the Campaign Against Racism and Fascism) the band was described as having a 'no-nonsense anti-racist politics and commitment to Islam' (*CARF*, 22: 6). In contrast *Melody Maker*'s early comments on the clip pointed to the violent nature of the images, recognized some degree of racism in Britain, but ended up repeating opinions that this was a country with 'no history of, or tolerance or capacity for, political extremism' (quoted in *CARF*, 22: 6). From comments like these, it would seem that the 'banning' of the *Dog-Tribe* video is understood by the music press as a response to Islamic extremism, and there is little care or concern that political statements can be so readily erased. Powerful symbolism, that scarf. Admittedly, later editions of *Melody Maker* articulated the growing youth mobilization against the CJA, and once provided space for both Nawaz and Fun^Da^Mental's Dave Watts to present critical perspectives on racism (the 22 October 1994 edition reported Nawaz's speech against the CJA outside Westminster City Hall on 19 October in a three-page article). Nevertheless, *CARF* catalogues a systematic deployment of the music press against the political militancy of the band: they point out that 'articles on Fun^Da^Mental in the music papers are now peppered with ridiculous diatribes on the threat of Islam, and defences of Western values' (*CARF*, 22: 6). Again exceptionally, *NME* managed an admirable discussion of *Dog-Tribe* in May which explained the track as being 'about members of the community who've had enough beatings, enough of their neighbourhoods being terrorized, and who've decided to fight back' (7 May 1994). This issue of *NME* also provided a list of names and offences of known BNP members.

In an interview with *CARF*, Nawaz pointed out that the politics of

Fun^Da^Mental is not a fashion statement, nor an attempt just to make
it big in the music business. The music provides a platform for a statement, in this case a video 'that should not have been banned' (Nawaz)
and should be played on daytime television to raise questions about
race violence in the minds of young viewers. Nawaz also points out
the importance of fighting imperialism and colonialism, which are 'all
part of racism' (*CARF* 22: 7). Any suggestion that this is Islamic 'fundamentalism' requires analysis of popular panics about the threat of
militant Islam, terrorism and violence that need to be unpacked in the
context of media-managed new imperialist demonologies and post-
Khomeini US warmongering. Rather than an exegesis of the meaning
of fundamentalism – a favourite neo-Orientalist academic pastime – it
would be preferable to develop critiques of media constructions of
'dangerous' others and the way this alibis new global instances of imperialist aggression and institutionalized racism together (the United
Nations in the Gulf and the CJA in the UK both as examples along
the same continuum). Such an analysis would need to investigate why
a video such as *Dog-Tribe* should be 'banned', and how the mechanisms
of 'banning' relate to new authoritarian turns and ongoing imperialisms.

So *Dog-Tribe appears* to be a dangerous text because of its portrayal
of militant Islamic 'fundamentalist' violence. No doubt this could engage
scholarly debate in another banal discussion about freedom of speech,
although significantly it did not. Academics were quick to jump to
Salman Rushdie's defence when it was a matter of an attack on an
honoured establishment writer, however progressive, but there is a difference when it is a matter of less literary popular-cultural examples of
silencing, and where it is the British state, not an Islamic foreign power,
doing the silencing. Impi D of Fun^Da^Mental hinted at a wider
agenda in an interview: 'You're not going to solve the problem [of
racism] by being civil about things. These people [fascists] don't make
an attempt at dialogue. We're saying stop whinging about freedom of
speech, because these people are not about free speech' (*Guardian*, 17
June 1994).

On paper the 'banning' seems to have been less a government decree
than self-censorship in anticipation of such a decree on the part of
MTV and ITV, the major television music video distribution outlets
(and crucially important for mainstream visibility). It was decided the
clip would be likely to attract an 18 certificate from the censor (under
the Video Recordings Act of 1985, a supplier can be prosecuted if the
video has not received an appropriate British Board of Film Classification certificate), although it is not clear that the BBFC has ever

viewed *Dog-Tribe*. ITV's *Chart Show* refused the clip, and MTV chose to show it only after 10 p.m. A showing on Channel Four's *Naked City* (June 1994), also after 10 p.m., made much of the 'banning' of the clip, and invited Nawaz and Sonya Aurora-Madan to discuss anti-racism issues. The treatment here, in the guise of a transgression of the 'ban', did nothing to disrupt panic reactions to televised violence. This is so even where the clip has a message considerably different from that of most banned or 18-certificate violent cinema or television films, or the widely approved Terminator style ('you said not to kill anyone', says Schwartzenegger as he fires two rounds from a shotgun into an assail-ant's knees. We all laugh. In Hollywood, white stars like Stallone are consistently seen blowing up buildings full of police without censure; indeed, they are cheered along). The point is that violent attacks upon Asian youth in Southall, east London, Bradford and other cities affect the whole community, including those under eighteen, so squeamish-ness about this violence, or the immediate practical necessity of self-defence, is nonsense.

Nonsense was piled upon nonsense in an escalation of white-noise silencing. Instead of a frank discussion of the politics of censorship in the context of racist Britain on *Naked City*, we were treated to simplistic and partial soundbites which offered little. In a letter to *Melody Maker*, Aurora-Madan complained of being 'asked token questions' on the show (*MM*, 23 July 1994) and that the fifteen-minute interview had been cut to two minutes: '...every valid point that I had made had been edited out and, to make matters worse, they wasted airtime showing *pretty* shots of me ... this sort of censorship is typical of what a lot of female musicians have to put up with' (*MM*, 23 July 1994). The inclusion of Aurora-Madan at one point referring to the 'fucking BNP' was also a token gesture on the part of the editors (intentionally outrageous, calcu-lated to shock, and so confirm the pretty Asian girl image). Aurora-Madan wrote: 'The media world is full of token questioning by people who don't really give a f★★★ [*MM*'s asterisks; see also pp. 148–9 above]. I am learning that I WILL be misrepresented' (*MM*, 23 July 1994).

To sum up. This silencing and misrepresentation of Madan (*MM* asterisks) is a parallel to the 'banning' of *Dog-Tribe* on television which was the avowed subject of the Naked City interview. This is further parallel to the silencing of Fun^Da^Mental's message in *Dog-Tribe* else-where within the mainstream public arena, and the historical failure of the white Left to hear the political concerns of the IWA and AYMs discussed in the previous chapter, or to address the racial aspects of the CJA. Despite the Left's limited inclusion of Asian bands in various political campaigns, it is common both for formations like the ANL and for MTV to fall into packaging and occlusion in this way. Academic and journalistic protest at censorship meanwhile are nowhere to be seen.

Of course, it would be naïve to suggest that Black musical cultural production is autonomous from an ever-expanding capitalist consumer culture, which increasingly neutralizes and sells back 'ethnicity' and cultural difference. Witness the recent MTV 'ethnic' fashion show *The Pulse* brimming with 'black' models, and over its closing credits playing the *Dog-Tribe* track without images ('What's the thing that makes a Black man insane' are the opening lyrics). The *Dog-Tribe* video has not been available for purchase in stores and had minimal coverage on screen. The novelty of banned videos doesn't seem to translate into bumper sales for Asians in the way, perhaps, that notoriety once did aid bands such as the Rolling Stones or Sex Pistols. Despite low exposure the Fun^Da^Mental album *Seize the Time* sold reasonably well in the stores and was reported at number fourteen in the national independent *Music Week* chart after five weeks (*Music Week*, 30 July 1994). Months after its release, 'Dog-Tribe' was used as a signature soundtrack for the MTV Europe video awards, again without the images (November 1994 and again in July 1995), while segments of the video clip itself were used several times in an MTV/Coca-Cola news item on Hip-Hop politics.

THE CRIMINAL JUSTICE ACT (DOG-TRIBE REPRISE)

How does something 'cultural' like a music video come to be banned for 'political' reasons? Apart from the 1985 Video Recordings Act, the most recent legislation under which a video such as *Dog-Tribe* might be banned is the Criminal Justice Act, and specifically clauses added in April 1994 after a truncated 'debate' on racial harassment (House of Commons, Official Report, Parliamentary Debates, *Hansard*, vol. 241 – all references to *Hansard* are from this volume unless otherwise noted). The clauses cite 'publishing etc. material intended or likely to stir up racial hatred' and showing videos which 'present an inappropriate model for children' as grounds for censorship or arrest. Although similar clauses may be found in other legislation (such as the Race Relations, Public Order or Video Recordings Acts), in the context of the Criminal Justice Act these clauses make issues of inequality and prejudicial interpretation and application of the law more explicit.

Feeling like I didn't have enough to get upset about, I thought a day in Parliament would be entertaining, and would offer a chance to listen to elevated debate about issues of concern to the nation from the most eminent in the land, font of the Westminster system. Forgive this facetiousness, it is nevertheless revealing to hear what is said in the halls of the state (of course a critique of essentialist notions of 'race' would demolish the parliamentary debate over racially motivated violence – but such would be to avoid the instructive aspects of the whole windbag exercise). The importance of the CJA does demand extended academic debate. That, thus far, it has not attracted general interest is only partly a function of the low level at which it was presented in parliament.

Amidst the 150-plus clauses of the Criminal Justice Act – all of which defy comprehension in their anti-people hostility, their massive expansion of police powers, their criminalization of youth, their anti-music, anti-fun, anti-everything Blitzkrieg – there was an interlude debate over the inclusion of amendments on racially motivated violence and harassment proposed by Labour member Joan Ruddock (Lewisham, Deptford).

Labour wanted to introduce new clauses into the bill which would increase the power of the courts to impose more severe sentences for crimes where it could be shown that racial hatred was a motivating factor in the crime. Certain obligations on the part of the police and the courts to investigate and report on racial factors, and a new offence of racial harassment were included. That Labour argued this amendment but abstained from voting on the passage of the bill as a whole suggests that they were more concerned to be seen to support anti-racist legislative tinkering than to defend the rights of the general population or specific communities such as ravers, travellers, gypsies, youth, minorities, common citizens, prisoners, immigrants… basically everyone. Mark Butler reported this as well as anyone: 'Anti racists [including Tony Blair (*sic*)] have provided the candy coating for proposals to increase police powers. Under these powers the police in places like east London can regularly harass white youths … and at the same time, they can continue to push around young Asians, this time on the pretext of clamping down on the 'racism' of Asian gangs too' (Butler in *Living Marxism*, 1994: 35). What was significant in the brief legislative hiatus of the amendments was the symbolic display (varieties of posture) of very fine sentiment and rhetorical flair which effectively achieved the opposite of what was required.

It was for the most part a tedious debate, even by parliamentary standards. At one point the Conservative Minister of State, Peter Lloyd, explained his move from support for anti-racist violence legislation being included in the bill with that wonderfully arcane banality 'a week is a long time in politics'. At other points Conservative members were at pains to point out their anti-racist credentials, but were on the whole adamant that no support for the Labour amendment was possible, and they proposed their own, severely truncated, amendment on the issue of publication of racist literature and increased penalties for race-related murder. Labour members made much of their desire to do 'something' about the increase of race attacks in Britain – the increase was also acknowledged by the Tories – but Labour's proposed legislation (to get the police to do something about it) was voted down 285 to 247. The Conservatives' amendment was ultimately accepted without debate the next day and achieved little new except for adding the crime of sending racist material through the post to the already immensely effective and ever-so-important anti-pornography postal regulations (brown envelope brigade).

The ironic summation was provided by Keith Vaz (Leicester, East) who said: 'we can all condemn racial attacks on fellow citizens, but the important thing is what we propose to do about them' (*Hansard*). This mighty insight raises yet again the question of the efficacy of legislative measures of the bourgeois state. Earlier in the debate David Sumberg (Bury, South) had railed against the 'evil in society' and the unacceptable rise of the 'hard right' in Britain (a country he characterized as having 'always been a tolerant, just and humane society – a society that has welcomed immigrants to its shores for many years'). The 'evil', it turns out a paragraph later, is that the existing adequate laws are not being enforced properly, and that there are enforcement loopholes. The evil was to be corrected by the Conservatives' amendment, rather than Labour's.

Labour's Gerald Kaufman (Manchester, Gorton) argued that those who become victims of crimes of property because they are Asian, Jewish or some other 'uncontrollable factor of their birth', whether they are rich or poor, suffer a more odious kind of crime. Kaufman related his recent visit to the Chief Constable of Manchester accompanying Pakistani constituents who were concerned that 'their wives could not go out shopping and their children could not go out safely'. At this point, Sir Ivan Lawrence (Burton) took the opportunity to deepen the analysis and introduce a more grand European world history dimension to the debate – surmisedly in response to Kaufman's specifically local flair – and in a suitable epic tone recounted the following:

> Racism, in all its forms, is an evil and destructive force in our multi-racial society. There is no doubt that it is spreading and that it has to be stopped. As the pressures build in the liberated eastern European countries following the break-up of the Soviet empire [there is no need to tell you which side of politics this guy is from] so ethnic divisions are building up all over Europe, often resulting in ethnic cleansing wars. Inevitably, we have seen a substantial increase in the number of refugees travelling from one country to another and immigration to countries which have not seen immigration on such a large scale before. So, too, will the pressures of racism inevitably grow and spread to the United Kingdom.

Is not this amazing? The threat, not even veiled, is that immigrants will want to come to Britain, and indeed these dastardly foreigners will bring their filthy communist racism with them. Except that the racism has escalated because of the fall of communism, which is a problem since I guess this means the blame might be stuck upon the new economic 'advances' of Eastern European capitalism, and so, it wouldn't be too difficult to surmise, these wars of ethnic cleansing are the consequence of the emergent free market ... but this is another story. Sir Lawrence of Burton continues:

> Britain must realize the likely extent of that evil [a rise in racism] and start to put up our defences as strongly as we can so that the worst excesses at least can be avoided and this nation can maintain its reputation for being tolerant and decent (*Hansard*).

It would, of course, be considered by many to be unfair to quote impromptu ravings by parliamentary pinheads and take them all too seriously. In this instance Sir Ivan was speaking on behalf of the Home Affairs Select Committee, or at least on behalf of a six-to-four majority of that committee, and he also used some of the same metaphors – 'tolerant decent nation', 'tackle the evil' – that the legislator from Bury, Mr Sumberg, had deployed. So this putting up of defences against the immigrating, ethnic cleansing, ex-communist hordes seems pretty much standard Tory line. Except that the Home Affairs Committee had not yet submitted its report. The report has been delayed, was hoped for before Christmas, but had been waylaid. It did manage reports in previous years, but since 1989 nothing. During which time, Sir Lawrence told us, 'there have been shocking attacks, murder and violence' and the committee had been taking evidence. What was to be done? The committee had not yet agreed recommendations – though it managed to stand – six to four – against the amendment under discussion.

But wait, Sir Lawrence has lost the amendment: in the midst of a discussion of clause 13 he admits, 'I cannot immediately find new clause

13, so I cannot answer…' Minutes later he is able to rise again, and I quote: 'I have now refreshed my memory about new clause 13. It may confuse the issue.' *Hansard* prints it so, verbatim, although perhaps there is something missing in the cadence, the nuances of the spoken word, the tone, which I can't convey here. Tone is always important, the same phrases can mean altogether another thing sampled otherwise, can beat to a different drum… Anyway, the issue at stake at this point in the proceedings is Clause 13 and the part that is specifically to do with whether or not a judge or a jury shall be empowered to determine whether a crime is aggravated by being a race crime. Matters of interpretation arise. To the point is the comment by Jeremy Corbyn (Islington North) who notes that the reporting of racial aspects of an attack are left to the discretion of the police. Similarly (referring to *Hansard*, 7 February 1994), Ms Ruddock notes that the police are 'not specifically requested to note whether they consider racial motivation a factor'. She asks why is the government bothering to do anything at all?

A letter sent earlier by the Home Secretary to the Lord Privy Seal provides an answer: there are 'intense public and Parliamentary pressures … for changes in the law' on racially motivated crimes. Why? The letter goes on to explain the Home Secretary's concern that 'the government's position is likely to become untenable'

> and at the very least open us to enormous criticism, especially once the urgent measures relating to stop and search powers I intend to introduce in the bill become public [this was before the Criminal Justice Bill was tabled in the house]. The proposed new powers are already being described in the minority press as recreating the discredited 'sus' law (letter tabled by Ms Ruddock).

Why Labour didn't make more of this admission during the passage of the CJB is not clear, but the government's motivation for doing something on racism, albeit only a watered-down amendment on powers of arrest in relation to racist publications, was exposed. The Home Secretary's letter continued: 'It is therefore important that the government take the initiative on racial crimes if it is to counteract the belief amongst ethnic minority communities that we do not take their concerns equally seriously'. The plan was to get the CJA and its new powers through under cover of an anti-racist smokescreen which would gain multilateral support.

So, for the government, 'initiative' means that the role of the police becomes all-important. It seems that the 'evidence of a very senior officer at Scotland Yard, Commander Allison', who had the ear of Sir

Lawrence, explained police concern that they had little power of immediate arrest to allow them to gather evidence – 'all sorts of forensic
evidence' (Sir L.) – in cases of distribution of racially inciteful literature.
Such increased powers would be of some use to the police. Sir
Lawrence puts it this way: 'If there is no power of arrest [in these
cases], by the time that the police arrive at the premises from which
they think the material is being distributed the birds have fled and all
the forensic signs of their culpability have dried up and disappeared'
(*Hansard*). (In contrast, just to keep the issue of self-defence in mind,
Trotsky recommended community actions that would summarily
'acquaint the fascists with the pavement' – no need to get out the
forensic squad here. And no 'by the time they got to the place where
they thought the distribution was...'. The relevant passage reads: 'The
tactical, or if you will "technical" task was quite simple – grab every
fascist or every isolated group of fascists by their collars, acquaint them
with the pavement a few times, strip them of their fascist insignia and
documents, and without carrying things any further, leave them with
their fright and a few black and blue marks' – 'Ultraleft Tactics in
Fighting the Fascists', March 1934.) When Sir Ivan talks about forensic
evidence drying up we could imagine that he has in mind clauses 45
to 50 of the CJA which give the police additional powers to take
bodily samples from persons, detained or not, with consent or not,
charged or not.[4]

The debate raged on and on, and it is hardly productive to reproduce
much more of its substance (or lack of). Two final curios: In search of
forensic signs: the Conservative amendment introduced new powers of
arrest and search, without warrant, while the Labour amendment argued
for a specific offence of racial harassment where a person, on racial
grounds, 'displays any writing, sign or other visible representation which
is threatening, abusive or insulting' (up to two years' imprisonment).
This last reference was to cover things such as the daubing of a swastika
on a wall (Barbara Roche, Hornsey and Wood Green) – which perhaps
could also be thought of as drying forensics. Whatever, Labour's motion
was voted down, the Conservative amendment was passed and joined
to the Criminal Justice Act, and it was sent off to the House of Lords
for its next reading after Labour abstained from the vote on the Act as
a whole.

The final curio from this debate was Sir Lawrence's reference to the
powers of the Home Secretary to ban, and of the police to impose
conditions upon, 'marches, processions and demonstrations' if it was
felt that these 'might result in serious public disorder, disruption to the

life of the community and so on'. He went on to note that the Act did
not cover marches and processions involving race hatred and 'therefore,
the police felt that they were not always able to respond to the community's concerns about marches by right-wing groups which did not,
perhaps, result in violence, but which contributed to a climate of fear
and hatred among the ethnic minority'. A subsequent amendment to
the Public Order Act was proposed so as to cover marches invoking
race hatred. Inverting the logic, Minister Lloyd objected that 'it would
be difficult to argue ... that a march of Nazi skinheads down Brick
Lane would stir the local population to racial hatred, but it may well
cause them fear and distress and provoke angry and violent reactions'
(*Hansard*). He thought the new clause did not give the police any
additional useful powers but would just 'confuse' their 'operational
judgement'. Sir Lawrence responded that he had in fact been asked to
include the clause by the police, and said that 'if *they* do not understand the present law, what on earth is the likelihood of the ethnic
minority communities in Britain understanding it?' The likelihood is
that they will understand that here Parliament is allowing the police to
dictate laws, while all concerned recognize they are horribly confused.
It was not a good day for democracy. Here is Parliament discussing
new legislation that will extend the material and physical might of the
forces responsible for racist attack upon Black people and the discussion circles around the painting of slogans and the question of posting
videos. A critique that would be adequate to an opposition to such
forces – the CS gas, the batons and surveillance cameras, but also the
arms manufacturies, the institutions of discipline and correction (school
and prison) and the ideological apparatus – needs to learn from the
self-defence work of those fighting this state. Quietism in the face of
such forces is forever inadequate.

. The Criminal Justice Act as a whole goes much further than this
minor skirmish in the politics of reformism. The incursion of legislative
power into more and more aspects of all of our lives – from what we
can watch on TV to DNA records – escalates. The new authoritarianism
insists that everything is the business of the state. The Act has paved the
way for increases in policing in the already over-policed urban areas of
Britain, it opens opportunities for a return to the late 1970s provocations of having police chiefs and ministers announce that all blacks are
muggers, and introduces and extends the targeting of any groups or
social formations that seem set to drift outside the containment of
capitalist market economics. It is this last that would explain the hostility of the Act towards otherwise small fry such as squatters, travellers

and ravers. These would need to be understood as examples of public organization and participation that were to be reclaimed, recuperated and reintegrated – by force if necessary – into everyday commerce. Hardt and Negri note that resistance to capitalism 'is no longer exercised simply in the old forms of trade union defence' in the large factories of industry, but in a period of greater politicization of all aspects of life 'new forms of political positioning and attack immediately address social levels of accumulation' (Hardt and Negri 1994: 210). If the commercialization of rave via House parties, and of squatters via housing co-ops, was insufficient to rope in alternative economies, then police repression would be deployed. With an analysis that began with such a viewpoint it would then be possible to understand how the attacks on rave were indeed a part of combating anti-capitalist activity, which unfortunately the conservative forces understood more readily than the ravers themselves. If there had been a more concerted linking-up and alliance amongst the different sectors targeted by the Act this might be a different story. In the end reformism has so far been able to prevail over any such formations.

The point of my earlier discussion of legislation is in part to illustrate the bankruptcy of reformism and the contemporary rightist gymnastics that are the dynamic of both sides of parliament. It would also be possible to show how the reformist calls of the non-parliamentary fake-left like the SWP and Militant are also counter-productive in the face of contemporary very-late-twentieth-century capitalism's requirements. The pseudo-management of 'race' in this legislative domain, like other reformist calls, seems always to result in more police powers. It is important to note a separation between anti-racist activity and anti-racist reformism – with this reformism fostered by late capitalism, and even integral to its productive relations (maintenance of an underclass in the Western democracies, and so on, despite obsolescence of trade-union/welfare state/liberal concessions). There is much more to be said on this – Westminster and democracy discourses should be examined not only for their rhetorical tropes and illusions of meaning, or, yet more tenuous, for active government effects (Parliament as simulacra), but also as organizational and motivational sites of definition even for those who profess not to believe in, or need to, work through the parliamentary experiment. I am, however, leaving this as an opening in a discussion that moves elsewhere. The point was to illustrate the contrast and contradiction of legislative debate over against the kinds of community activity articulated by certain Asian groups.

COMMUNITY DEFENCE AND
INTERNATIONALISM

What I want to do in this third section is take up the issue of community defence as presented by Asian musicians and activists in the context of anti-racism and the Criminal Justice Act. I am equating the silence of academics on the 'banning' of *Dog-Tribe* with silence on the most important parts of the CJA, and suggesting there are echoes of this in regard to the practicalities of combating racist violence today. This section takes up the Left press and the work of bands like the Kaliphz and Asian Dub Foundation in an attempt to open and extend a space for political writing about music that doesn't simply avoid these troubles.

At a 1994 YRE (Youth against Racism in Europe) conference in Germany, debates about the relationship of activists to the police, and tactical differences over community-organized defence versus legislative controls, consumed much time. Militant Labour from Britain and their co-thinkers the Voran Group from Germany and the Gauche Revolutionnaires/Jeunesses Communistes Revolutionnaires (JCR) from France argue that the cops are 'workers in uniform' and are a potential ally in the fight against fascism. Spartacist League (SL) cadre at the conference pointed out – in line with Marxist orientations drawn from the classics – that the police were 'a body of armed men' (Lenin, *State and Revolution*) who were 'in the service of the capitalist state' (Trotsky once wrote, 'The worker who becomes a policeman in the service of the capitalist state is a bourgeois cop, not a worker' – *What Next* 1932). Trading insults and pamphlets the Militant/Voran group were exposed by the Spartacist League as offering support for the social-democratic SPD and British Labour in the guise of an anti-racism that offers nothing to the community except more police. Militant's role in the Tower Hamlets fight against the BNP, where they campaigned for Labour, the party which abstained in the vote on the Criminal Justice Act, confirms the SL's position as described in the pamphlet *Militant Labour's Touching Faith in the Capitalist State* (August 1994). Perhaps calling the cops the 'paid goons of the capitalist rulers' (SL) tends towards rhetorical colour rather than analytical precision, but in the context of immediate struggle against racist attacks by the police, the state and fascists, this is acceptable terminology. A slightly more reasoned presentation of this sentiment can be found in the Revolutionary Communist Party affiliated Workers Against Racism (WAR): 'In a society like Britain, where racism is woven into the very fabric of the nation, upholding "law and order" means upholding racist institutions and practices' (*WAR News*, 12: 6).

Issues such as this raise questions about organization in the community and the need to do more than either anti-Nazi carnivalgoers or Labour and Conservative legislators. The view of the legislature as completely bankrupt is difficult to refute as all the legislation seems to amount to is variation in the modes of repression available to the state. In the video *Dog-Tribe* it is clear that singular symbolic gestures are considered insufficient – Nawaz is beaten as he puts a 'Nazis Out' slogan on the wall at the beginning of the clip, while in the middle of the narrative a politician is seen to ignore Nawaz's petition (a petition against the CJA was 'left on table' at the final reading, while the Act itself was passed on to the House of Lords and into law). In the parliamentary debate Labour politicians kept on saying the government had to send a message out to the community that it cared. That is, a message of reassurance of order – of stability and the status quo, of care, for votes, for individuals, the eternal practicals. Labour will not organize defence. Kaufman's visit to the chief constable concerning shopping is almost excessive for Labour. It is no surprise that practical activity must be taken by the community itself.

In reviewing a Fun^Da^Mental gig in June 1994, David Stubbs wrote in *MM*: 'I'm at once troubled and inspired by the revelation that it doesn't matter a f★★★ [*MM*'s asterisks yet again] what good intentions people like me have from now on. What's gonna happen will happen' (*MM*, 16 July 1994). The point is not whether or not audiences, white, black or Asian, think it's good or not, the urgent issue is that racial violence against Asian youth happens every day and something is being done... has been for a long time.[5] What is prominent among the various Asian bands that work closely with anti-racist self-defence groups is an awareness of the everyday complexities of face-to-face racism. There is a difference between making appealing statements in the press, showing placard and poster support for anti-racism in demonstrations through London's main streets, or uttering mantra-like acknowledgements of the need for the inclusion of anti-racist education in the school curriculum, and the rather different practicalities of estate-based anti-racist defence, support of those subject to police or workplace persecution, and the immediate confrontation of active fascist militants in towns like Rochdale. The no-nonsense approach to anti-racism is a far cry from the popular mobilizations for protest marches and festivals that are the preserve of Britain's orthodox anti-racism. While there are few youth in Britain today who would express explicit racist propaganda as per the BNP, Combat 18 or other fascists, and while most youth will be happy to say they believe in, and are even happy to campaign for, anti-racism, there is still little that such feel-good reassurances can provide for those subject to fascist and/or police attack. The blunt solution of the Rochdale band the Kaliphz would not find widespread approval from the softer elements of anti-racist badge-wearers. The lyrics of their 1994 release 'Hang 'Em High' do not rely on subtlety, stating that the 'remedy for white supremacy' is to 'kill the BNP and the Klan in Tennessee':

An eye for an eye, a tooth for a tooth,
a knife for a knife and a life for a life.
Hang 'em high, hang 'em high,
hang 'em by the neck until the mutha-fuckers die
...I'm no pacifist, I'm a pistol-packing Paki-fist.

(Kaliphz, 'Hang 'Em High', Semtex 1994. Words by Choka, Sniffa Dawg, 2Phaan. Published by Perfect Songs.)

The Kaliphz often seem caught up in a version of macho Gangsta rapping that is testosterone-fuelled and *Boyz n the Hood* aggressive, yet their record in opposition to British fascist groups is considerable. Where militancy and clout are concerned, it seems the Kaliphz have far more sophistication that any of the blood-and-honour fascist bands of the BNP, National Front and Combat 18 circuit. The Kaliphz 1995 album release (with a US label) stands them on the verge of international commercial success which will hammer home their tough message. Their immediate political rivals from the Rochdale branch of Combat 18 are in disarray.[6]

The anti-racist group that works most closely with the Kaliphz is Anti-Fascist Action, and it is AFA who consistently criticize avowed Left groups such as the ANL for calling upon Labour councils and the Conservative Party to ban the BNP, to refuse membership to fascists in the Conservative Party, or to reject lease applications for premises. These are criticisms also made by the Revolutionary Communist Party and the Spartacist League under the debate title 'No Platform?' (the question mark is significant), although resolved in differing ways – with the RCP turning towards a critique of institutional racism and imperialism, and offering the powerful slogan 'ban nothing – question everything' (T-shirts available by direct debit), and the Spartacist League calling for militant action (in joint action with...).[7] The RCP questioning of the ANL focus on Nazis requires them to play down fascist violence in ways that cannot endear them to those who are actually attacked, and yet the ways in which the ANL tactic of lobbying politicians invites further repressive force upon itself is clear. More police power. The major problem with the 'No Platform' stance (with no question mark) of the SWP and like groups was not just the contradiction that had oppositional groups pleading with the government to implement censorship. Although the small clutches of BNP members needed to be dealt with, the repressive apparatus of the state and the conditions that permitted the fascists to exist – the protection they received at Welling, for example – and the more extensive, legitimized racist violence of the police and the courts and other institutional racisms were in no way addressed by 'No Platform' calls.

To the question 'Should the BNP be banned?', put by an *i-D Magazine* journalist, Hustlers HC replied: 'To ban the BNP would make martyrs of them and they would play on it massively. Moreover, if they are forced underground, they will become more dangerous. Better the devil you know' (*i-D Magazine*, January 1994 – phenomenal, Asian rappers quoting Kylie Minogue). What is evident in interviews with these musicians is a consciousness of a zone of political engagement that cuts across the narrow focus of anti-racist groups to take on a cultural politics that encompasses everything from the names they are called, to international issues, or issues of gender. On gender they take up the complicated issue of arranged marriage and argue against jumping to Eurocentric conclusions about it, in terms of names they play against stereotypes and clichés. Hustlers HC worry about acceptance by the Hip-Hop crowd, evoking a tendency toward forms of cultural cringe that manifest as headlines, as in Hip-Hop Connection (September 1994), that play on variations of 'Turban Species' and 'Sikhing to Destroy' (nobody expects the music press to be all that creative: other clever coinages include 'GenerAsian X' and 'Goonda Rap'). Hustlers HC hustle to disrupt expectations. There is now an almost standard narrative in live reviews which starts with a question like 'Wha? Why are these Sikh guys all hanging around on stage?', which then leads into 'When we started playing, everything was quiet', and the dénouement, 'by the time our set was finished the crowd was wild for more, really kicking'. This is a classic breakthrough set, but Hustlers also worry that because of this novelty effect, their message is not getting across. Their attempts at a cultural politics that addresses much more than racism require a complex series of steps where they say, 'we don't see ourselves as ambassadors for the Asian community' but 'racism is an important subject to tackle because it affects our everyday life' (*Eastern Eye*, 4 October 1994), and their approach to everyday life is also more laid-back than that of Nation Records labelmates Fun^Da^Mental, by design: 'we don't talk about racism everyday, we just wanna have fun' (Hustlers, *NME*, 15 October 1994, quoting Cyndi Lauper). Another Asian posse, the Asian Dub Foundation, are closely involved with east London Bengali youth and their track 'Jericho' expands the priorities of defence to a general political consciousness:

> The music, we use it, we're making a stand,
> we wouldn't call this a green and pleasant land
> a conscious response is what we demand
> challenge the system and those in command
> express your opinion, it's your domain
> if you fail to do this, you're partly to blame
> My heart is beating no retreat
> the battle continues
> we'll suffer no defeat
> this war you've been waging
> it's time we were raging
> in our minds and on the streets
> sample this
> it's an education
> the sounds of the Asian Dub Foundation
>
> (Asian Dub Foundation, 'Jericho', *Facts and Fictions*, Nation Records 1994. Words by A. Das, J.A. Pandit, Savale, Zaman. Published by QFM/Warner Chappell Music)

In tracks such as this Asian Dub Foundation take up the theme of self-defence in the context of a broad political narrative that combines migrant and anti-colonial sentiments in a progressive confrontational stance. Here, and in videos like *Dog-Tribe* by Fun^Da^Mental, or in the more blunt 'Trotsky's-pavement' squadist approach of 'Hang 'Em High' by the Kaliphz, Asian musicians recognize that the issue is one of how to organize responses to everyday street and institutional racist confrontation in local and global contexts, and they attempt to convey this message to a wider public through their music. The question remains one of who hears these messages (academics, leftists, anti-racists, journalists, the 'Asian' community?). An example of how this work differs from the Rock Against Racism carnivalism of the ANL/SWP might be Asian Dub Foundation's participation in the 3 September 1995 Newham Unity Festival organized by one of the longest-serving and best-known anti-racist local community groupings, Newham Monitoring Project. In a recent issue of *CARF*, the latter's reasons for using music as a part of its work was explained:

In the past, Newham Monitoring Project has criticized the 'ANL syndrome': passing off anti-racist concerts in black areas, attracting thousands of people but leaving little lasting effect, as huge anti-racist mobilisations. The Unity festival is different. The venue is in the heart of Canning Town, a predominantly white working-class area seen by the BNP as fertile ground for recruitment. And the Unity festival isn't a one-off, but part of Newham Monitoring Project's long-term work in south Newham around issues such as housing and employment (Piara Powar in *CARF*, August 1995).

Other featured bands at this event were the Kaliphz and Fun^Da^Mental, expressing their commitment to, and support of, local organizing strategies that cut across white–black divisions and which seek to organize the working classes against the racist provocations of the fascists and against systematic exploitation in terms of lack of housing and employment and so on. This sort of engagement combines the best aspects of carnivalism and hard-edged community self-organization as well as cross-sectoral alliance work.

There are Left initiatives that also offer more than the 'ANL syndrome'. The magazine of the Revolutionary Internationalist League (RIL), *Revolutionary Fighter*, comes out strongly with banner headlines, in huge block sans serif font, declaring the need to 'Organize Defence Now!' The work of this group also centres mostly around east London and the Bengali community of Tower Hamlets. In summer 1994, the magazine stated:

> *Revolutionary Fighter* has campaigned for Worker/Community defence over the past year as the only response to make the streets safe. We know the police will do nothing except harass us. We know that all the marches, speeches and protests by themselves can't drive the racist attackers off the streets … Black and Asian youth have no alternative but to organize and defend themselves.

The argument of RIL is that the youth of these areas are already forced to defend themselves against attacks every day. 'Anti-racists and socialists must help to organize this defence, involving wider forces to prevent the youth from being isolated or criminalized by the racist state':

> The question is not: should young people defend themselves or not? The real point is that defence must be organized. Already school students and youth defend themselves but when it's done in an unorganized way they are more open to attack and the police arrest them for carrying offensive weapons or for some other crime. The youth will not wait for others to agree to defence patrols before defending themselves, but if it is not organized, if structures are not set up to co-ordinate activities, link up different youth, and if there is not

a wider political campaign amongst the working class to help organize defence, then the youth will remain isolated, picked up by the police and picked off by the racist thugs (*Revolutionary Fighter*, 3).

Militant Labour's response to this old-style rhetoric was not to see that there was a serious and urgent need to act along these lines, but to suggest a council-sponsored conference to discuss matters. Subsequently RIL has come under attack from the Labour council for their support of the Langdale 4 (Bengali students arrested for an alleged attack on a known racist at Poplar High School) and has attracted hostility from Militant and from the SWP in the shape of reformist support for anti-Left legal persecutions. The legal apparatus strengthened by the Criminal Justice Act avails itself of anti-Left collusion to maintain its racist order. Workers Power members do call for a 'serious approach to organized self-defence' (*Workers Power*, November 1994) when they attend ANL conferences, but it is not clear what practical steps they have made beyond a critique of SWP media campaigns. To the credit of the SL, the *Workers Hammer* came out strongly in support of the RIL, while pointing out that the RIL's community defence proposals were inadequate without the support of 'genuine workers defence guards' (*Workers Hammer*, September 1994). Urgency and immediacy on the one side couched in militant workerist rhetoric against Militant's cringing bureaucratic surveillance and avoidance on the other. Given this breach it is potentially the role of concerned and equipped critics to provide the required initiatives and explanations for work that will make community defence proposals feasible – or at least make these a subject of wider discussion beyond the nether pages of the Left press – but most members of the complacent intellectual middle class prefer instead to sit back without even defending their own declining work conditions in the universities, let alone respond to actual everyday violent attack organized against members of the community. Stop-and-search and police anti-crime campaigns at least drew some academic attention first time around in the 1970s, but so much for the sophistication of post-Marxism, when today only the remaining custodians of old rhetorics speak true to power. It was up to the Spartacist League to draw out the more systematic implications of the reform process that was called the Criminal Justice Act – in September 1995 it named police commissioner Condon's Operation Eagle Eye a 'racist dragnet' targeting black youth in London. The SL said: 'Even before Operation Eagle Eye, young black men were ten times more likely to be stopped than their white counterparts. But now backed up by the Criminal

Justice Act the cops feel they can go swanning into any place they please, swinging their truncheons with impunity' (*Workers Hammer*, September 1995). Few others noted the links between the racist elements of the CJA and ongoing police persecution, despite sufficient evidence to make the link, and high profile criticism of Eagle Eye in the press. Instead of linking the mobilizations against the CJA to the ANL campaigns and then extending it to Condon's outrageous initiatives, much of the Left used the 'mugging' issue as another discrete campaign that could operate as a recruitment drive. The cynicism of those who campaigned against the CJA without any long-term strategy was exposed by Nawaz who noted not only that the racist elements of the CJA had enabled attacks on Blacks by police, but also that at the very time these attacks took place much of the white Left had abandoned the campaign, leaving only the committed sound system groups, road protesters, squatters, anarchists and Black community groups – the opportunist groups having picked up a few newly politicized recruits and moved on to the next big thing.

Is it a failure of nerve on the part of middle-class radicals and academics that characterizes their piecemeal and short-term contributions to single issues? Or are there other reasons for their refusal to support Asian self-defence? The scripted and choreographed academic responses to the issues of defence can be anticipated and sidestepped. The question of violence obviously opens upon the terrain of morality and liberal notions of communal harmony. Enlightenment tolerance is as much the liberalism of academic 'anti-racists' as well. Phil Cohen notes that Rattansi and Gilroy 'have argued the case for new strategies in anti-racist education that avoid … its "moral symbolic and doctrinaire forms"' (Cohen 1992: 62). It would be a lesson well learned by all that certain dearly held positions close down opportunities for action. There are certain protocols of justice, of justifiable force, that come into play when the question of violence is raised (see Benjamin, Derrida, Girard, and so many others) and these are, more often than not, far away removed from the questions, evidence and interpretation that are the preserve of law. The question of evidence – also a favourite of academia – is traceable here to Sir Ivan's forensic investigations. Along with evidence come questions of judgement, interpretation and decision – in legalese, of 'ruling'. What kind of violent knowing is it that must investigate all that is sent in the post, and intimate bodily samples? Is there a relation between the samples of the forensic squad and the sampling of *Dog-Tribe*? One authorized by power, the other censored? Engagement with questions of interpretation are demanded when the televisual and justice are conjoined, and vex us as in the LAPD police defence trial where 'samples' of the Rodney King video are 'analysed' and excused frame by frame to exonerate thugs, and we are left as watching couch potatoes while a human being gets mashed. Further questions here would interrogate the media and the forums in which the 'message' of bands such as Fun^Da^Mental and Hustlers HC are disseminated: video, television, international satellite, technologies of communication and the ways in which scholarly interest in these technologies rarely moves beyond safe questions about access.[8] Instead this questioning could explore the role of technologies such as the camcorder and mobile phone in political work and the relation of these forms to institutional structures. Does, for example, the use of video cameras as the Hustlers HC suggest ('you could drive around with a video camera') imply a 'touching faith' in the court system that experience might indicate was unwarranted? Is the surveillance of the streets such a great idea? Why move to a *Clockwork Orange/Videodrome* world characterized by the prospect of Sony-equipped surveillance squads roaming the streets (chanting 'war on drugs, war on drugs' – apologies to Pynchon) while the rest of the population cower in secured suburban bunkers watching live-feed transmissions beamed in from those very same squads (courtesy of the technologies developed by the leisure industry such as Sports-Cam™). Similarly, concern about surveillance and dysfunctional aspects of community defence will be raised, and need to be addressed, in terms of gender and conservation – specifically the policing of identity, allegiance and conformity which may arise and include such concerns as the recuperation of runaway daughters and the tar-and-feather approach to collaborators.[9] Such matters are of course a problem for all organizational forms, and are no less prevalent – are indeed more systematic in many ways – on the part of the state. These important concerns should be delegated to discussions on organizational discipline and democratic centralism – on which there is a considerable literature. It should be noted that nobody raises the problems of police violence or the violence of the state and of law in the same ways as is common when moral outrage and tabloid vexation provokes unthinking criticisms.

The possibility of defence groups moving from macho posturing to more aggressive gender and community policing is an issue that raises somewhat psycho-social questions about proposing a militancy which, while linked to organized self-defence groups, will also be taken up and circulated beyond these groups through mass media. The effect of the articulation of a militant refusal of Asian victimologies has political effects that cannot be ignored, least of all within Asian communities themselves, and in terms of relations with Afro-Caribbean communities and white ones. However, what seems significant in the cultural politics of Fun^Da^Mental as regards Asian identity is that after a period characterized by assertions of Asian specificity in the UK (which can probably be dated from the Rushdie controversy and from when commentators like Hall and Gilroy began talking about Black *and* Asian), there now seems to be a reassertion of the earlier Black politics from a position of greater surety and strength, though there are those who will remind us that this strength was always present, simply unrecognized in the face of media stereotypes about passivity. Rather than consign such developments to old fears about macho militancy or ill-discipline, new alliances can be identified, as some writers recognize. The conscious dialectical movement of Asians back to a Black politics offers other parallels: talking about the difference between media representations of Asian women (as passive, quiet) and African women (loud, brash), bell hooks argues the necessity of publicly naming solidarities with one another against such stereotypes (hooks 1994: 218). In the *Dog-Tribe* video another solidarity is displayed (but not named), as the Asian woman sitting quietly by the graveside is later seen joining in the trashing of the BNP office. The participation of women's organizations in anti-racist campaigns will be evident to anyone who has attended any of the rallies for, to mention only a few: Justice for Joy Gardner (a black woman killed by police in her home; the police were not prosecuted), the Free Satpal Ram Campaign (imprisoned for defending himself from white racist attack), the Brian Douglas campaign (killed by police using the new LAPD-style long truncheons) and the defence campaign for Amer Rafiq (who lost an eye in police custody in Manchester after Eid 1996), and so on. The presence and work of women organizers and speakers in campaigning is vast and immeasurable compared to their invisibility and apparent 'passivity' in mainstream media representations.

These possible alliances open wide questions that offer a future project only hinted at in *Dog-Tribe*. The need for the formation of new alliances emerges at a time when some argue the coming of a 'total subsumption' of everything to the production of new world order capitalism. Here all social, political, and cultural formations are 'subsumed' to the production of value, subsumed to the formation of a coming community, with all its cultural 'differences' in terms of race, class, gender. Within this complex the commercialized production of meaning, identity, spaces, everything, is orchestrated for what Marx called the 'real subsumption' of life to production – a stage that comes after the imposition of an organizational form of capitalism upon 'otherwise non-capitalist' things. Today, all projects tend towards an organization that produces all life – from leisure to education to formal 'work', and including criticism and analysis, music and sex – in ways that are integral components of a seamless global factory. Whatever the final assessment of this analysis, and its further elaboration beyond the work of Antonio Negri and Félix Guattari 1990 (*Communists Like Us*) and Hardt and Negri 1994 (*Labor of Dionysus*), it is important to consider the implied programme of Fun^Da^Mental's video/lyrical productions in this context. Some wildly general points about this context can be made (very quickly): with the winding back of the welfare state buy-off of the West's workers, racism escalates. White workers were enticed to develop a vested interest in the system – a trick. Racism keeps the working class divided, and the so-called middle classes are also similarly dissuaded from political initiative and alliance against ever more invisible profiteers in a rampant social factory where everything is geared towards global production. Capitalism in crisis relies upon superprofits from a restructuring which designates hi-tech production to the expensive Western labour markets and moves mass production to Third World sites. The necessary costs of development include the education of elite workers in the West (no longer a geographical category), an ever larger service sector, and deployment of forces of subjugation (new authoritarian controls) in this new world order. Concomitant requirements include: fortress Europe and the expulsion of immigrant labour no longer needed; martial law/Criminal Justice Act/Operation Eagle Eye; the UN as world police and the moral rearmament of imperialism; First World science development/automation; Third World production/intensive labour; heightened communication, information and transportation flows; competitive state privileges.

Yet within any total subsumption of culture into capitalism, the production of escape clauses, nooks and crannies of dissimulation, diversions and dysfunctions offers momentary respites which we should hope to extend, elaborate, valorize – even as so much of this is inevitably absorbed and folded within the factorium (which indeed needs resistances as a kind of motor force). Subversion is temporary, alliances are fluid. By new lines of alliance we might refer to those demarcations usually accepted and approved but which might be usefully transgressed – the lines that divide music and politics, the white Left and Asian political groups (Fun^Da^Mental do this), the lines between Bhangra and post-Bhangra, or between Bhangra and Hip-Hop, between diaspora and local politics, between technology and tradition. All these are the context in which the politics of *Dog-Tribe* is one part of a resistant social formation generating alliances that remake and renew the possibilities for Left political practice today, and perhaps grounding differences and knowledges in a political struggle that fosters those lines of escape, new assemblages, wrex mikes.

Regrettably, most pious academic discussion of racism avoids the practicalities and requirements of everyday anti-racism – beyond attendance at one or two carnivals each year – concentrating instead upon neat structural polemics within the tradition, policy initiatives and refinements, and proposals for still more carnivals and conferences. This is not to say there is not a role for these sophisticated 'interventions'. Of course. But where are the defences of self-defence? Where is the critique of the Criminal Justice Act? Where is the outcry against the censorship of *Dog-Tribe*? What is going on? Don't tell me that these issues are not the preserve of academics too – what is cultural studies about if not the contest of culture? It is surely up to intellectual workers to link these issues together in ways that facilitate co-ordinated actions, is it not? The parameters of academic engagement allow certain kinds of contestation and debate but not others – a more sceptical evaluation of the possibilities of scholarly consideration of racism would note that these parameters were co-ordinated more by competition for places and advancement than by any politics. After all, what can fine words do in practice? Harmonious calls for tolerance and no violence reiterate conservative moralities and the status quo – in what one activist called 'repetitive bleating' from the bourgeoisie (August 1994). Academic abstention in the face of this terror ignores the life-and-death confrontation that simply, bluntly, must be engaged now. The list of the names of the dead is not a rhetorical device, but indicates the extent to which passivity and complacency have allowed a retreat from critical engagement on the part of comfortable intellectuals. The task is to wake up from this stupor – this book is not simply an essay in cultural studies of the Left in the UK or some journalistic report from the culture zone. What is at stake, and what small contribution this text might attempt, is a reconfiguration of the parameters that sustain anti-racist racism. By anti-racist racism I mean the failure of academics to do anything beyond presentation of feel-good statements that end up fuelling reformist calls for more police. Vigilance is a difficult price to pay to ensure that paranoid law-making disguised as good deeds does not alibi further attacks. Vigilantes do have a defence, but the place of *Dog-Tribe* has been usurped by the white noise of the censor, the white noise of reformism, and the white noise of complacency. Instead, educational and transformational initiatives within an internationalist framework might counter racist violence not with isolated and spontaneous fighting, but with a defence programme that is anti-racist, anti-capitalist and anti-sectarian and that extends into new lines of alliance against various and multiplying global examples of imperialism, exploitation and persecution. The materials for any organizational co-ordination of such alliances need to be produced in association with the ready fighters and activists. One of the issues this chapter attempts to raise is the question of what to do about the failure of academic anti-racism. It only begins to make a space for elaboration of answers. *Dog-Tribe*, at least in this reading, sounds out that space. Within limited parameters such a discussion can provide possible incentives for movement into practical activity. Informed perhaps by the considerable resources and theoretical arsenal that the institutions' disciplinary academia provide – even post-Marxism and postmodernism, post-structuralism, post-feminism (and post-early-for-Xmas) – there are numerous approaches that have current favour and might be refashioned and deployed here. Is it sufficient to point to the need for this engagement, and to follow the path of some, while encouraging more? To declare the need to provide a defence of defence squads, of anti-racist anti-capitalist organization, of those cultural and political workers engaged within such struggles? The trick here (in order to end this chapter and leave for other urgent tasks) would be to claim limitations of space...

NOTES

1. Writing this chapter was made easier by the members of the Transl-Asia Project and Charterhouse Reading Group in Manchester: Musa Ahmed, Meeta Rani Jha, Prita Jha, Sanjay Sharma, Virinder Kalra, Tej Purewal, Shirin Housee, Uma Kothari, Kinni Kansari, Curtis Liburd, Sean McLoughlin, Lynn Humphrey, Bobby Sayyid, Tim Eadensore, Eli Wong, Damien Lawson, Chris Raab. Also many thanks to Ben Ross, Angie Mitropoulis, Susan Fry, Emma Grahame, Barnor Hesse, Esther, Aki and Simon at Nation Records, Wenonah Lyon, Pnina Werbner, Rebecca and Neil from the RCP and Melanie from the Sparts. Red Salute.

2. Additionally, the Act offered the following: a return to the discredited sus laws of stop and search, at the discretion of a superintendent or inspector who suspects violence is 'imminent'; abolition of the right to silence; attacks on travellers (unauthorized movement, unauthorized homelessness); increased fines for drug use (class C cannabis, £2,500 fine); privatization of prisons (entrepreneurial incarcerations); more 'secure training centres', for young offenders, from age 12; increased police power to take bodily samples, without consent, intimate and non-intimate divisions, saliva, pubic hair, semen (a DNA database came into operation early in 1995); obscene telephone calls surveillance; more police powers;

prevention of terrorism (random search without suspicion); prisoner drug tests; scalper crackdown; security for mainstream party political conferences (public purse excise to fund the paranoid wherever they meet); council application for prohibition of trespassory assembly; aggravated trespass in the vicinity of the hunt; impounding vehicles; impounding of virtual space (tekno division); restrictions on bail; offence of research that aids terrorism (*Who's Who?* section); revision of Race Relations Act, no room for gypsies (Roma family incarceration unit); Stonehenge clause – annual hippie cull; several varieties of anti-party law (in preparation, in attendance, on the way to a rave – repetitive beatings); more police powers; more police.

3. I think it is very important that the scarf of organization does not replace the scarf of international political solidarity, but joins it.

4. For the purposes of the Act an 'intimate sample' means: (a) a sample of blood, semen or any other tissue fluid, urine or pubic hair; (b) a dental impression; (c) a swab taken from a person's body other than the mouth. Non-intimate sample means: (a) a sample of hair other than pubic hair (dreadlock sample); (b) a sample taken from a nail or from under a nail (unwashed sample); (c) a swab taken from any part of a person's body including the mouth, but not from any other body orifice; (d) saliva (punk gobbing sample), etc. Previously the most intimate bodily orificial samples could only be taken in cases of serious offence – murder, rape – now such samples will be allowed for any recordable crime, including offences like faredodging, shoplifting, or listening to repetitive beats in a field at night with ten friends.

5. I am not going to review the literature on community defence here, nor the legal cases that establish self-defence as a defence in law. The former is only really available in the occasional and small press – although see *Race Today* any issue, but especially 'Charting the Asian Self-defence Movement', *RT* 10(6): 128-131. In 1990 Paul Gordon wrote a Runnymede Research Report on the legal record on self-defence. This report took up the Bradford 12, Newham 7, Newham 8 and other well-known/not well enough known cases.

6. Combat 18, the most prominent fascist militia in the UK, at present seems to be in national decline and confusion, despite occasional outbreaks of violence and its members' continued cowardly practice of targeting the periphery of Left demonstrations to pick off individuals. There is some debate as to their actual numbers, their blustering hype and their organizational coherence – *Dispatches*, Channel 4, 25 October 1994. Yet they have managed considerable intimidation for their small presence. Significantly, C18 feature on the dub version, the instrumental version, and in live performances of 'Dog-Tribe', recorded from a message they left on a Youth Against Racism answerphone: 'C 18 is watching you, you communists. Nigger-loving Paki cunts. Fucking dickheads, we're gonna hang you for burning the British flag' ('Dog-Tribe – people of the sun mix') – note here the conjunction of racism, nationalism and red-baiting hysteria, typical of so many anti-communist, rightist, prejudiced scum.

7. I must note, with emphasis, that I am not attempting a survey of the various positions of the myriad trotocracies and fiefdoms of leftist debate in the UK as such would be exhausting, and possibly very dull for those not transported by the subtleties and nuances involved. It is sufficient to acknowledge the

seriousness with which these debates are engaged – the struggle is grim – and to hope that anyone wanting such a survey will read the texts themselves and will, with fingers stained from that black ink specially produced for the socialist press, excuse this clumsy *en passant*.

8. I have addressed some of these issues in a chapter called 'Adorno at Womad: South Asian Crossovers and the Limits of Hybridity-talk', in Pnina Werbner and Tariq Modood (eds.), 1996 *Debating Cultural Hybridity: Multi-Cultural Identities and the Politics of Anti-Racism*, Zed Books London.

9. These points were made by Emma Grahame and Angie Mitropoulis.

PART FOUR

PHANTASMAGORIC TERRAINS

8

VERSIONING TERROR:

JALLIANWALA BAGH AND THE JUNGLE

Koushik Banerjea and Jatinder Barn

The dust of the garden says to every particle in the orchard
Don't you remain indifferent to the ways of the elements
Its sapling has been watered with the blood of martyrs
Don't ye grudge to shed tears for the budding...[1]

Welcome to the garden, the bagh, where the peaceful social order of
Baisakhi is subjected one fateful day to authorized colonial destruction:
the garden becomes a jungle of cavorting and distorted limbs; a place
of wholesale terror where the 'native' brown body becomes the site of
massive disruption, the focus of an oxymoronic colonial gaze and the
precious container of mythology and folklore. Jallianwala Bagh, Amritsar,
1919.

Survey the wreckage of diaspora.

The sentence breaks – oh my gosh, 'it's agony in your body' – arms
manically swivel, bassheads drop diasporic science and 'native' performance is remythologized near the old imperial city's outer limits.
The jungle in this distended, disparate incarnation is host not just to
the spectral, febrile excesses of the post-colonial imagination but to the
everyday horrors of white 'steel in the hour of chaos'. Death continues
to stalk the natives but 'science' is now their ally. Drum'n'bass beats
time on the city where for the Asian diaspora it is terror as usual.
London, 1995.

Imagine the bagh, a walled garden safe from the encroachment of a
militarized exterior. It is Baisakhi, a thanksgiving for the bountiful
harvest. Many had come to take a dip in the holy water surrounding
the Golden Temple, the Sikhs' holiest shrine.

On the afternoon of 13 April 1919, Brigadier General Reginald Dyer walked his small party of native troops through the streets of Amritsar arriving at the narrow entrance to a dirt quadrangle called the Jallianwala Bagh. Skip to a different version in a domestic imperial setting three quarters of a century later. It is Diwali, a celebration of light before the bleak winter months in England. Metropolitan carnivalesque, in the trappings of an Asian Christmas, assumes its nocturnal form in the spaces of a London dance hall to a soundtrack culled from the vaults of Bollywood and frenetic drum'n'bass patterns. An accelerated volley of staccato treble announces the arrival on stage of Karl-Kani-clad native insurgent for a Gaillardean session of rhyme'n'nonsense in suburban south London. Long after the last academic is safely ensconced in his authorless, rudderless historical vault, 'faceless white suburbia' is host to its most theoretically inimical tenants or, to give them their 'correct' title, 'youth of the South Asian diaspora'.

Marking space has become a life-threatening (or life-preserving) business for British Asian folk in consequence of the veritable litany of racial exclusion, intimidation and murder that underscores the everyday existence of the diaspora. The psychodynamics of contested urban space has offered a rich vein of disquiet to be fruitfully tapped by vocal as well as softly spoken British 'patriots' whose nightmare of being 'swamped' by alien hordes provokes heated debate and the occasional murder. Consider the families of Gurdip Singh Chaggar, Altab Ali, Quddus Ali and Rohit Duggal, to name but a few. Respect the probity of their racial witness. It is openly disrespectful to conflate the white terror of invisibility (of 'being swamped') with the poetics and practices of diaspora.

And in Amritsar? After a moment's hesitation on account of the entry to the bagh being too narrow for his armed cars and their mounted machine guns to pass through, Dyer stepped into the bagh and stood on a raised platform just inside the entrance. There, from his panoptical position, he saw a large number of people, some sitting and listening to the speakers, others sleeping, still others playing cards and chatting amongst themselves with only half an ear on what the speakers were saying. Within seconds of his entry he had surveyed the scene with his trained eye. Deploying his troops to the left and to the right of the entrance he gave the order, as he blithely remarked, for his troops to open fire. He had shouted no warning.

The successful strike is eulogized by a community under siege. Dyer has saved them from unspeakable horrors. Horrors unspoken of since the mutiny. The white women and children are safely if uncomfortably enclosed in the fort.[2] Dyer is flushed, swelling even, in his own prowess. Stiff as a mahogany sideboard, encouraged in his upright postures, and accompanied by Miles Irving, he addresses a crowd on their responsibilities, (see Furneaux 1963: chapter 7). He has performed his duty, his horrible duty. And it hurt him more than it hurt them. Obliged by the dictates of reason to deliver a didactic blow, he is ready to soothe the pain and ease the suffering of their weary bodies provided of course they can make their own way to the hospitals.[3]

The sermon is not yet complete. Before the terrorized population he assures them of his intent to deliver, if need be, further blows. As he is a 'man of his word' there could be no doubt that he would fulfil his promise. He had done so many times before. He would perform such a duty with the utmost vigour be it on the playing fields of England or the battlefields of India. 'I am a soldier,' he proclaims. And as a soldier, 'I will go straight.' He would not deviate to the right or to the left. If they wanted war he was ready. If they wanted peace (on his terms of course), he was ready. They must not listen to the *badmashes* on the street. They must open all their shops at once. A state of normalcy is returned, never mind that the emergency visited on huge populations by the English incursions is a subsisting state of normalcy (see Furneaux 1963: 89).

And all the time, in his mind he churns over what the Manja Sikhs are thinking. Already the tour of reassurance has commenced. It is always already playful. Are these relations defined by Nicholnsingh Sahib's taking of *Amrit*.[4] They took him to be one of their own. *Amrit* is given also to Dyer. They chuckle as he says he will not be able to give up his snout. He must, they insist, but then they relent. He adds to the *Amrit*, and is assured by their assurances. Regaled in saffron robes and adorned by Karpan and Kadah he comes out in the wash a Sikh. There is more than a suggestion that this is a modernist battle for individual masculine subjectivity. It is not, however, a postmodern pantomime, a dressing up in each other's clothes, which seems about as radical as 'Aki-stani' (aka Aki Nawaz of Fun^Da^Mental) responding with radical chic posturing in concert to an earlier tape-recorded death threat from the neo-fascist organization Combat 18 with a risible: 'I don't think so!' Rather, we suggest, skipping the almost carnivalesque aura of the ceremony leaves us here with the management of disorder. Dyer needs to feel comfortable with the 'natives'. In the event of discomfiture there is a ready management strategy that he can employ to disperse their unsettlingly 'threatening' poses. It is worth remembering that Dyer taught military law and tactics at Chakrata, according to his biographer, from 1901 to 1908. Familiar with military techniques, he first of all manoeuvres to integrate the threat posed by the perceived masculinity of the Sikhs within the overarching masculinity of the white *sahib*, thereby dispersing their subversive potential and reaffirming the natural superiority of a now even sturdier and stiffer-backed general (see Dawson 1994).

Suburbia awakes to the sound of drum'n'bass hardstep mapping its more than imagined geography from bedroom junglism to the certainties of dancehall. Consider, though, what lies in between. These are, after all, the same vengeful streets stained with the blood of Rohit Duggal and Stephen Lawrence. The self-appointed guardians of an emblematic British sovereignty have graciously burdened themselves with the thankless task of postponing the onset of barbarity from British streets. These proud children of Kipling remain unsullied by their duties both to the nation and to the natives as they step up their efforts to rid the 'green and pleasant land' of its most inimical tenants. Myth making is once again reliant on life taking as the fiction of a 'pure' British nation is invoked by its loyal subjects to justify the inexhaustible practices of racial terror. And at its heart thrives the spectacle of an exaggerated white masculinity, paralysed by fear of erasure and momentarily empowered by the rights (rites) conferred upon the giver by acts of extreme violence against the apparently encroaching 'Eastern hordes'. Under this state of normalized emergency, what Michael Taussig has called 'terror as usual', those fears of white dissolution within an infinite blackness are played out in the most bizarre and terrifying narratives with horror as their definitive corollary.

Consider for example the way in which the cultural (that is, linguistic, culinary, sartorial, musical, literary) productions of the various black diasporas in England have always been colonized and appropriated by a white working class with an insatiable penchant for privileged cultural consumption never matched by a similar fondness for flesh-and-blood black folks. The 'purity' of this mythical British nation predictably fails to exemplify its norms, as these are for the most part constituted in the uneasy, if hybrid practices of the everyday where the metropolis holds court to a reworking of colonial power relations.[5] Intriguingly, this compelling spectacle of a most British of fusions can be conflated all too unproblematically with the most vicious forms of white supremacy. The slippage from hybrid consumption to assertion of a virulent ethnic particularity occurs with such frequency that its concomitant function of engendering terror in the hearts of the 'natives' becomes the normative condition of most white/Asian urban encounters. Surely there is nothing arbitrary about the targeting by racists of the 'new' trading posts of exchange – the grocers, corner shops, sub-post offices, video marts and eating houses – for the vagaries of graffiti, intimidation and arson. Diasporic knowledge reveals Gary Bushell's chirpy brand of 'new patriotism' of the 'I'm not a racist, I'm a patriot' variety as anathema to those many Asian folk who have experienced 'British patriotism' first-hand.[6]

The faltering logic that is unable to see the conflation between a nation and its narration is blind too to the (union)-jack-booted loyalisms of a quaintly xenophobic Bushell. The cheeky cockney can cheerfully lay exclusive claim to the hallowed turf of 'the Krays' and then suffer selective amnesia in the small matter of cockney plurality. Psychic erasure is his answer to the spectre of homegrown talent whose brown bread is browner than usual. Hence the new 'holy war' being waged on Britain's streets by Bushell's diverse cadres against the 'polluting' menace of an 'Eastern mob'.

The point is not the sheer inaccuracy of Bushell's allegations. Rather it is their ability to galvanize the fears and insecurities of many white Britons faced with increasing political disenfranchisement and massive post-industrial economic decline. Slum administration has supplanted colonial authority yet the 'newly' racialized character of the apparently archetypal 'inner city' remains the catalyst for the most brutal forms of authoritarian hierarchy. The dissolution of the British colonies has fuelled calls for 'carceral' policing in the former metropolitan centres and the repatriation of so-called 'immigrants'. This, then, is the back-drop against which Bushellite echoes reverberate.

Time to get real. The white working classes have always had a penchant for 'paki-bashing' even in the good old days of (nearly) full employment, allegedly compliant natives and uninterrupted white cultural hegemony. Remember Gurdip Singh Chaggar and Altab Ali. Insist on their remembrance. Cast your mind back even further to the brutal colonial sanctions that ensured sustained Indian subsidy of the ailing Lancashire textiles industry. Respect the ultimate sacrifice of those Indian workers starved first of work and then of life. And then there is the small matter of 'operation eradication' at Jallianwala Bagh. The phat historical litany of abuse is testimony to that continuing 'holy war' so beloved of Bushell and his forgetful ilk. Perhaps now is a good time for some gentle reminders.

Though many postmodern metanarrators are prone to forget it, sustained white inhabitation and appropriation of black cultural institutions have not short-circuited the appeal or the implementation of

white-supremacist politics on British streets.[7] Indeed it can be persua-
sively argued that London, for instance, is the site of the most acute
forms of white racism and syncretic black musical cultures and these
continue to thrive both because of, and in spite of, their proximity to
each other. Urban leisure spaces have functioned as public arenas in
and around which aggressive racism is manifested, although often contested by vernacular, expressive culture, particularly in the form of sound
systems. Whilst some work has conceptualized these spaces as an 'alternative public sphere' (Gilroy 1993b) there has been little discussion of
how the cultural dynamics of sound systems are qualified by their
proximity to the practices of racial terror. We would suggest that a
more informed understanding of the twin processes of intense racial
conflict and creative cultural expression in London could be helpful to
a more critical reading of South Asian sound-system performance.
Consider for a moment the way in which crews like east London's
Asian Dub Foundation and west London's Hustlers HC offer powerful,
critical commentaries on the immediate local conditions in which their
musical performance originates (Chapter 2). Particular histories of
migration and experiences of white Britain permeate the lyricism of
Hustlers HC's diasporic parable of love, life and terror, 'Big Trouble in
Little Asia', as it strikes a narrative chord at the heart of a 'community
of interpretation'. If we are forever mindful of the reality that cultural
and political borders are not necessarily congruent, it follows that
syncretic textual strategies are not merely additive; rather, they counterpoint cultural elements in a space of clash and interchange. Thus the
interpretive community alluded to is composed within a dialogic forum
established around the strictures of race and community and marked by
a process of 'naming'. Bounded by a critical antiphony and enjoined
within a digital diaspora it is all too easy for us to sidestep the thorny
issue of how such a constituency mediates the everyday exclusions of
'multi-racist Britain'. Crucially, are we to engage in a reified version of
cheerleading composite with a banal optimism regarding issues of
cultural hybridity and replete with a politics of syncretism?

Just as 'fuzak' draped over unfussy breakbeats is not an impassioned
advocacy of 'Jungle', so the insatiable 'liberal' desire to see the rene-
gade culture of street rebels should not become the arbiter of legitimation when issues of cultural authenticity and reproduction are at
hand. The tireless translation of liberal particularities into supposedly
apolitical universalities has already created an unhealthy climate of
censure and proscribed debate wherein the impoverished options are
between a thoroughly disingenuous essentialism and an angst-ridden

anti-essentialism. Thus for the moment it is more instructive to return to the bagh.

When General Dyer stood there, unbending, on that fateful afternoon in 1919, what did he see that so infuriated him that he would wreak such vengeful havoc? The horrific carnage has been meticulously recorded many times before. Less well documented are the apparently trivial yet utterly crucial details of the build-up to the devastation. It was Baisakhi, as we already know, and people were relaxing, playing cards, chatting and listening to the speakers. However, one activity in particular has assaulted the good general's aural sensibilities and left its audibly catastrophic signature ringing in his ears. The good general had issued a proclamation, on 12 April 1919, to the citizens of Amritsar. It read thus:

> The inhabitants of Amritsar are hereby warned that if they will cause damage to any property or will commit any acts of violence in the environs of Amritsar *it will be taken for granted that* such acts are due to the incitement in Amritsar city and offenders will be punished according to military law (Datta 1969: 94).

He issued another version in the morning of the thirteenth, but this time he went through the city, accompanied by the superintendent of police, the deputy commissioner and others. The town crier shouted Dyer's warnings at various places in the city. But the party felt the harshness of the midday heat and returned to the Ram Bagh. In the wake of the general's procession another, harsher sermon followed: pure unadulterated Dyer steel. 'The mob' called upon people to dance to their tune. Their leaders shouted that people should assemble in the garden that afternoon. Guran Ditta and Balo, Datta tells us, went round the city and beat out their tune on an empty steel tin. With promises of appearances by prominent local leaders, Balo and Ditta announced that people had nothing to fear, dismissing Dyer's proclamation as an empty bluff (Datta 1969: 96).

Consider for a moment the small but Rabelaisian party of Punjabi men ceremoniously issuing mimicked calls to order to the mocking accompaniment of a dholki. Dyer's nervy symbiotic relationship with the Manja Sikhs is at once jeopardized as the myth of Hindu inactive, panactive, effeminate masculinity is shattered. The spell is broken. No more the absolute ruler of an unquestioned domain (was he ever?), the classically trained, Sandhurst-educated colonial master will never again command the authority born of an exaggerated masculine ethos. This mockery as part of the everyday is what is so galling to Dyer. His voyeurism, which could simplistically privilege and legitimate (as alterity) a version of Sikh masculinity, was wholly unprepared for the simple yet hugely disruptive Hindu hands on the drum and magically farcical proclamations in the air. The moment of reckoning is past and the slaughter that will follow should be seen not as 'a moment of madness' as certain commentaries have been quick to suggest;[8] rather it should be read as the fearful sanction of a regime whose political pederasty in India has at last achieved unequivocal public exposure. The machinations of a militarized god have been cleansed of their deceit as if the subject of a purification rite at any ghat. Thus not even the transplantation of a savagely 'feudal' England within India's colonial heart has managed to subsume far older traditions of dissent and stoical disruption. As Spivak reminds us, a seamless narrative of synthesis can hardly undo or even make it possible to understand the 'systemic violence of colonialism', which depends for its very existence on normalized relations of terror.

The tainted soil of Jallianwala Bagh bears witness to a lethal anti-phonic exchange. Parody, farce and horror are very much the guiding principles of this drama. Manly proclamations of intent by Dyer are answered by an ultimately implosive creativity dispersed through the mockery of those 'other' male voices and the metonymic certainty of the drum. Yet the call of this bassline pulse of rebellion is met with the most extraordinary, sustained volley of staccato treble machinegun fire as 'order' is temporarily 'restored' to the mutinous bagh through the imposition of massive amounts of disorder. This is the apocalyptic jungle where a momentary silence masks the shock and the 'sorrow. The authority of the good general was never more paradoxical.

Sample the modern metropolis once more. Voyeuristic white masculine discourses around 'cool black subjectivity' rarely attempt to hide their distaste for perceived Asian 'effeminateness' and in fact are reliant upon such dialectical conceptualizations for their legitimacy. The most enduringly addictive constructions of blackness in general and black masculinity in particular within this angst-ridden neo-colonial psyche are the swagger of 'the hustler', his brooding malevolence and heightened sexual prowess. So begins a white-owned 'radical black subjectivity' enjoying such illustrious patrons as Jack Kerouac, Norman Mailer, Madonna and East 17.[9]

Notions of the 'cool black subject' have often heavily impacted upon the legitimation of particular forms of cross-racial affiliation in urban Britain. Simon Jones's ethnographic text *Black Culture, White Youth*, is useful as an exploration of this phenomenon in Britain's second city, Birmingham, and highlights the way in which such dialogues are subject to a heightened masculinist discourse. For instance, white respect for young blacks most often emerges from acknowledgement of the latter's perceived sporting or combative skills as 'good footballers or tough fighters'. Similarly, black cultural elements such as the polysemic qualities of black speech and the perceived militancy of Reggae in the dancehall tradition are shown to hold special allure for working-class whites.

Our caveat concerns the ambiguities of such patterns of affiliation. Such vagaries assume added significance when it is recognized to be a sign of white privilege to encounter and perceive blackness exclusively through the primary definition of apparently oppositional black cultural forms. It is only as hegemonic that whites can appropriate black creativity for their own opportunistic ends while simultaneously being complicit in the practices of racial terror. The alarming inconsistencies in the 'rationales' provided for patterns of appropriation and affiliation legitimate comparative preferences within a discourse of difference. Thus while the very 'alienness' of Afro-Caribbean cultural practices is cited as integral to white attraction and appropriation, that same white constituency subsequently justifies virulent anti-Asian prejudice and violence through commonsense perceptions of Asian culture as 'different and alien'. Bizarrely, a further discursive slippage then proceeds to perceive similarities between white working-class culture and key aspects of Afro-Caribbean culture. Thus the parallel discourses of a chauvinistic white racism and sustained appropriation of black cultural forms assume the flexibly disseminated dynamics of a cultural racism which underpins the culturally specific racial imagery of British urban life. So while the public realm may be transfigured by powerful cultural formations in the heartlands of the British metropolis, the imperative is to provide an analytical narrative that fully explores the contested spaces between blackness and Britishness in all their contradictory splendour. Musical syncretisms may well disclose the dynamics of cultural syncretism, yet everyday narratives of hierarchical terror demand a rethinking of the cultural possibilities of diaspora.

The Manichean landscape plotted through a masculinist binary lens becomes the site of fearful insecurity as the albeit temporal certainties afforded by its exclusionist practices are challenged, like the good general's command, by those 'other' voices. Familiar tropes of feminized Asian masculinity and thoroughly alien cultural proclivities are destabilized by the unequivocally critical presence of Asian youth across Britain. Historical configurations of power and knowledge generate an assymetry within the relativization of culture and nation whereby whiteness is encoded as a norm and blackness is particularized as the precursor to its reification. More importantly the city becomes the prime site

both for the contestation and perpetuation of such polarities as combative constituencies, and ideas are increasingly spatialized. It is worth
noting that 'postmodernity', supposedly characterized by the end of
margins, does not circumvent the physical and psychic fallout of racial
hegemony nor the mechanisms that uphold them. In the spirit of
C.L.R. James we may reasonably ask, therefore, whether the boundaries
between privilege and disenfranchisement are really remapped by
cultural strategies under these conditions.

The attractive prospect is that 'new' cultural practices offer a critical
cognitive mapping in which transnational culture and technology are
used to democratize space and shatter binary models of urban development. Our contention is that fragmented cultural forms such as Hip-
Hop, Ragga and more recently Jungle whilst homologizing cultural
disembodiment simultaneously empower a transformative journey to
the safe spaces of the known, frequently the absolute. Consider Hip-
Hop nationalism as a condition of Rap hybridity rather than as an
aberration and you begin to get the picture.

Interestingly, the raw, stripped-down percussive minimalism favoured
by much Ragga, Hip-Hop and Jungle has failed to erase the crudely
constructed struggle between two enduring black musical traditions, of
opulent fusion and drum'n'bass definition. Tellingly, the semantic code
most frequently invoked to clarify this apparently ruff/smooth dialectic
belongs to a thinly veiled racialized agenda which in another age would
have offered a reasonable narrative accompaniment to the scientifically
enlightened zealots of craniometry. Ponder, if you will, the subtleties
of this language which suggests the neat conflation of white hands
with handy science. Enter this mythical, cyberkinetic jungle and the
path to fulfilment is clearly marked. Here the willing trekker is assaulted
by a prescriptive literature of signs whose crusading zeal masks an ill
interior.

'The Information Centre' charges Ragga influences with bringing
crack into clubland and ruining the post-rave unity vibe. Happy white
House is pitted against the marauding 'darkbeats' of Jungle and whilst
white youth are happy to consume this 'devilish' new product away
from the 'dark spaces' of dancehall, the nightmarish visions of en-
dangered white womanhood at the soundclash are allowed to flourish
in the finest traditions of Jim Crow. It would seem that disruptive
'native' hands threaten the very integrity not just of mainstream Western
musicality but of that even older Western prerogative of determining
the patriarchally ordered nature of society.

Rewind to the bagh where a burgeoning horror is swelling the ranks of the terrorized and the fallen. No more the. instruments of pleasure during Baisakhi, these are the spectacular bodies of panic, flight and distortion pursued by the relentless staccato chatter of a mortal colonial sanction. And on the face of the executioner a different kind of terror. Let us freeze time and stalk the shadow of Walter Benjamin as we call a temporary halt to unqualified notions of historical progress. What, then, is the linearity (lineage, even) of the carnage wrought by Dyer?

Let us invoke the possibilities of a Sandhurst-educated gentleman. Dyer is the product of the classical military academy and this bears no small relation to the nature of the massacre at the bagh. To elaborate, if it is the case that childhood experiences are often replicated during adult life then it is fair to suggest that the militarized code of conduct imbibed by Dyer the boy is a guiding principle for Dyer the general. Imagine the dominant patrician ethics at work here: the premium placed on an exaggerated, unflinching, stoic inscription of masculinity. Now reconsider how such boyhood martial relationships within the academy abjure the relationships of Dyer's adulthood without. We are already aware of the good general's begrudgingly fearful admiration for what he perceives to be the archetypal martial 'race', the Manja Sikhs. That this is reliant upon a cogently split, desirous imagination which has equally quantified Hindus as a hopelessly effeminate, unthreatening 'other' is ultimately Dyer's undoing. For when he registers the ludic strains of Hindu rebellion being played out in front of him that fateful afternoon, his only concern is not to show anything that can be construed as weakness by the Manja Sikhs. There can be no concessions, not even the *possibility* of concessions to these *badmashes* gathered in the bagh; otherwise, like the patrician scoutmaster who fails to discipline his charges, his tenuous authority over his Punjabi domain will have been fatally weakened.

Hence Dyer's particular *performance* of masculinity, born of this fear of humiliation, of being laughed at, and manifested in the most brutal of the options available to him – massacre.

Back to the future and to the pressing question: what constitutes a jungle safari? Frantz Fanon eloquently reminds us that: 'the settler makes history and is conscious of making it ... the history of his own nation in regard to all that she skims off, all that she violates and starves' (Fanon 1961: 40).

'The jungle' was where those settlers would go to track down, admire and then eradicate 'wild' beasts; it was the primordial site for that most colonial of all sports, 'the hunt', a place to pit modern craft against primitive fire. Here was the spectacle of the 'good white man' fallen amongst natives only to redeem his noble fiefdom from the savagery of the subalterns. Here, too, his adoring 'memsahib' swoons in the hope that lustful native hands have been assuaged, at least for the moment.

Now picture this. Nearly a century has elapsed and in the farthest, febrile reaches of the 'popular' imagination 'the beast' is very much alive and well and daring to venture into the heart of the modern metropolis. Its brooding presence searches out the darkness and its stormy eyes register the great white hunter in the shadows as he prepares for one final onslaught.

'Jungle! Ah London Sumting Dis!' Chevignon, Osh Kosh and Karl Kani vie for primacy in the fuck-off queue which, gorged, snakes its inevitable way around the Astoria's historic bloc. A few miles away in the 'garden of England', those who would 'keep Sunday special' remain blissfully ignorant of this latest most graphic of outrages. For the young men and women massing outside the Astoria represent the spectre of a designer-clad native insurgency in the world's oldest imperial capital. This is the multi-headed, polyphonic beast which inspires dread and admiration in the gaze of the good island people. And what of the hunter, the gatekeeper to civilized society? Alas, our noble warrior is to be found within the gates of his suburban stronghold, arms manically swivelling, dragon stout aloft uncomplicatedly reciting the most unexpected of mantras: 'It's not a black thing, it's not a white thing, it's a London some'ting dis!'

What has brought about such an extraordinary proclamation of intent? We may point to recent boundary crises being experienced by certain sections of thoroughly ambiguous white youth as previously efficient binaries are eagerly interrupted by the practices of diaspora. We may even speak of the new 'public' cultures of diasporic youth or of a reconfiguration of the everyday within the contingency of British social relations. The suspicion remains, though, that there is something even more primal at work here. Ah, yes, the small matter of white, supremacist, capitalist patriarchy (to punchphrase bell.hooks) being held to ransom by a community of urban British renegades. Well, sadly, not quite, but there are hopeful stirrings.

Take the legendary 'Sunday Roast' sessions at London's Astoria whose critical presence lay in its ability not just to routinely serve a fierce selection of bass-neck frequencies but also to place icons of Englishness

– like the roast dinner – in the service of an emergent, recombined sense of youthful identity. Or the pugilistic destructions of mercurial Sheffield-born boxer, Prince Naseem Hamed, delivered to a Jungle soundtrack. Or the hardcore Afro-Asian constituency of a sound system like This Generation and the eclectic outdoor carnival blitz generated by A. Desai's dextrous deckwork.

Pause for a moment and recall the way in which Jungle's richly syncretic textures are reworking old flavours and a curious paradox begins to appear: the very notion of syncretism is itself the product of a hegemonic discourse of assumption, reliant upon the over-zealously conceived fluidity of cultural exchange, as if this is unsullied by the existing inequities of productive, distributive and consumptive networks. Indeed, the mobility of goods, ideas and peoples within a transnational economy may actually exacerbate rather than diminish the fault lines of class, race, gender and religion and raises important issues around dis-location and the shifting concerns of capital. Even postmodern directives envisioning the global ubiquity of market culture assume a new stage of capitalism in which culture and information are the key sites of contestation. Transnational capital, say its advocates, insists that cross-cultural transformations evoke the possibility of a non-essentialist approach to identity and culture. They conveniently omit to mention, however, that the racialized 'native' body has been subjected to a sustained history of the most appalling mental and physical abuse as well as to the 'cultural erasure' entailed in aesthetic stigmatization. Under such circumstances it seems reasonable to suggest that it is only through the recovery and rearticulation of that history that we realize those other syncretic possibilities not damaged by conflation with theft or unacknowledged appropriation. (This assumes added urgency in view of the fact that the psychic fallout of racial hegemony has ensured the silence of most postmodern thinkers concerning this discrepancy be-tween ideas of global emancipation and global systems of exchange.)

The dissonant modalities of a popular cultural form like Jungle implicitly problematize the process of 'translation'. A further cautionary note is likewise sounded by the ceaseless commercial impulse of a new cultural imperialism to commodify, package, reproduce and legitimate versions of exotica, of otherness to be engaged in a consumptive terror. Here, cultural capital allows the consumer to purchase an 'interpretive' knowledge of 'alterity', mediate dislocation and make the supposedly marginal palatable. Translation becomes the performative function of terror, as 'otherness' is analytically captured and 'preserved' in the third space of the museum. Anwar Abdel Malik sees in this process the potential for postmodern theory as the 'hegemonism of possessing minorities' (quoted in Shohat and Stamin 1994: 135). The paradox, then, of post-structuralist theory is that it nourishes through its activism the very totalizing myths it seeks to disrupt. Indeed the paralysing post-structuralist erasure of historical subjectivity does more, in theory at least, to disappropriate black, British youth of their cultural identifications than any doom-laden Powellian prophesies.

In an age of electronic Orientalism, images of the backward Asian as coy virgin and as demonic unbottled genie proliferate in the British media and by extension the public imagination. Hence the primary definition of a plurality of Asianness through pathological discourses around Islamic identity and a crude politics of victimology. Notwithstanding the frail premises of such parlance, its ability to reactivate a particular paranoid rationality owes much to the fetishization of technology as ideology where high-tech industry is allied to a contemporary instrumental rationality to generate a pervasive psychopathology. Within these 'modern' technoscapes perhaps we can rethink prosthetic ideas of mechanically reproduced participatory democracy by taking on board Les Levidow's suggestion that: 'If we are to subvert such reification of our collective social labour, then we will need somehow to dereify technology, to appropriate its potential for mediating social relations between people' (Levidow 1994).

The implication of tropicalization is clear. Whilst paradigmatic notions of synthesis complicate attempts to recover and authenticate traditional notions of 'the real', the conjunctive energies harnessed by technology may actually embellish interpretively conceived nationhoods. Within this diffuse landscape diasporic aesthetics are increasingly seen to occupy 'a ludic space of cultural specificity that challenges all holdings of British authority' (*Territories*, 1984, directed by Isaac Julien), and so it is with Jungle.

Overintegrated conceptions of deficient Asian physicality, a surfeit of cunning and negligible, if 'weird', cultural presence have long characterized what some have uncritically viewed as the wholly contingent social relations of the British city. In the domains of popular culture a similar electronically mediated Orientalism has been wheeled out every time the currency of such Dada-speak has been queried. 'They don't want to integrate, they just want to keep their ways' we are told by the acolytes of Ray Honeyford at home, at work or at play. The implication, in time-honoured Orientalist fashion, seems to be that a good dose of 'creolization', 'mestizaje', call it what you will (masala, ji?), would save us from our own (more often white folks') savagery and drag us kicking and screaming into the age of (post-) modernity.

Such advice sits uneasily with the assertion that identity and experience are most often mediated, narrated, constructed and confined to spirals of representation and intertextuality. Consider the attempts made to tarnish Jungle with an essentialist brush as if the very notion of 'community' were illegitimate when employed to recover a sense of diasporic agency rather than to locate the 'origins' of young offenders and 'illegal immigrants'. Parochial liberal panic is rarely more obvious than when British Asian populations revocabularize the territorial holdings of Britishness in all their ambiguities. Even those who at first appear sympathetic to Asian interventions within public cultural domains are subsequently found wanting in their desire to legitimate such activity by drawing parallels with paradigmatic models of oppositional, black cultures, as if the unique currency of such strategies is their ability to reinscribe the anterior moments of black, cultural discourse. Hence mimesis supposedly becomes the language of alterity and Apache Indian the standard-bearer of British Asian cultural production. The point is not the musical merits or demerits of this former sheet-metal worker; rather it is the way in which he is personified as holding a monopoly on the musical production of the diaspora. Creolization in the case of British Asians would appear, then, to hold the pitfall of homogenization. Plurality is sounded out in favour of a more politically expedient notion of hybridity and the sonorous voices of dissent are debilitatingly labelled 'simplistic' or the multi-purpose 'fundamentalist'. It is as if the antiphonic exchanges of Britain's diasporic populations have been a one-way street of Asian appropriation, reinscription and corruption. There is no mention in this dialogue of the 'rotification' of popular culture and its subsequent erasure in the search for a less diluted originary moment.

Consider some of the vagaries of Hip-Hop as movement outlined by 2Phaan Da Alien of the Rochdale Rap crew Kaliphz:

> The old crew was originally called New Conscious Kaliphz ... because we had a slight political tinge to things, but it was like more to do with the flavour of what was going on around then. We did our first show in London to about 22,000 people – just two of us – and it was scary. People just wasn't ready for Pakis rapping. They kept trying to push us off into being something else.... The Indian people have been down with hip-hop from day one but it's the same with Hispanic guys (in America) who got pushed out, not because of the people that was in it. When the media latched onto it, they didn't see the Hispanic side of it. The same with us. There was a lot of Indian

breakdancing crews and we were just as good as anyone else. We were part of the whole scene but nobody wanted to pay any interest.... Now, Indian people are the flavour of the month.... We ain't about that.... So forget Bhangra and hotter than vindaloo and all the usual reference points... (press release, Media Village).

We don't for a moment doubt the veracity of Hip-Hop's Africalogical, griotic roots nor the inherently publicly political character of black expressive cultures built around an instinctive antiphony. Nor do we take issue with the association of the term 'Jungle' as a descriptive musical genre with a district of Kingston, Jamaica, whose official title of Tivoli Gardens belies its connotation in 'yard' terminology as 'the jungle'. We may be reminded of that other ferociously deceptive garden and its sublime terrors but there is nothing problematic about such transplantations. What is questionable, though, is the haste with which the consignment of such emblematic figures as Steve Kapur, UK Apache and for that matter Naseem Hamed to exclusively black traditions implicitly regulates and devalues the many musical notes of the diaspora.

The idea of antiphony, for instance, needs to be absolved of its fettering assumptions and reinvisioned as governing the highly emotive, deeply ecstatic call-and-response patterns of Kirtan and Qawwali – the devotional musics of the South Asian diaspora.

Shidi and sadhu drum patterns and the inner technologies of such music offer a further rebuff to those for whom 'darker than blue' could never mean brown. And the polyphonic patterns of the Keralan chenda drum or the baul drumming of Bengal are nothing less than a musical score for the everyday narratives of diasporic ingenuity and performance. So too the accompaniment of the dholki as the organizational impulse of Baisakhi and its folkloric overture, Bhangra. From Kishore Kumar to Kaliphz and beyond, the refabulation of the drum lends substance to a picture of consistent if contingent antiphonic practices at the heart of Asian diasporic cultural performance and refuses the censorious, if seductive, allure of a hapless binary logic in the narrative location of such forms.

Our contention is that acknowledgement of such practices may offer a less blinkered approach to issues concerning hybrid metropolitan performance and the spatial prerogative of racial safety. Let us return for the moment to a case in point, south London's 'original nuttah', UK Apache. Tooting-based Apache, whose output with retiring digital *Wunderkind* Shy FX has already resulted in several Jungle 'anthems', has created a stir of a different kind away from but intrinsically belonging to the traditions of dancehall, in his refusal of a thoroughly spiteful, essentialist version of Britishness promulgated by the neurotic manifesto of white supremacy. His scathing dismissal of such 'politics' is contained in his unequivocal assertion that:

'Jungle … 'cos it's from England, right, I can really relate to it because I'm born here … I'm from England, from London, and nobody can't tell me that I'm not from here. At one time I was going around like ashamed of being British and the, like, Jungle's drawn me back to my roots because though … I'm half Arab, half Asian I can relate to those countries only up to a point; well, like, when I talk to my children, I can't talk to them about where my dad's from because my life has not been there, my life has been in England, in London. I can talk to them about Balham, Tooting, where I'm from so if you're born in England be proud of it and don't make nobody tell you no different, no BNP or anything like that' ('Jungle Fever', BBC2, October 1994).

The Junglist Massive offers scant reward in a digitally-enjoined heterotopia for the hateful posturing of white supremacists. Moreover the particular narratives of Asian Junglism help to define the totemic performance of an 'original nuttah' like UK Apache in the face of disabling dichotomous polemics which owe more to old-skool hysteria than new-skool creativity. Substitute 'yellow' peril for 'brown' and you get the picture. But perilous to whom, we may ask, and why? Forget Gangsta Rave and its clichéd assumptions about the primary definition of youthful black, British life. White youth still exercise their option to rework such narratives as part of a privileged cultural 'dialogue' with what they see as their black 'counterparts'. The point is not whether black folks were ever consulted about their 'contribution' to this particular exchange. Rather it is the way in which white men have valorized their appropriations from and demonization of black males within a cultural domain. 'We can fear and respect dem badaass niggers and even see heightened tropes of our own virility in their muscular, attitudinal prowess.' The necessary postcript is of course that it is still the inherently superior moral, ethical and cerebral stature of white societal values that sets whites apart from these 'savages'.

Crude reductionist politics operates at this level. A homogenized black masculinity is prized and feared as personifying the archetypal, old-skool 'masculine' qualities of detached cool, languid machismo and heightened sexual prowess. Whites who are able to access such perceived 'tropes' are seen to occupy a unique space 'at the cultural crossroads' as interlopers into an imagined blackness. That there are genuinely altruistic white appreciations of ubiquitous black cultural forms is not in doubt. What is doubtful though is the haste with which such fluid identifications are cited as the blueprint for an 'emergent' cultural politics.

Cross-fade in time to the revealing image of Dyer awkwardly imbibing his ceremonial 'inscription' into an eminently expedient pantheon of Sikh masculinity. In spite of his 'objections' to the conversion, such as the incommensurability of a life without his snout and the obligatory short back and sides, both sides are able to reach a 'happy' compromise and Dyer's initiation is ensured. Regaled with Karpan and Kardah, Dyer's grand gesture of goodwill is thrown into stark relief by what has gone before it. It is only days since the massacre at Jallianwala Bagh and already the tour of reassurance is under way. The good general, ever pragmatic in his Faustian performance, has concluded that his best, his only chance of survival rests on his ability to resurrect his supposedly special 'martial' relationship with those Manja Sikhs. Even at this stage he still believes that the failure to achieve this rather than the devastation at the bagh is what will unseat him from his colonial perch. And it is not without precedent that he has such faith for he is eminently aware of the 'case' of 'Nikalseyn Sahib': General Nicholson – famed for his part in quelling the 1857 popular uprising, known by Western historians as the Indian Mutiny with the most brutal force – subsequently went specifically 'native' and 'converted' to Sikhdom in an oft-cited ceremony (Colvin 1929: 202). The redemptive possibilities of pragmatic conversion would then have seemed limitless to Dyer as he contemplated his crumbling fiefdom. Just as he earlier 'takes it for granted' that it is his duty to punish the 'insurrectionists' at the bagh, so he now assumes that a 'mimetic' gesture to placate the Sikhs will assure his future. Indeed his eventual 'fall' from grace owes more to the grand pragmatism of the British colonial authorities than to any sanction against the hybrid poetics of terror.

Thus our 'emergent' politics of transgression is revealed as old wine in new bottles. Norman Mailer's 'white negroes', Jack Kerouac's masturbatory fantasies and the 'radical' charades of Madonna and East 17 do not individually or collectively short-circuit the mechanics of racial terror. Their unflagging refusal to acknowledge how the privileged terrains of their discourse problematize uncritical notions of a fluid cultural politics further discredits such opportunism. For cultural forms are not produced in some sort of vacuum; rather they emerge from and provide narratives for the everyday negotiations of diaspora. Just as bell hooks encourages us to see the all-American story of 'philistine gangsterism' retold in the drive-by narratives of Gangsta Rap, so we should not view Jungle as an aberration from a national fabulation across the ocean.

If the new location of culture is the studio and the new cultural historians are the engineers then Jungle's multilayered fusions coupled with its drum'n'bass minimalism at once refuse the romantic valorization of aura whilst reinscribing anterior modes of address which may not easily lend themselves to mimetic appropriation and opportunistic theft. Consider how sophisticated sampling technology disrupts the fetishization of a particular performance aesthetic as well as those assumptions in the way that technology is practised about who we are. It has even been suggested that what we are witnessing is a new feudalism within which the DJ as trickster plays the role of 'reality hacker'. This is diasporic science which dismisses pragmatic white branding of masculine currency on a performatively imagined black subject and unsettles corollary notions of Asian mimicry or invisibility. On the vexed question of invisibility a significant detail emerges. Whilst playfully eclectic sampling and dynamic, if infrequent, MCing (mike-chanting) can draw on the vast catalogue of diasporic science corralled in the dense archives of, for instance, Studio One, griotic traditions, and Bollywood, there would appear to be no equivalent cultural resource for white junglists. With this in mind it is not difficult to see how the 'Information Centre' frequently charges Jungle with operating as a cultural virus, eating away at that popular fiction of a pure British cultural heritage. In which case we are bound to ask: what is the body being attacked and what is the body being preserved?

When Asian Junglism comes to voice, the melodious tales of love and life transformed by the exertions of Bollywood into 'filmi' classics are recombined with ballistic bass and exploding drum patterns owing an equal debt to the firebrand traditions of Bengali Baul as to those of phat, Caribbean dancehall. The narratives of celluloid fantasy become the talks of London sound scribes in the imaginative renderings of contemporary urban geography. Think about it when the disorientation of Lata Mangeshka and Mohammed Rafi gon' clear has passed and 'Thanda Panni' has worked its therapy. Copping instrumental licks from Shankar and Zakir Hussain simply fleshes out the sensation and further eschews white chauvinistic politicking. And herein lies that most Dyeresque of terrors – the fear of white invisibility. Distressed by the energizing statements of Asian Junglism a beleaguered tract of white British youth resort with murderous vigour to the ever-ready option of racial terror. Disseminating hierarchical versions of masculinity remains integral to the effective operation of such a policy. More disturbingly, 'The Information Centre' is increasingly reliant, in these supposedly subtle (post)modern times, on a more pernicious strategy of legitimating the misinformation born of dangerous subterfuge. Thus the dualistic 'gaze' which subtly arranges the heterogeneity of Junglist output into frighteningly homogenous patterns. 'Radicalism' is not seen by enough commentaries in Jungle's seamless capacity for fusion as both historical reinscription and recovery of interpellative agency. Rather it is dubiously granted its narrative location in proliferating white-produced instrumental overtures which in any case borrow heavily from the lavish traditions of 1970s Jazz Fusion, Detroit Techno, Garage and almost any other contemporary Afro-American, diasporic popular musical form that you care to mention. Tellingly, 'critics' like Simon Reynolds charge the black producers of more instrumentally oriented Jungle with making it 'sound more like "proper" techno and less like its own baaad self ... infected with the funkless frigidity and pseudo-conceptual portentousness of Trance Techno.... Overall, everything that (this) is applauded for bringing to Jungle actually detracts from its ferocity' (*Wire*, June 1995).

What is even more worrying than the usual registration of liberal 'disappointment' with (and disapproval for) sophisticated Jungle are the implied definitions of black cultural expression that have presumably been unsettled. Only an ossified idea of black cultural roots could allow for the legitimation of ferocity as authentic and sophistication as the inappropriate musings of a 'wannabe' culture. Thus in one fell, if slack, swoop we are treated to the unnerving spectacle of the 'comforting' qualities (for whites) of myths of uncultivated, noble savages labouring on musical metropolitan plantations. The yearned-for ferocity of the jungle must never be in any doubt else the overseeing function and implicit civility of whiteness may be irreparably wrested of its Faustian pretensions. The other significant observation to be made here is that Asian Junglism is notably conspicuous in its absence from such white-sponsored 'discussion.'

All of which demands recognition of the inherently unequal systems of exchange to which cultural flows are subject and the discursive imbalances that this disparity empowers. And the 'original nuttah'? He continues to offer energetic performative reminders to verbose white constituencies of the enduring debt their ambiguous cultural identifications owe to the critical presence of Britain's black diasporas. That version of white supremacy so beloved of Dyer and his contemporary white charges teeters 'on the verge of a nervous breakdown' as its dialectical assumptions of a specifically rooted masculinity are continuously disrupted by the parodic performances of gender that are played out in the 'new' Jungle diasporas of London dancehall. National history can no longer credibly assume the privileged currency implied by 'history of the nation' as the terrifying traditions of modernity are made explicit in rhyme and verse by sagely scribes recalling savage times.

> Lo! let our sorrow be thy battle – gauge
> To wreck the terror of the tyrant's might
> Who mocks with ribald wrath thy tragic plight,
> And stains with shame thy radiant heritage!
> O beautiful! O broken and betrayed!
> O mournful queen! O Martyred Draupadi!
> Endure thou still, unconquered, undismayed!
> The sacred rivers of thy stricken blood
> Shall prove the five-fold stream of Freedom's flood,
> To guard the watch towers of our liberty.[10]

Sarojini Naidu's impassioned plea for justice in the wake of the massacre at Jallianwala Bagh demands above all else that the blood of the 'martyrs' not be bleached from the selective historical remembrance of 'the garden'. After all it is only the stains on the ethereal landscape of the bagh that raise the spectre of 'ungentlemanly' colonial savagery and its febrile fictitious accompaniment of a threatening, jungle-bound 'other'. Dyer's didactic posturing lends weight to this apocalyptic sketch: we are told that his hybrid composition of tenderness and terror was for the 'natives'' benefit. It was to save them from their own savagery. The garden as mythical residence of a quintessentially English idyll cannot be permitted to lose its paradisiacal flavour. If the *badmashes* were allowed to 'triumph' here then heathen profanity would have superseded the 'civilizing mission' of a colonial god, and 'paradise' would never be quite the same again. The only boundary between man and beast was the jungle and it was Dyer's profound conviction that his terrifying sanction was a last resort to prevent (Indian) man from 're-verting' to his beastly condition. 'It's a home-rule, pantheistic thing, you wouldn't understand' cried out the ungrateful natives, or so the story goes. They would rather return to their 'jungle' creed of monkey-worshipping, ghatt bathing and 'childlike' incompetence in the management of 'home affairs'. For the good general and his ilk this is a retreat from a state of 'civility' and it is only the demands of progress that oblige the colonial call to arms.

We have already dwelled on the essentially pragmatic nature of such imperial analysis and its parallel discourse of militarized terror. What needs to be stressed, as Edward Said has memorably emphasized, is that the idea of the jungle not only empowers imperial terror but simultaneously becomes its functioning reality. Thus the desire to see the jungle as the site of 'wild' insurrection is conflated in the colonial mind's eye with the actuality of the bagh. Baisakhi and its accompanying narratives of mimicry, impersonation and celebration are registered as a dangerously debilitating presence in the heart of the colonial 'garden': the 'purification rite' that follows is viewed by 'the authorities' as no more than an irritating obligation.

Three quarters of a century later and the loose-limbed 'terror' of the jungle is audibly transferred to a sonic soundscape via 'deep' bedrooms and New Age mercantilism. Yet it continues to be stalked by the fears borrowed from an earlier colonial setting. The dislike of jungle translates into fear of the Alien Ruffneck, of the Rudeboy from the council estate who's supposedly spoilt the peace-and-love vibe and the dream of trans-tribal unity. Jungle, so this racist myth goes, is what killed Smiley (Kodwo Eshun, *i-D Magazine*, May 1994).

Remembering 'Smiley's' ecstatic prominence as the symbol of a drug-related, happy (white) rave scene from 1989 onwards is useful. It allows us to think about the overtly racialized symbolism of utopia. Even digitally engineered utopias are apparently ruined by the natives. Their science is seen as bad science. It is Jungle that disrupts the ordered progress of British culture . Or so the story goes. Intriguingly there is no mention of how terror killed Smiley and a whole lot of black folks too. Such selective amnesia also ensures the projection of 'native-free' cultural zones policed by the strictly hierarchical nature of 'English/ Foreign' classifications. 'Native' produce is readily consumed as the precursor to its erasure yet its illicit properties are frequently invoked to justify its cultural exclusion. 'Smelly Pakis' cannot be allowed to assume the mantle of Asian Junglists otherwise the interior furnishings of the 'cultural department' will never again be a white masculine settlement where 'playful eclecticism' indulges cultural theft and the mortal recoil of 'civilizing' terror.

NOTES

We dedicate this piece of writing to our respective parents for all their help and support.

1. The Urdu poet Iqbal, quoted in V.N. Datta (1969: 171–2). The following account is indebted to a number of studies of the Amritsar massacre, though we make extensive use of Datta's work, the most prominent among them.

2. The story of white women and children suffering the indignities of everyday life in India during their time in the fort are set out for us in the anonymous contribution made in 1919 to *Blackwood's Magazine* by 'An Englishwoman'. To give readers a feel for the conditions our anonymous Englishwoman has to put

up with we need to include part of her testimony. We would suggest that this provides a useful link with our notion that it is openly disrespectful to conflate the white terror of invisibility with diasporic practices. For instance, she 'remembers': 'At midnight we turned in, but daylight seemed to come before we closed our eyes. The outlook was not pleasant for women who had never known a day's real hardship before; they found themselves suddenly stripped of all the decencies and comforts they had come to look upon as necessities, and surrounded by the miseries of dirt, heat and overcrowding. There was no sanitation; everything depended on the servants, who had not yet been organized. There was no privacy, and we had to hide under our bedding to dress ourselves. Sixteen people shared one small room for the first three days, and those who had no rooms were really better off. There were no beds, no proper bedding, no mosquito nets, no fans and hardly any lighting. No one had any small personal possessions or any change of clothing. The place was infested with sandflies, and the stagnant water of the moat bred the most virulent kind of mosquito. We did not know when we should get supplies of fresh food or milk, and as there were only twelve cups and about twenty plates, distribution of what food we had was difficult. One could summon up courage to face these conditions oneself, but the presence of so many babies and children made the situation really serious. One baby had developed typhoid fever that morning, and they all had requirements which could not be met' (*Blackwood's Magazine*, April 1920, p. 444).

Swamped in indignities, in the nightmare vision of restless slumber without the barriers provided by a closely woven gauze, she is really rather afraid of being ground into the dirt. Bearing down on her, the heat, the overcrowding, the immensity of the infestations, all the unreasons that resist her organizational imperatives impel her 'saviour', General Dyer, to pursue the orderly path with whatever means are at his disposal.

3. The reference to the wounded and dying at the bagh making their own way to the hospitals comes from the good general's replies to questions put to him by the Indian members of the Hunter Committee of Inquiry, set up to investigate the disturbances throughout parts of northern India in 1919. See Report of the Committee Appointed by the Government of India to Investigate the Disturbances in the Punjab etc. Cmd 681, 1920 p. 116. The following exchange took place:

Q: 'After the firing had taken place did you take any measure for the relief of the wounded?'

A: 'No, certainly not. It was not my job ... the hospitals were open and the medical officers were there. The wounded only had to apply for help. But they didn't do this because they themselves would be taken in custody for being in the assembly. I was ready to help them if they applied.'

4. From a few scattered comments in Sir Henry Cotton's autobiography we learn that Nicholson, another military man in colonial India, trained in a hard school, not flinching at meting out summary justice. He ruled, we are told, with a proverbial rod of iron. So much so that in Cotton's view what he called the cult of Nicholson Sahib became a fetish. Interestingly, Cotton adds that methods resorted to in the Punjab have never carried over well in the rest of the country, only ever being a potential source of danger when applied generally. If the cult

of Nicholson is thought of as a fetish', the extravagant almost pathological invest-
ment in the rod displays an obsessive concern with the native's body as a source
of libidinal gratification. In this case the desire is satisfied through every strike of
the whip, through every thrust of the rod. Yet if every act of summary justice is
a manifest satisfaction of libidinal desires, it simultaneously contains a number of
fearful elements. The pre-eminent fear in this case, as indeed in others, is that of
disorder, one of the underlying themes of which is the supposed threat that the
stiff-backed man of Empire will be undermined by a version of native masculinity (see Cotton 1911; Dawson 1994).

    5. We are thinking here of those many and varied white folk who have
converted through ritual into modern 'English' custom the unusual and often
excessive practice of alcohol consumption as the prelude to a late-night visit to
that most diasporic of inventions the 'curry house', and the fiercely defiant in-
take of a sizzling so-called vindaloo. Its particular significance, we would suggest,
lies in that peculiar hybrid performance so beloved of all British patriots which
temporarily relinquishes the mantle of purity for the literal consumption of a
spiritually and gastronomically challenging Other. Here, there is a heightened
conflation of those familiar masculinized tropes of abuse, consumption and
expulsion where a sense of normalcy is returned via the cathartic, if painful,
process of physical expulsion of the strongly spiced product, the legacy of disruptive 'native' hands.

    6. Gary Bushell has vigorously promoted his 'populist' version of British
nationalism for over two decades, both as a columnist (for the *Sun* newspaper)
and as a much-fêted media pundit and self-appointed cultural critic. He remains
one of the staunchest advocates of the 'fictitious' and vehemently racist television
character Alf Garnett.

    7. The sustained references to white supremacy and white racisms are
implicitly useful here. They assume the existence of alterior forms of black
supremacy and racism. We find it instructive to consider the ways in which these
forms clearly disrupt the certainties of white supremacy and are most often seen
as locked in a symbiotic relationship. The anxiety and arrogance of such a binary
opposition is rightly scorned and we revel in its continuous disruption.

    8. See Furneaux (1963), who is only one of the more vocal in suggesting
Dyer's madness; thus, for example, as Dyer was standing with his men on the
platform in the Bagh he had a rush of blood to the head.

    9. Beat poet Kerouac projected his clichéd racial fantasies onto Charlie Parker;
Norman Mailer is famed, amongst other things, for his advocacy of a politics of
mainstream subversion empowered by the 'transgressive' white Negro; Madonna's
aping of a particular black performative aesthetic as passport to 'radical chic' is
scathingly exposed by bell hooks (1992), amongst others – see her essay: 'Madonna
– Soul Sister or Plantation Mistress?'; all-white teen pop combo East 17 have
achieved mainstream stardom without ever acknowledging their wholesale colo-
nization of black British linguistic, sartorial or musical styles.

    10. Sarojini Naidu, 1919, quoted in Datta (1969: 172).

9

NEW PATHS FOR SOUTH ASIAN
IDENTITY AND MUSICAL CREATIVITY

Raminder Kaur and Virinder S. Kalra

Me say me gone go make a movie mon over India,
plane a where me catch a Indian air-liner
Place a where me land dat a Amritsar, who meet me no de Prime minister
Who a rush me baggage no a fe her father, who kiss me Gandhi daughter
Me there in de country like a big movie star, jump pon a taxi dem a call a
     riksha
Pass Bombay and a Khalistania, de people meet me dem a no de producer
Make one film with de one Amitabh, make another one with de one
     Rekha
Who sing de song Lata-Mangeshka, who play de music no Ravi-Shanka
Come take it from de youth bare-back rida,
me chatta pon de mic like you could of never
So each and everyone mon come follar me mon, dip your knee cork out
     your botty
De style a where you do are Bhangra jockey...
Your pound and dollar say dat a rupee, your firewater say dat a desi
You want a glass a water say dat a parnee, me want me chalice say dat a
     hookie
Me pull out me rizzla and me sensi, dey say Wild Apache mon you a
     umalee
Come take it from de youth mon fe everybody,
you no say dis a youth have de authority
Me play it fe de White, de Indian and de Yardy.

            (Apache Indian, 'Movie over India', Island
            Records 1993. Published by MCA)

Prominent artistic productions such as the pop song, 'Movie over India',
the drama *Tartuffe*, and the film *Bhaji on the Beach,* are only the most
well-known and commercial end of what is a spectrum of expressive

activities. Though located in Britain, they cannot be described or contained with reference to particular national boundaries.[1] The narratives entailed in these productions criss-cross various parts of the globe linked by histories of colonialism and migration. Such travels necessitate a transnational focus of study when considering related formations of identity and creativity. The interplay between these processes of globalization and localization are particularly pertinent when considering musical cultures.[2] The crucible from which our concerns arise involves a number of factors. In sum, the tense social and political climate of early-1980s urban Britain charged a creative turmoil in which South Asian youth amongst others, building on their experiences, forged new cultural forms. Music presented an accessible and universal forum for articulating this dynamic social flux. These expressions have been facilitated by the increased rate of musical flows around the world, correlate with technological developments. Simultaneously, the commercially driven search for novelty, symptomatic of the rapacious pop industry, has both filtered the more radical elements and channelled the more acceptable forms to a wider audience.

A central purpose of this chapter, as of this book, is to initiate a debate around the identification 'Asian' from the particular perspective of the production of youth music cultures. By concentrating on the arenas inhabited by South Asian diasporic artists and consumers we attempt to destabilize such rigid terms of identification, and propose other alternatives. After laying out a theoretical tract for localized and transnational forms of identity, we go on to focus on the ethnography of a particular musical culture, highlighting the complexities entailed in such identity and musical formulations.

SOME BR-ASIAN CONSIDERATIONS

The term 'Asian' has no consistent historical or global use. In the USA, the term by and large refers to people from Japan, Korea, China, and Vietnam. People who trace their ancestry back to the Indian subcontinent tend to be categorized as 'Indian' or 'East Indian'. Gayatri Spivak reflects on the use of the term 'Indian' in the USA: 'Subterfuges of nomenclature that are by now standard have almost (though not completely) obliterated the fact that, that name lost some specificity in the first American genocide' (Spivak 1993: 54). In the British context, in popular parlance the term 'Asian' has come to specify immigrants from the Indian subcontinent. Similar problems of inconsistency are encountered when considering the term 'black'. In the USA, the widespread use of the term 'black' refers to those of African descent, and its valorization was a consequence of the civil rights movement of the 1960s. In 1970s Britain, however, 'black' came to refer to all those groupings that experienced racism and shared a colonial past, thereby including the category 'Asian'. A satisfactory terminology to describe those occasions when racism actually does unite disparate cultural and social groupings in a resistive way is still anticipated. Whilst acknowledging the need for an examination of the dissolution of a discursive Black subject, it is still the case that the term 'Black' can be used, particularly in the sense developed by Gilroy in *The Black Atlantic* (1993a). Referring primarily to expressive cultures, Gilroy locates 'Black', simply, in those processes of displacement and creative tension encompassing the Americas, the Caribbean and Europe.

In the discussion of musical forms, it has to be recognized that popular music is not simply a reflection of socio-political situations, but is involved in a series of dynamic interactions – sometimes reflecting, constituting, or subverting, at other times tangential, reactionary and, occasionally, anarchic. Certain nodes of identification can be located within the flux at any particular moment in time, illuminating the role of music in identity formations, actual or potential. When considering musical productions, we wish to propose the contingent term defining those of African and Afro-Caribbean backgrounds in Britain as 'Blak' (Gilroy 1993a: 81), and for those of South Asian backgrounds resident in Britain we propose a new term: 'Br-Asian'. This latter construction refers to the complex subject positions of migrants and their offspring settled in Britain with links both imagined and material to South Asia. It is intended to be an open term, beginning the exploration of shifting identifications and representations. The over-used and poorly defined category 'British Asian' is problematic as it essentializes both terms, as well as hierarchizing the former against the latter. Further, it does not fully convey the various and sliding subjectivities that come into play in response to historical, social and political vicissitudes. Our theoretical categories need to be closer to the ethnography from which they come, as a strategy to counter universalizing categories. In so doing, we recognize the contingent status of all theoretical and nominal constructions, whilst not denying the accuracy of these categories for particular analyses.

As an illustration of sliding subjectivities, it is possible to note occurrences of youth of a Gujarati or Bengali background identifying with Bhangra bands which use Punjabi as their lyrical language. Typically, Bhangra is seen as emblamatic of Punjabi identity: collective memory recalls Bhangra as a male folk musical dance performance, celebrated in rural settings, particularly at the bringing in of the harvest at Baisakhi (the Punjabi New Year on 13 April). Men dressed in brightly coloured cloths wrapped around their waists, *lungis*, embroidered waistcoats, flamboyant turbans, and bell-straps on their ankles sang and danced to a loud percussion provided by one or more drums, dhol or the smaller version, dholki. The dancers accompanied the rhythm with vigorous movements of the shoulders and feet, hands gesturing and usually held aloft over the head. For some time now Bhangra has also been performed at celebratory occasions such as weddings and birthday parties in Britain. Bhangra in this context refers to the modernization of a Punjabi male folk form of dance and music. In many cases, the 'traditional' traits of Punjabi lyrics, the use of the dholak rhythm and antiphonal styles of singing are retained but combined with electronic instrumentation such as synthesizers, drum machines and electrical guitars. In contemporary Britain, the multiple use of languages, whether Bengali, Urdu or Gujarati, does not act as a barrier to a sense of solidarity in identifying with displaced South Asian-derived musical cultures; this then instantiates the new form of identification which we have called Br-Asian. This identification is in no sense fixed, bounded or cohesive at all times and places; and nor is it limited only to musical identifications – it also finds expression in the reception of Indian popular films in Britain, and in the print media of which the wide circulation of the weekly English-language paper, *Eastern Eye* is a good example.

For any particular situation there are two basic opposing vectors or trends of identity formation. One is that of correspondence, where ideas of a shared past, similar backgrounds or comparable present-day circumstances are stressed. The other is that of difference where, either through antagonism, resistance or cultural superiority complexes, particularities are stressed. These need not be rigid oppositions. We might find a complicated entwining of the vectors as personal inclination and situation emphasize one more than the other – latticed identities that might be rigid for one situation but loosen up for others. Thus we have an oscillation of the one and the many, the fixed and the unfixed, the essentialized and the de-essentialized, the particular and the hybrid, in constant processes of suturing and fracturing. In certain cases, however, identity formations are still firmly structured by convention and regulation. This is particularly apposite to the question of gendered identities in Br-Asian musical production. Here, women exemplify less interaction with the public 'space' of their locale. More often than not, they continue to be represented with reference to their conceptualized place of origin – that is, symbolic of Punjabiness or Indianness – as chief bearers of culture or representative of Oriental exoticism. Hence, in the patriarchal context of musical production, women's expressions of identities persist in more fixed and bounded parameters than is evident for the case of men.

The term 'Br-Asian' is forwarded as an analytical tool from which it is possible to consider identity formations in the particular locality of Britain, whether it be in their exclusivist or hybridized variations. By acknowledging the impossibility of complete categorization in theory and in practice, 'Br-Asian' is intended both to be disruptive of the centre–margin relationship and to destabilize fixed notions of Asian identities, stressing their contingency on historical and spatial moments. As a hyphenated form of identification, 'Br-Asian' contains possibilities for splintering as it does for the formation of other alliances. The question of regional affiliation and the degree of religious and caste consciousness act as breakable joints in this categorization; common subjection to racist oppression and criticisms of mainstream society serve as platforms to align with other marginalized groups. To develop fully the conceptualization of 'Br-Asian', we need to acknowledge the permeability of such terms in view of the fact that this categorization is intimately linked across the globe to other hyphenated identities.

PLANET BOL

Our argument in relation to popular musical culture around the globe questions the marginality of Br-Asian musical productions to the mainstream music market. In the process, we delineate a non-Western-derived global mapping of ideas, products and people. It is frequently argued that Black global music (including Soul, Reggae, Ragga, Afro-American Rap and their Euro-American versions) is accepted as the mainstream. On the question of youth musical culture, it could be reasoned that black is certainly not at the margins but underwrites much of Western popular music ('Birthrights: Crossing the Tracks', BBC2, 2 August 1993), in relation to which other musical cultures are considered as the incomprehensible outsiders. This issue of incomprehensibility is illustrated by the following account: Henry Louis Gates argues that there is a short-sightedness within European literary canons and critiques when discussing Black narrative traditions: 'These admittedly complex matters are addressed, in the black tradition, in the vernacular, far away from the eyes and ears of outsiders, those who do not speak the language of tradition' (Gates 1988: xx). In this valuable effort to redress European hegemonic intellectual and cultural practices, recent theorists of Black culture and history have revealed certain short-comings, in that they become the outsiders to other 'languages of tra-dition'. For instance, in the consideration of Rap a number of its features have been aggrandized, particularly the supposedly unique traits of antiphonal styles, and the self-promotion of the artist in the lyrical text. Callahan writes, 'Call and response is a distinctively African and African American form of discourse' (Callahan 1992: 78), and Cornel West notes, 'A distinctive feature of these black styles is a certain pro-jection of self – more a persona – in performance' (West 1989: 72).

As a counterpoint to such propositions, we observe that there has been a long tradition of the use of antiphonal styles or *boliyaan* in 'traditional' North Indian folk music/dance performances, which are central to the production of the musical event, as with Bhangra and Giddha.[3] *Boliyaan* refers to a musical text of call-and-response couplets, within which *bol* describes a single couplet. The modern versions of these forms have continued the antiphonal style with many groups using at least two singers in call-and-response interactions. Second, the pro-jection of the author or performer of poetic/music texts has had a long-standing presence in North India.[4] The appearance of these similar stylistic forms is not simply to imply a replacement of Afrocentrism with 'Asiancentrism', as we do not argue for a unique or essential 'Asianness' that needs to be addressed and located; rather we look to the continuities and discontinuities, the parallels and differences, within various narrative texts. Nor do we set out to establish or control a canonical narrative tradition that may act to exclude inherent margin-alized groups and uphold the status quo. Rather, by taking a transverse and transnational focus on cultural flows, we intend to avoid the afore-mentioned pitfalls.

Since the emergence of the Hindi popular movie at the very begin-nings of the twentieth century, the filmic product has traversed national boundaries in terms of production, content and distribution networks. Simultaneously, it has cannibalized folk music forms within the sub-continent and circulated them in mutated form to its far-flung audi-ences. The rapid onslaught of communications technologies particularly since the 1980s has seen an acceleration of these transnational and intranational movements. Additionally, since the mid-1980s satellite tele-vision has radically transformed the pace of media cultural flows. Since 1995, Europe has begun to receive Zee TV (formerly TV Asia in the West), which is re-broadcast in North America – with programming scuttled from television and movie broadcasting in India and Hong

Kong. Global movements are also noted in the print media, where magazines and newspapers such as *Cineblitz* and *Stardust*, published in India, and *The Asian Age*, simultaneously published in New Delhi, Mumbai, Calcutta and London, are in the vanguard of publications that cross national boundaries.

To chart the relevance of the above to musical phenomena there is a need to account for the shifting centres within the South Asian diasporas. In this process we begin to expose the limitations of the very notion of diaspora. We note that technological innovations, amongst their other effects, have played a key part in allowing minority-group cultural productions to transgress nation-state boundaries and communicate with others. Global media and telecommunications, and the flow of sound structures divorced from their place of manufacture, have provided for a greater interconnectedness and interdependency for minority groups. To begin the exploration of this phenomena, we propose the imagined spatial arena of Transl-Asia not as a fixed area of the world but rather a continuous movement of imagined and actual arenas. To a greater or lesser extent, South Asia is one of the many reference points of Transl-Asia, but not necessarily its originary location. Our contention is that the understanding of diaspora privileges a place of 'origin', that is of an unchanging and stable nature, whereas the term 'Transl-Asia' is intended to prioritize the notion of space, which 'highlights histories of domination and the production of difference and hierarchy, as well as imaginative social practices' in its various locales (Axel 1994: 17). We do not wish to replace the notion of origins with something else, namely, the 'space' of localized post-migrant cultures as in 'Br-Asian', but to note the interactive dynamics between 'place' and 'space'.

To develop this argument further, we note Homi Bhabha's comments:

> Culture as a strategy of survival is both *transnational* and *translational*. It is transnational because contemporary postcolonial discourses are rooted in specific histories of cultural displacement.... It is translational because such spatial histories of displacement – now accompanied by the territorial ambitions of global media technologies – make the question of how culture signifies, or what is signified by culture, rather complex issues. It becomes crucial to distinguish between the semblance and similitude of the symbols across diverse cultural experiences – and the social specificity of each of these productions of meaning as it circulates as a sign within specific contextual locations and systems of value (Bhabha 1992: 47).

The constellation of spaces within the concept of Transl-Asia might include changing configurations between parts of South Asia, Europe,

North America, the Caribbean, East Africa, Australia and the Far East. The localization of *symbols*, in our case musical forms, might take on variant associations according to the social, geographical and historical contexts. This chapter considers this phenomena mainly in relation to Br-Asian musical forms, whilst acknowledging how this production is articulated by an ever-intense to-ing and fro-ing between other places in Transl-Asia. The significance of Br-Asian musical production has been the pivotal role it has played in constructions of other localized hyphen-ated Asian identities. To appreciate the changing waves created by Br-Asian musical productions we have to trace the travelogs of both artists and consumables (cassettes, records and compact discs). It becomes apparent that Br-Asian musical developments initially placed Britain at the core of Transl-Asia. However, this is not a fixed centre but one in oscillation with other centres such as Toronto (Canada), Mumbai (India), Jallandhar (India) and California (USA). In each case as musical in-novation develops, technology interacts with and dissipates it around Transl-Asia; which term here describes an arena of cultural flows, not entirely geographically grounded nor always nationally bounded, but constantly on the move charting out new spatial configurations.

MUSICS ON OUR DOORSTEPS

The theoretical terrain traversed above will be brought to bear on the development of the musical scene in Britain, as well as to address parallels in other localities. In the early 1980s, the reverberations of modernized Bhangra began to be felt in the heart of one of the Br-Asian residential quarters in Greater London, Southall. A prominent band that began to experiment with synthesizers and drum machines was Alaap, who later, along with the sound engineer Deepak Khazanchi, were instrumental in setting the ball rolling in terms of providing a new blend of Bhangra sounds. Like many other Bhangra groups, Alaap began by performing at celebratory occasions, mainly weddings. Largely they performed for the *baraat*, the male assembly, although amongst certain sectors of the community both men and women might come together in hired halls to the accompaniment of Bhangra. The groups were appreciated for the quality of their musical sound alone rather than being enmeshed in particular celebratory occasions – beginning the process of the commodification of music into a sound-object. Hindi film song also had a strong influence on this new British style, indicating a reversal of the post-1950s phenomenon of Hindi film culture cannibal-izing regional musics. Now Bhangra bands, diasporic offsprings of regional musical performances, cannibalized Hindi film tunes as well as the latest sounds in Western dance music. This dynamic is not surprising if one also considers that the Bhangra bands tapped into a cassette industry already providing Hindi film music.

One can find parallels with other musical global flows. As mentioned before in this book, Gilroy (1993a) has noted the musical interchange between the countries of North America, the Caribbean and Britain. John Storm Roberts (1973) has described the musical round trip between Africa, the Caribbean and Latin America. Roberts notes that musical styles 'originally' from Africa were creolized in places like Cuba as a result of the presence of related communities, and then went 'home' to influence the development of popular music on the African continent. Similarly, British-based Bhangra music went 'home' to influence the development of popular music in the Indian subcontinent, resulting in the signing of Indian film music contracts for Br-Asian groups such as Alaap, D.C.S. and Golden Star. However, we diverge from Roberts's argument in that we do not wish to prioritize an originary location for the various musical cultures that we are interested in but to decentre the place of Punjab/India in our tracts. In this case, the music disrupted the simplistic notion of 'home', with Br-Asian musics developing their own dynamics in the socio-musical landscape of Britain itself. Britain became the centre for musical export to such places as Kenya, Canada and the Caribbean. In these journeys, consumer goods play as important a role as live music. For instance, whilst weddings in Britain were playing host to live bands, in California audio tapes of their music were accompanying the wedding party. This is just one facet of a complex series of loops happening on a transnational level we have called Transl-Asia.

Modernized Bhangra of the 1980s filled a demand amongst Br-Asians, enabling them to enjoy a musical genre that was at once modern yet different from mainstream pop in such a way as to express their transmuted identity in innovative ways. However, although initially the Bhangra scene allowed for a Br-Asian identification particular to Britain, by the end of the decade the centrality of Bhangra to this formation began to subside. There were several factors in this deflection. Many youth began to express a disaffection with the Hindi film costuming – usually sequins, spangles and white trousers – of the generally middle-aged performers. Consequently, bands with younger, British-born members whose ages and tastes were closer to those of their audiences began to emerge, as was the case with Anaamika, the Sahotas, and Achanak. Furthermore, complaints about Bhangra's untrendiness, linguistic barriers and lack of 'socially meaningful' lyrics began to surface. In addition, there was ambivalence towards the distorted and essentialist view that Asian youth should have some kind of 'natural' affiliation towards Bhangra.

Out of these fractures of musical identifications came other cultural expressions inspired by a wide range of sources. A recent example of what Hebdige (1987) calls cut'n'mix – to describe sound editing procedures as well as the relations between identities and music – is the way that the Bhangra traits of Punjabi lyrics and dholak sounds have been mixed with the dancehall Rap genre known as Ragga. It is notable that the dynamics of musical interchange in Blak and Br-Asian margins has resulted in the likes of Bally Sagoo's remixes with Bhangra tracks, Ragga patois and other dance sounds. The creolization between the two musical forms is commonly referred to as Ragga-Bhangra, and the performers as Ragga/Bhangramuffins. They are an assertion of the meeting of black musics and Bhangra traditions with their own musical histories and reference points. The marginal position of Br-Asian music relative to the mainstream has undergone a rapid transformation since the commercial success of Apache Indian since 1992. The musical style that Apache initially projected owes much to the Bhangramuffin phenomenon.

It is instructive to use the case of Apache Indian to investigate subject positions we have outlined above, and in the process highlight the contingency and permeability of such nominal terms. What we have is a suspension of categories impinging on essentialist notions of British, South Asian and black. Br-Asian allows us to open up these essentialist terms of identification to explore related socio-musical phenomena. Apache illustrates that Br-Asian is at once about centres of post-migrant populations such as Handsworth (Birmingham) and Southall, but also involves a wider reading which takes into account posses, patois, and Ragga. Effectively, Apache refracts the experiences of Br-Asian youth; and Apache's Ragga patois, his Jamaican orientations, and his Reggae affiliations exhibit the inherent potential for disruption within any forms of singular identification. They demonstrate the ability to form alliances with others, within, through, and without national borders.

There is a fusion and confusion of boundaries, aptly illustrated by the juxtapositions of transnational and translational symbols, for example, Mahatma Gandhi and the Indian flag juxtaposed with the colours of Rastafarian Africa on Apache's *No Reservations* album cover. Musical flow in Transl-Asia is exemplified by the song 'Moving On' which was initially about Hindu–Muslim communalism in India. It was then swiftly altered to expose racism in Britain two days after a British National Party candidate was elected into power in Tower Hamlets, London, in 1993.

Apache's recognition of the marginality of Transl-Asia is expressed when he represents himself as the musical pioneer who is breaking into the international music scene:

> One thing I am trying to do for the whole of the Indian people and the whole of the Western people and the White press in England and America is [to show] that Indian people have got a lot of talent. But the problem is that people like Michael Jackson, Elvis Presley and Whitney Houston are stars for the whole world. Indian stars, Indian singers and Indian actresses and actors should be stars for the whole world, not just Indian people (Apache Indian, interviewed in BBC2's 'Birthrights', 1993).

Through commercial success, Apache has managed to push the parameters of Transl-Asia to penetrate global mainstream music. The video of the single 'Make Way for the Indian' is set in New York, and in musical terms is in the Rap genre. Entry into the American music market has increasingly become a prerequisite for global commercial success. This single is evidently Apache's attempt to widen his audience.

Two points can be added to our reading of the Apache Indian phenomenon. The first is that Apache is not the total sum of Br-Asian musical productions – in fact he is just the tip of an iceberg. Within Br-Asian circles, conventional Bhangra bands as well as the more radical troupes (such as Fun^Da^Mental and Kaliphz) present polychromatic subject positions in terms of their constituents, alignments, and audiences. The work of these musicians has been explored more fully in other chapters of this book. Second, women still remain peripheral to Apache's lyrical address, either contentiously invoked as symbolic of Indianness, as in 'Arranged Marriage' – 'dressed up in a *sari* and sweet like *jalebi*' - sexualized for the male gaze, or not mentioned at all. Such chauvinistic bearings are at the intersections of conservative tendencies within multinational music houses and certain types of Br-Asian music. We now wish to go on to explore the areas around these prominent crossroads.

GIDDHA ON IT

So far our attention has been focused on a primarily patriarchal set of practices evident in musical cultures. We need to expose inherent asymmetries, where empowerment by a re-evaluation of cultural productions such as modernized Bhangra has not considerably reflected or affected the position of women. Affiliation to modernized Bhangra is not in any way gender-specific with regard to the consumption of musical forms and live performances. Here women tend to associate with the musical forms in a manner that exemplifies a diverse array of subjectivities. In terms of musical production, however, Br-Asian women's subjectivities lie more towards essentialist rather than hybridized forms. Bhangra and later Br-Asian developments marginalize women in narrative and industry. In conventional Bhangra texts women tend to appear as 'fit and fashionable temptresses' to be watched, teased, commented upon and owned – for example, there are explicit references to the woman as the outsider married into the family such as the *bhabi* (sister-in-law) and *nooh* (daughter-in-law). This is different from the whore/wife dichotomies one might find in Black Rap (hooks 1991), for instance, but inevitably is similar in that the representation of women is stereotypical and of a limited focus. In contradistinction, one of the spaces in which women's musical production and performance are controlled by themselves is in the performance of Giddha. Characteristically, this involves a circle of women with two women in the centre leading with their sung phrases or *bols*, to the rhythm of hand-clapping and in some cases a dholki drum. These performances, whilst generally having a harmonious grace, may periodically slip into unrestrained bawdiness as *bols*, and gestures about a whole range of risqué topics are comically indulged in. Some of these performances may involve subversion of gender expectations as women dress up as men and ridicule their behaviours.

With the professionalization of Bhangra since the mid-1980s, Giddha has tended to take a back seat due to the combined factors of relative lack of approval, motivation, and opportunities for women performers in the public sphere. None the less, a few women such as Kamaljit Neeru, Parmjit Pammi, and Sangeeta broke out into wider professionalized music circles as singers in the 1980s Bhangra scene. The image that is presented is that of a very clean-polished persona and song narrative, very much at odds with the character of Giddha performances. This is also exemplified since the mid-eighties in the circulation of video cassettes of sanitized Giddha performances. These videos have served various purposes – to instruct, to preserve the form, to innovate in *bols* and dance steps, and to publicize the musical performance. The significant point here is that whilst a new space for musical performance and participation has been created, it has relied on a more rigid formula than Bhangra. This form of presentation is not geared for the mainstream music market, and the music continues to be seen as symbolic of Punjabi Indianness, corroborating our argument about women's limited range of assumed subjectivities.

Nevertheless, changes are apparent in Br-Asian circles, where women also are demanding a space to articulate their views. Their agency is highlighted by the uncompromising positions taken up by the likes of Radical Sista and Imtiaz Hussein, and the collaborations of the poet Joyoti Grech with soundtracks provided by Annirudha Das. These developments demonstrate that Br-Asian women are beginning to address issues of gender and race for themselves, in an effort to challenge oppression both at a Br-Asian level and at a wider societal level. More commercial singers such as Sasha have a complicated relationship to these changes, in that they may be both producers and products of identification in what remains a patriarchal musical system. Rather than subverting patriarchy, their voices might even end up confirming the status quo when love songs speak of male dependency, and when the portrayal of the female body continues to be fetishized.

VANGUARD SPEARS TO THE BEAT

We wish to point to some of the possibilities for the development of the terminology we propose: namely 'Br-Asian' as a particular localization of global cultural flows in some way or another related to South Asia, expressed in the socio-musical scenario of Britain, and 'Transl-Asia' as the space that connects imagined and actual experiences and cultural forms around the world, perhaps linking up Br-Asians with Can-Asians and South Asians.[5] Our primary focus has been on expressive cultures, particularly music. However, the understanding of other social and political formations may be enhanced by the approach we have presented. If we consider the development of organizations such as the International Sikh Youth Federation, Young Muslims (UK) and the World Council of Hindus in Britain, each share the central concern of constructing essentialist religious identities, Sikh, Muslim and Hindu respectively. In the process, we note, they seek to eradicate the splintering along caste and regional lines that are manifest in their organizations and the everyday interactions they have across these boundaries. Alignments in terms of caste, religion, and region of affiliation are latent ruptures which are recognized in the conceptualization 'Br-Asian', but not so apparent in relation to particular fixed identities such as Muslim, Sikh, Indian, and Pakistani. Our approach allows us to acknowledge the essentialist elements whilst not losing sight of the de-essentialized fractures for the British post-migrant context. 'Br-Asian' allows us to

note the hybridity inherent in all identifications. Therefore, there might
be at least two levels of debate: one that clings to an essential nature of
an exclusivist category, and the other that opens up to form new possibilities of alliances. These vectors might operate to variable degrees,
simultaneously, or at different points in narrative texts. This politics of
identity, which is self-reflexive and recognizes how identities are con-
textually responsive, has been noted with respect to the 1995 street
violence in Bradford, when it was clearly expressed that this was a
(Br-)Asian struggle against police harassment – and not an issue about
'Muslims' as reported by mainstream media (*Eastern Eye*, 16 May 1995).

The concept of Transl-Asia applies more neatly to the socio-political
arena. Implicit to events such as the Golden Temple insurrection (1984)
and the destruction of Babri Masjid (1992) are flows of information,
goods and people around Transl-Asia. This movement is similar to the
musical journeys described above. We can thereby account for political
figures and organizations that are not necessarily centred in the subcontinent even though their primary concerns may be oriented in that
region. This is best illustrated by the fact that the Jammu and Kashmir
Liberation Front was founded in Birmingham in the 1970s, and by the
fact that the self-styled leader of Khalistan, Dr Jagjit Chauhan, is a
resident of London spearheading an organization with branches in
Canada, North America, Germany and Malaysia. These groupings have
branches throughout the world and their policies and practices are
reflective both of their locality and their concerns with South Asia. The
decentring of nation-states that Transl-Asia implies is one premise upon
which such transnational political mobilizations can be productively
explored.

The emphasis on musical production seeks to divert attention away
from the anthropologizing glare which enshrines categories such as
biraderi, caste, and inter-generational conflict when considering South
Asians in Britain. Br-Asian and Transl-Asia are vanguard spears of a
new theoretical approach which intends to pierce, wound and lay to
rest 'traditional' objectifying categories. The implications of this change
in theoretical tools are widespread: it enables us to slash out new paths,
new routes by which to challenge media and other ideological formations and their reliance upon unproblematized 'ethnic' categories.

NOTES

This chapter has appeared in public in various forms: at the 'Outside In – Maintaining Marginality at the Centre' workshop at the School of Oriental and African Studies, London, in May 1994 and at the Punjab Conference at Coventry University in June 1994. Thanks for comments to Ali Rattansi and Tej K. Purewal. Virinder S. Kalra would like to thank the British Cotton Growers Textile Workers' fund for financial support.

1. The pop song 'Movie over India' launched Apache Indian into the public eye in 1991. *Tartuffe* (1990) was one of the first British South Asian related theatre pieces to be sponsored by the National Theatre and to tour internationally. The play was adapted and performed by Tara Arts Theatre Company. *Bhaji on the Beach*, directed by Gurinder Chadha, was a major film success for Ambi Films in 1993.

2. See Featherstone (1990), Appadurai (1990), Harvey (1989) and Giddens (1991) for arguments concerning concepts of localization and globalization. In this chapter, we take globalization to refer to cultural flows around large parts of the world, including the movement of people, technology, media, and other cultural productions. Localization is the transformation of global flows in interaction with the socio-political landscape of a particular area. The term 'musical cultures' is not in any way taken as a fixed, bounded relation of categories, but used as an expression of convenience to further our main theoretical argument.

3. Giddha is the female counterpart to Bhangra, also commonly performed at Punjabi weddings.

4. The two most popular writers of Punjab are good examples: see *Heer* by Warish Shah (1991) and the *Kafian* of Bulleh Shah (1993).

5. Can-Asia was the name given to the Canadian festival of Asian film, held at the Canadian embassy in London in 1991.

REFERENCES

Appadurai, A. (1990) 'Disjuncture and Difference in the Global Cultural Economy', in Featherstone, M. (ed.) 1990 *Global Culture: Nationalism, Globalization and Modernity*, Sage, London.

Awan, S. (1994) 'Bhangra Bandwagon', in Burton, K. (ed.) 1994, *Rough Guide to World Music*, Penguin, London.

Axel, B. (1994) 'Place and Displacement, or Have Trope... Will Travel'. Unpublished paper. University of Chicago.

Back, L. (1994) *X Amount of Sat Siri Akal: Apache Indian, Reggae Music and Intermezzo Culture*, South Asia Seminar Series, ICCCR, Universities of Manchester and Keele, UK.

Baldwin, J. (1995) *Sonny's Blues and Other Stories*, Penguin Books, London.

Balibar, E. (1994) *Masses, Classes, Ideas: Studies on Politics and Philosophy Before and After Marx*, Routledge, New York.

Bambury, C. (1992) *Killing the Nazi Menace: How to Stop the Fascists*. Socialist Workers Party pamphlet.

Banerji, S. (1988) 'Ghazals to Bhangra in Great Britain', *Popular Music* 7(2): 207–13.

Banerji, S. and Baumann, G. (1990) 'Bhangra 1984–8: Fusion and Professionalisation in a Genre of South Asian Dance Music', in Oliver, P. (ed.) 1990, *Black Music in Britain: Essays on the Afro-Asian Contribution to Popular Music*, Open University Press, Milton Keynes.

Bauman, Z. (1993) 'Racism, Anti-Racism and Moral Progress', *Arena Journal* N.S. 1: 9–22.

Baumann, G. (1990) 'The Re-invention of Bhangra: Social Change and Aesthetic Shifts in a Punjabi Music in Britain', *World of Music* 32(2): 81–95.

Baumann, G. (1994) 'Dominant and Demotic Discourses of "Culture": Their Relevance to Multi-Ethnic Alliances', paper presented at a conference on 'Culture, Communication and Discourse: Negotiating Difference in Multi-

Ethnic Alliances', ICCCR, Universities of Manchester and Keele, 9–12 December 1994.

Bender, G. and Druckrey, T. (eds) (1994) *Culture on the Brink – Ideologies of Technology*, Seattle, Bay Press.

Bengali Housing Action Group (1978) *Race Today* 10(5): 109.

Bhabha, H. (1990) 'The Third Space', in Rutherford, J. (ed.) 1990, *Identity*, Lawrence & Wishart, London.

Bhabha, H. (1992) 'Freedom's Basis in the Indeterminate', *October* 61, Summer.

Bhabha, H. (1994) *The Location of Culture*, Routledge, London.

Bhuchar, S. (1989) 'I'm British But...', *Bazaar* 8: 9, South Asian Arts Forum, London.

Bonnett, A. (1993) *Radicalism, Anti-racism and Representation*, Routledge, London.

Bourne, J. (1987) 'Homelands of the Mind: Jewish Feminism and Identity Politics', *Race and Class* 29(1): 1–24.

Boyne, R. and Rattansi, A. (1990) 'The Theory and Politics of Postmodernism: By Way of an Introduction', in Boyne, R. and Rattansi, A. (eds) 1990 *Postmodernism and Society*, Macmillan, London.

Brah, A. (1992) 'Difference, Diversity and Differentiation', in Donald, J. and Rattansi, A. (eds) 1992, *'Race', Culture and Difference*, Open University and Sage, Milton Keynes.

Callahan, P. (1992) *The African American Grain: The Pursuit of Voice in Twentieth Century Black Fiction*, University of Illinois, Chicago.

Callinicos, A. (1993) *Race and Class*, Bookmarks, London.

Chambers, I. (1994) *Migrancy, Culture, Identity*, Routledge, London.

Chow, R. (1993) *Writing Diaspora: Tactics of Intervention in Contemporary Cultural Studies*, Indiana University Press, Bloomington.

Clifford, J. (1992) 'Travelling Cultures', in Grossberg, L., Nelson, C. and Treichler, P. (eds) 1992, *Cultural Studies*, Routledge, New York.

Cohen, P. (1992) 'It's Racism What Dunnit: Hidden Narratives in Theories of Racism' in Donald, J. and Rattansi, A. (eds) 1992, *'Race', Culture and Difference*, Open University and Sage, Milton Keynes.

Cohen, P. and Bains, H. (eds) (1988) *Multi-racist Britain*, Macmillan, Basingstoke.

Cohen, S. (1980) *Folk Devils and Moral Panic: The Creation of the Mods and Rockers*, London, Methuen.

Colvin, I. (1929) *The Life of General Dyer*, Blackwell, London.

Cotton, H. (1911) *Indian and Home Memories*, T. Fisher Unwin, London.

Datta, V.N. (1969) *Jallianwala Bagh*, Lyall Book Depot, Ludhiana.

Dawson, G. (1994) *Soldier Heroes: British Adventure, Empire and the Imaginings of Masculinities*, Routledge, London.

Decker, J. L. (1992) 'The State of Rap: Time and Place in Hip Hop Nationalism', *Social Text* 34, 11(1): 53–84.

Deleuze, G. and Guattari, F. (1980/1987) *A Thousand Plateaus: Capitalism and Schizophrenia*, University of Minnesota Press, Minneapolis.

Denselow, R. (1989) *When the Music's Over*, Faber, London.

Dhammi, O. (1992) 'Home Is Where the House Is', *Bazaar*, 22: 28, South Asian Arts Forum, London.

Dhondy, F. (1978) 'Teaching Young Blacks', *Race Today*, 10(4): 80–86.

Donald, J. and Rattansi, A.(eds) (1992) *'Race', Culture and Difference*, Open University and Sage, Milton Keynes.

Duffield, M. (1987) *Black Radicalism and the Politics of De-industrialization: The Hidden History of Indian Foundry Workers*, CRER, University of Warwick.

Evans, L. (1995) *Women, Sex and Rock'n'Roll: In Their Own Words*, Pandora, London.

Fanon, F. (1961) *The Wretched of the Earth*, Penguin Books, Harmondsworth.

Featherstone, M. (ed.) (1990) *Global Culture: Nationalism, Globalization and Modernity*, Sage, London.

Ferguson, R., Gever, M., Minh-ha, T. and West, C. (eds) (1990) *Out There: Marginalization and Contemporary Cultures*, New Museum of Contemporary Art, New York.

Fisher, M. (1995) 'Indie Reactionaries', *New Statesman and Society*, 7 July 1995.

Foucault, M. (1975/1982) *Discipline and Punish: The Birth of the Prison*, Penguin, Harmondsworth.

Frith, S. (1978) *The Sociology of Pop*, Constable, London.

Frith, S. (1990) 'Hip Hop', in Reynolds, S. (ed.) 1990, *Blissed Out: The Raptures of Rock*, Serpent's Tail, London.

Furneaux, R. (1963) *Massacre at Amritsar*, Allen Unwin, London.

Fuss, D. (1989) *Essentially Speaking: Feminism, Nature and Difference*, Routledge, London.

Gates, H.L. (1988) *The Signifying Monkey: A Theory of African-American Literary Criticism*, Oxford University Press, Oxford.

Geertz, C. (1984) 'Anti Anti Relativism', *American Anthropologist* 86(2): 263–78.

Giddens, A. (1991) *Modernity and Self-identity*, Polity, Cambridge.

Gillespie, M. (1995) *Television, Ethnicity and Cultural Change*, Routledge, London.

Gilroy, P. (1987) *There Ain't No Black in the United Jack*, Hutchinson, London.

Gilroy, P. (1988) 'Cruciality and the Frog's Perspective: An Agenda of Difficulties for the Black Arts Movement in Britain', *Third Text* 5: 33–44.

Gilroy, P. (1992) 'It's A Family Affair', in Dent, G. (ed.) 1992, *Black Popular Culture*, Dia Centre for the Arts, Bay Press, Seattle.

Gilroy, P. (1993a) *The Black Atlantic: Modernity and Double Consciousness*, Verso, London.

Gilroy, P. (1993b) *Small Acts*, Serpent's Tail, London.

Gilroy, P. and Lawrence, E. (1988) 'Two-Tone Britain: White and Black Youth and the Politics of Racism', in Cohen, P. and Bains, H.S. 1988, *Multi-racist Britain*, Macmillan, Basingstoke.

Giroux, H.(ed.) (1994) *Between Borders: Pedagogy and the Politics of Cultural Studies*, Routledge, London.

Gordon, P. (1990) *Racial Violence and Harassment*, Runnymede Research Report, London.

Grossberg, L. (1994) 'Introduction: Bringin' It All Back Home – Pedagogy and Cultural Studies', in Giroux, H. (ed.) 1994 *Between Borders: Pedagogy and the Politics of Cultural Studies*, Routledge, London.

Guattari, F. (1995) *Chaosmosis: An Ethico-aesthetic Paradigm*, trans. Paul Bains and Julian Pefanis, Power Publications, Sydney.

Hall, S. (1988a) 'New Ethnicities', *Black Film British Cinema*, ICA, London.

Hall, S. (1988b) 'New Ethnicities', in Donald, J. and Rattansi, A. (eds) 1992 *'Race', Culture and Difference*, Open University and Sage, Milton Keynes.

Hall. S. (1991) 'Old and New Identities, Old and New Ethnicities', in King, A.D. (ed.) 1991, *Culture, Globalization and the World System*, Macmillan, London.

Hall, S. (1992) 'What Is This 'Black' in Black Popular Culture?', in Dent, G. (ed.) 1992, *Black Popular Culture*, Bay Press, Seattle.

Hall, S. (1995) 'Black and White Television', in Givanni, J. (ed.) 1995, *Remote Control: Dilemmas of Black Intervention in British Film and TV*, British Film Institute, London.

Hardt, M. (1993) *Gilles Deleuze: An Apprenticeship in Philosophy*, University of Minnesota Press, Minneapolis.

Hardt, M. and Negri, A. (1994) *Labor of Dionysus: A Critique of the State Form*, University of Minnesota Press, Minneapolis.

Hardy, P. and Laing, D. (1995) *The Faber Companion to Popular Music*, Faber & Faber, London.

Harron, M. (1989) 'Pop as a Commodity', in Frith, S. (ed.) 1989, *Facing the Music: Essays on Pop, Rock and Culture*, Mandarin, London.

Harvey, D. (1989) *The Condition of Post-modernity: An Enquiry into the Conditions of Cultural Change*, Blackwell, Cambridge, MA.

Hazareesingh, S. (1986) 'Racism, Cultural Identity: An Indian Perspective', *Dragon's Teeth* 24: 4–10.

Hebdige, D. (1979) *Subculture: The Meaning of Style*, Methuen, London.

Hebdige, D. (1987) *Cut'n'mix: Culture, Identity and Caribbean Music*, Methuen, London.

Hewitt, R. (1986) *White Talk Black Talk: Inter-racial Friendship and Communication amongst Adolescents*, Cambridge University Press, Cambridge.

Hiro, D. (1971) *Black British White British*, Eyre & Spottiswoode, London.

hooks, b. (1991) *Yearning: Race, Gender, and Cultural Politics*, South End Press, Boston.

hooks, b. (1992) *Black Looks: Race and Representation*, South End Press, Boston.

hooks, b. (1994) *Outlaw Culture – Resisting Representations*, Routledge, London.

Hutnyk, J. (1996a) 'Adorno at Womad: South Asian Crossovers and the Limits of Hybridity-talk', in Werbner, P. and Modood, T. (eds) 1996 *Debating Cultural Hybridity: Multi-Cultural Identities and the Politics of Anti-Racism*, Zed Books, London.

Hutnyk, J. (1996b) *The Rumour of Calcutta: Tourism, Charity and the Poverty of Representation*, Zed Books, London.

Hutnyk, J. (1996c) 'Media, Research, Politics, Culture', *Critique of Anthropology* 16(4): 417–28.

Jameson, F. (1984) 'Postmodernism, or the Cultural Logic of Late Capitalism', *New Left Review* 146: 53–92.

Jameson, F. (1991) *Postmodernism, or The Cultural Logic of Late Capitalism*, Verso, London.

Jones, S. (1988) *Black Culture, White Youth – the Reggae Tradition from JA to UK*, Macmillan, London.

Kaplan, A.E. (1987) *Rocking Around the Clock: Music Television, Postmodernism and Consumer Culture*, Routledge, London.

Knowles, C. (1992) *Race, Discourse and Labourism*, Routledge, London.

Land, N. (1992) *The Thirst for Annihilation: Georges Bataille and Virulent Nihilism*, Routledge, London.

Levidow, L. (1994) 'The Gulf War Massacre as Paranoid Rationality', in Bender, G. and Druckrey, T. (eds) 1994, *Culture on the Brink – Ideologies of Technology*, Seattle, Bay Press.

Lipsitz, G. (1994) *Dangerous Crossroads: Popular Music, Postmodernism and the Poetics of Place*, Blackwell, London.

Lusane, C. (1993) 'Rap, Race and Politics', *Race and Class* 35(1): 41–56.

Marcus, G. (1989) *Lipstick Traces: A Secret History of the Twentieth Century*, Harvard University Press, Cambridge MA.

Marx, K. (1865/1950) 'On Proudhon', *Selected Works*, Vol. 1, Foreign Languages Publishing House, Moscow.

Marx, K. (1898/1950) 'Wages, Prices and Profit', *Selected Works*, Vol. 1, Foreign Languages Publishing House, Moscow.

McGuigan, J. (1992) *Cultural Populism*, Routledge, London.

McRobbie, A. (1994) *Postmodernism and Popular Culture*, Routledge, London.

Mercer, K. (1990) 'Welcome to the Jungle: Identity and Diversity in Postmodern Politics', in Rutherford, J. (ed.) 1990 *Identity*, Lawrence & Wishart, London.

Mercer, K. (1992) 'Back to My Routes', *Ten 8, Spring*, 2(3): 32–39.

Mercer, K. (1994) *Welcome to the Jungle: New Positions in Black Cultural Studies*, Routledge, London.

Messina, A. M. (1989) *Race and Party Competition in Britain*, Clarendon Press, London.

Modood, T. (1988) '"Black", Racial Equality and Asian Identity', *New Community* 14(3): 397–404.

Modood, T. (1990) 'Muslims, Race and Equality in Britain: Some Post-Rushdie Reflections', *Third Text* 11: 127–34.

Modood, T. (1994) 'Political Blackness and British Asians', *Sociology*, 28(4): 859–76.

Mukherjee, B. (1991) *Jasmine*, Virago, London.

Mukherjee, T. (1988) 'The Journey Back', in Cohen, P. and Bains, H. (eds) 1988 *Multi-Racist Britain*, Macmillan, Basingstoke.

Mungham, G. and Pearson, G. (1976) *Working Class Youth Cultures*, Routledge, London.

Negri, A. (1988) *Revolution Retrieved: Selected Writings on Marx, Keynes, Capitalist Crisis and New Social Subjects 1967–1983*, Red Notes, London.

Negri, A. and Guattari, F. (1990) *Communists Like Us*, Semiotext(e), New York.

Neiyyar, D. (1988) 'Bhangra', *Bazaar* 5:6, South Asian Arts Forum, London.

Noor, N.S. (1983) *Punjabis Living in England*, Issue 2, proceedings of the 1982 Progressive Writers Association conference. (Translated by by V.S Kalra.)

O' Brien, K. (1995) *Hymn to Her: Women Musicians Talk*, Virago, London.

O' Brien, L. (1995) *She Bop: The Definitive Story of Women in Rock, Pop and Soul*, Penguin, London.

Oliver, P. (ed.) (1990) *Black Music in Britain: Essays on the Afro-Asian Contribution to Popular Music*, Open University Press, Milton Keynes.

Omni, M. and Winant, H. (1986) *Racial Formation in the United States*, Routledge, London.

Perks, R. (1987) 'The Making of a British Asian', *Oral History* 15(1): 67–74.

Piccone, P. (1976) 'Review of Helmer: The Deadly Simple Mechanics of Society', *Theory and Society* 3(2): 135–8.

Raphael, A. (1995) *Never Mind the Bollocks: Women Rewrite Rock and Roll*, Virago, London.

Revolutionary Communist Tendency (1978) *Under a National Flag.*

Reynolds, S. (1990) *Blissed Out: The Raptures of Rock*, Serpent's Tail, London.

Reynolds, S. and Press, J. (1995) *The Sex Revolts*, Serpent's Tail, London.

Roberts, J. S. (1973) *Black Music of Two Worlds*, Penguin Books, London.

Rosaldo, R. (1993) *Culture and Truth – the Remaking of Social Analysis*, Routledge, London.

Rose, T. (1994) *Black Noise: Rap Music and Black Culture in Contemporary America*, Wesleyan/University Press of New England, London.

Ross, A. and Rose, T. (eds) (1994) *Microphone Fiends: Youth Music and Youth Culture*, Routledge, New York.

Russel, R. and Shamsher, J. (1978) 'Punjabi Poetry in Britain', *New Community* 7(3): 291–305.

Said, E. (1978) *Orientalism*, Penguin, London.

Savage, J. (1991) *England's Dreaming: Sex Pistols and Punk Rock*, Faber & Faber, London.

Sayyid, B. (forthcoming) *A Fundamental Fear: Eurocentrism, and the Emergence of Islamism*, Zed Books, London.

Shah, B. (1993) *Kafian*, New Book Company, Jallandhur.

Shah, W. (1991) *Heer*, Nanak Singh Pustak Mala, Amritsar. (Translated by A.S. Kang and K.S.Suri.)

Sharma, S. (1994) 'Who's in the House: The Cultural Politics of the New Asian Dance Music', South Asia Seminar Series, ICCCR, Universities of Manchester and Keele, November 1.

Shohat, E. and Stam, R. (1994) *Unthinking Eurocentrism*, Routledge, London.

Sidran, B. (1995) *Black Talk*, Payback Press, Edinburgh.

Sivanandan, A. (1982) *A Different Hunger*, Pluto, London.

Southall 23 April 1979 (1980) Report of the Unofficial Committee of Enquiry. National Council for Civil Liberties, London.

Southall: The Birth of Black Community (1981) Campaign Against Racism and Fascism, Institute of Race Relations, London.

Spartacist League (1994) *Militant Labour's Touching Faith in the Capitalist State.*

Spivak, G. (1988) 'Can the Subaltern Speak?' in Nelson, C. and Grossberg, L. (eds) 1988, *Marxism and the Interpretation of Culture*, Macmillan, London.

Spivak, G. (1993) *Outside in the Teaching Machine*, Routledge, London.

Stephens, G. (1992) 'Inter-racial Dialogue in Rap Music', *New Formations* 16: 62–79.

Street, J. (1986) *Rebel Rock: The Politics of Popular Music*, Blackwell, London.

Sweeny, P. (1991) *Directory of World Music,* Virgin, London.

Swedenburg, T. (1992) 'Hommies in the 'Hood: Rap's Commodification of Insubordination', *New Formations* 18: 53–66.

Taussig, M. (1992) *The Nervous System*, Routledge, London.

Tomlinson, J. (1990) *Cultural Imperialism,* Pinter, London.

Virilio, P. (1984/1989) *War and Cinema: The Logistics of Perception,* Verso, London.

Visram, R. (1986) *Ayahs, Lascars and Princes: Indians in Britain 1700–1947*, Pluto, London.

West, C. (1989) 'Black Culture and Postmodernism', in Kruger, B. and Mariani, P. (eds) 1989, *Remaking History*, Bay Press, Washington.

Widgery, D. (1986) *Beating Time: Riot 'n Race 'n Rock 'n Roll*, Chatto & Windus, London.

Yuval-Davis, N. (1992) 'Fundamentalism, Multiculturalism and Women in Britain', in Donald, J. and Rattansi, A. (eds) 1992, *'Race', Culture and Difference*, Open University and Sage, Milton Keynes.

Žižek, S. (1989) *The Sublime Object of Ideology,* Verso, London.

Žižek, S. (1993) *Tarrying with the Negative,* Duke University Press, Durham NC.

MAGAZINES/NEWSPAPERS

The Asian Age
CARF
Daily Mail
Eastern Eye
Face
Fight Imperialism, Fight Racism
Fighting the Nazi Threat.
Guardian
Ghazal and Beat
Hip-Hop Connection
i-D Magazine
Independent
Living Marxism
Melody Maker
New Musical Express
Observer
Race and Class
Race Today
Red Action
Red Pepper
Represent
Revolutionary Fighter
Select

Sling-Shot
Sniffin' Glue
Soul Underground
Sounds
Straight No Chaser
Time
The Times
Time Out
WAR News
The Wire
Workers Hammer
Workers Power
Zigzag

ORGANIZATIONS

AFA	Anti-Fascist Action
ANL	Anti-Nazi League
ARA	Anti-Racist Alliance
AYM	Asian Youth Movement
BNP	British National Party
CARF	Campaign Against Racism and Fascism
CPI	Communist Party of India
CPI(M)	Communist Party of India (Marxist)
CPI(M-L)	Communist Party of India (Marxist-Leninist)
IWA	Indian Workers Association (GB)
NF	National Front
RAR	Rock Against Racism
SL	Spartacist League
SWP	Socialist Workers Party
SYM	Southall Youth Movement
WOMAD	World of Music and Dance

INTERVIEWS

Asian Dub Foundation 3 August 1994, at the Community Music Centre, Farringdon, London.
Sonya Aurora-Madan at Savage and Best Plugging, London 4 August 1994.
DJ Ritu, Nitin Sawney and Vikas Malik at Club Outcaste, London 13 June 1995.
Anjali Bhatia, Voodoo Queens at Too Pure Records, London, 9 August 1994.
Fun^Da^Mental, Astoria, London 20 July 1994.
Tejinder Singh, Cornershop at Wiija Records, London 23 March 1995.
Left Forum conference, School of African and Oriental Studies, University of London, 23 March 1995.

DISCOGRAPHY

Achanak (1990) *PaNACHe*, Nachural Records.

Achanak, Safri Boys et al. (1993) *Hoye Hoye Kiss*.

Achanak et al. (1993) *East 2 West: Bhangra for the Masses*, Nachural.

Apache Indian (1993) *No Reservations,* Island.

Apache Indian (1995) *Nuff Vibes*, Island.

Apache Indian (1995) *Make Way for the Indian*, Island.

Asian Dub Foundation (1994) *Conscious*, Nation.

Asian Dub Foundation (1995) *Fact and Fictions,* Nation.

Azaad (1989) *Drum'N'Dhol*, Multitone.

Aziz Mian (n.d.) Various, EMI Pakistan.

Babara Mason (1983) *Another Man*, West End.

Babylon Zoo (1996) *The Boy With the X-Ray Eyes*, EMI.

Bally Sagoo (1994) *Bollywood Classics*, Columbia.

Bally Sagoo (1994) *Bollywood Flashback*, Columbia.

Bally Sagoo (1994) *Chura Liya*, Columbia.

Bhujhangy (1989) *Bhujhangy (Ra)*, Keda Studio Series.

Bindu, DMF et al. (1993) *Culture Clash*, Multitone.

Bittu et al. (1993) *Extra Hot 9*, BMG.

Keni Burke (1982) Rising to the Top, BMG.

Terry Callier (1990) 'I Don't Want to See Myself Without You', Acid Jazz.

Shiela Chandra (1991) *Shanachie*, Shanachie.

Oliver Cheatham (1983) Get Down Saturday Night, MCA.

Chocolate Milk (1975) *Actions Speak Louder Than Words*, BMG.

Cornershop (1994) *Woman's Gotta Have It*. Wiija.

Cornershop (1996) *6 am Jullander Shere*, Wiija.

De-Lay (1995) *Vibes Alive*, Outcaste Music.

Det^ri^mental (1995) 'Xenophobia Cooking', Vinyl.

Fun^Da^Mental (1993) 'Countryman'/'Tribal Revolution', Nation.

Fun^Da^Mental (1994) 'Dog-Tribe', Nation.

Fun^Da^Mental (1994) 'Gold Burger', Nation.

Fun^Da^Mental (1994) *Seize the Time*, Nation.

Fun^Da^Mental (1995) 'Nother India', Nation.

Fun^Da^Mental (1995) *With Intent to Pervert the Cause of Injustice*, Nation.

Junior Giscombe (1983) 'Mama Used to Say', Mercury Records.

Leroy Hudson (1978) 'Closer to the Source', Curtom.

Hustlers HC (1994) *On a Ride,* Nation.

Indian Lion (1995) 'I Won't Give Up Till I Get It', Multitone.

Kaliphz (1995) 'Hang 'Em High', London.

Kaliphz (1995) *Seven Deadly Sins*, Payday.

Kavita (1996) *Believe*, Keda.

Love Unlimited Orchestra (1973) 'Love's Theme', Pye Records

James Mason (1992) *Sweet Power Your Embrace*, Luv'n Haight Records.

Curtis Mayfield (1974) 'To Be Invisible', Curtom.

Maze (1981) *Joy and Pain*, Capitol.

Maze (1985) *Back in Stride*, Capitol.

Maze (1985) *Twilight*, Capitol.
Monsoon (1982) 'Ever So Lonely'.
Nusrat Fateh Ali Khan (1989) *Shahen-Shah*, Real World.
Nusrat Fateh Ali Khan (1990) *Mustt Mustt*, Real World.
Nusrat Fateh Ali Khan (1991) *Ali da Malang*, Oriental Star Agencies.
Nusrat Fateh Ali Khan (1993) *Qawwal and Party Jhoole Laal*, Popula.
O'Jays (1983) *Put Your Heads Together*, CBS.
Panjabi MC (1994) *Another Sellout*, Nachural.
Lou Reed (1978) *Street Hassle* (includes 'I Wanna Be Black'), RCA.
Pharoh Sanders (1972) *Upper Egypt*, ABC.
Nitin Sahwney (1995) *Migration*, Outcaste.
Malkit Singh et al. (n.d.) *Pump Up the Bhangra*, n.p.
Sabri Brothers (1990) *Ya Harib*, Real World.
Various (1993) *Bally Sagoo in the Mix*, Mango.
Various (1992) *Dhol Blasters*, Saint Records.
Various (1992) *Womad: Ten Years*, Real World.
Various (1978) *Bhangra Power*, Multitone.
Linda Williams (1979) *Elevate Your Minds*, Arista.
XLNC (1995) *Out On Bail*, Multitone.

FILMOGRAPHY

'Birthrights: Across the Tracks', BBC2 2, August 1993.
Territories, dir. Isaac Julien, 1983.
I'm Not British But... dir. Gurinder Chudha, 1990.
The Late Show, BBC2, 12 October 1994.
Rhythm and Raag, Interface Video Productions, 1992.
Identical Beat, dir. Smita Malde, on Asian Dub Foundation, 1994.
Walking Away with the Music, dir. Shafeeq Valini.

ABOUT THE CONTRIBUTORS

Koushik Banerjea is a freelance writer based in London. He is currently working on a novel.

Partha Banerjea is a psychiatrist working at the Maudsley Hospital, London. His interest in soul predates his interest in medicine.

Jatinder Barn, a lawyer, is at Goldsmiths' College, University of London, writing on Jallianwala Bagh, the Amritsar disturbances of 1919 and techniques of colonial governance and violence.

Mukhtar Dar is a film-maker, youth worker and political activist in Manchester.

Shirin Housee teaches at the University of Wolverhampton and is currently writing on tourism and representations of Mauritius.

Rupa Huq divides her time between researching youth culture at the University of East London and being an all-round· (wannabe) media whore.

John Hutnyk is the author of *The Rumour of Calcutta: Tourism, Charity and the Poverty of Representation*, Zed Books 1996.

Virinder S. Kalra is. Working, playing and other things around and about research life. Bored by white, usually male, academics, he is interested in counterhegemonic theory and practice.

Raminder Kaur is doing research on art, religion and nationalism at the School of Oriental and African Studies in London. She is a (script) writer and artistic director of Chandica Arts Company.

Ashwani Sharma teaches in the Department of Cultural Studies at the University of East London. He is currently researching in the area of post-colonial Indian film and radical politics.

Sanjay Sharma teaches at the University of Manchester and is doing research on pedagogy and cultural difference.

INDEX

Achanak, 38, 148, 153, 225
Acid Bhangra, 33
Acid House, 65
Acid Jazz, 76
Action Committee against Racial
    Attack, 133
Afrika Bambata, 83
Alaap, 38, 84, 90, 94, 104, 224, 225
Ali, Altab, 133, 194, 197
Ali, Ishaque, 133
Ali, Quddus, 150, 153, 194
Ali, Tariq, 139
Allison, Commander, 171
Anaamika, 225
Anti-Fascist Action (AFA), 146, 147,
    148, 159, 177
Anti-Nazi League (ANL), 131, 132,
    134, 136, 137, 138, 139, 140, 141,
    142, 143, 144, 145, 146, 147, 148,
    152, 153, 159, 167, 177, 178, 179,
    180, 182
Anti-Racist Committee for the
    Defence of Asians in East London,
    132
Anti-Racist Alliance (ARA), 145, 146,
    147
Apache Indian, 3, 6, 9, 15, 33, 36, 41,
    63, 66, 67, 72, 77, 79, 161, 207,
    217, 226, 227
Arora, Paul, 46, 151
Asian, as category, 7, 40, 41, 47, 54,
    219

Asian Dub Foundation, 5, 32, 42, 43,
    47–51, 64, 68, 69, 77, 79, 145, 149,
    157, 175, 179, 198
Asian Kool, 64, 75, 77, 79, 161
Asian Rap, 33, 161
Asian Youth Movements (AYM), 129,
    132, 136, 145, 149, 153, 166
Astley, Rick, 63
Aurora-Madan, Sonya, 71, 74, 147,
    166
Awan, S., 78

Babylon Zoo, 29
Back, Les, 35, 36, 37, 40, 67
Balo, 199
Bambury, Chris, 142
Banerji, S., 64, 66
Bangladeshi Youth Movement, 133
Bass Clef club, 89
Baumann, G., 34, 35, 36, 37, 64, 65,
    66, 74
BBC, 78; Radio One, 93, 94, 95;
    World Service, 72
Beatles, 62
Benn, Tony, 140
Beverley, Frankie, 119, 121
Bhabha, Homi, 55, 223
Bhangra, 3, 6, 7, 25, 26, 33, 34, 35,
    36, 37, 38, 39, 40, 41, 54, 55, 61,
    62, 63, 64, 65, 66, 70, 74, 76, 77,
    78, 79, 82, 83, 84, 85, 86, 89, 96,
    99, 101, 102, 139, 185, 208, 219,

220, 222, 224, 225, 226, 228
Bhangramuffin, 33, 79, 226
Bhatia, Anjali, 72, 73–4
Big Life Records, 97, 103
Black, as category, 7, 39, 41, 42, 47, 51, 62, 118, 149, 209, 218, 219
Black Panthers, 51, 53
Blacka-D, 51, 68, 127, 164
Blair, Arnold, 105
blues, 9
Bollywood remixes, 27, 28, 33, 66, 71
Bomb the Bass, 71
Bombay Jungle, 65, 66, 75
Bonnett, A., 142
Bourne, Jenny, 43, 44
Br-Asian, use of term, 219, 220, 221, 224, 226, 229
Bradford 12, 133, 134, 135, 149
Bradford Asian Youth Movement, 132
Breakdance, 83
British National Party (BNP), 47, 67, 98, 144, 146, 148, 163, 164, 166, 177, 178, 180, 184, 209, 227
Bushell, Gary, 197
Butler, Mark, 168
Buzzcocks, 139

Callahan, P., 222
Callier, Terry, 113
Callinicos, Alex, 141
Campaign Against Racism and Fascism (CARF), 149, 164, 179
Carey, Mariah, 102
Carne, Jean, 106
Centre for Contemporary Cultural Studies (CCCS), 62
Chaggar, Gurdip Singh, 132, 194, 197
Chambers, Iain, 18, 21, 22
Channel 4, 166
Chauhan, Dr Jagjit, 230
Cheetham, Oliver, 105
Chitrakar, Ishwar, 130
Chocolate Milk, 114
Chudha, Gurinder, 32, 63, 67
Clapton, Eric, 137, 138
Clash, 139
Clinton, Bill, 156
Cobra, 35
Cohen, Phil, 67, 182

Columbia Records, 77, 91, 99, 100
Combat 18, 148, 163, 177, 195
Communist Party of India, 130
Communist Party of India (Marxist), 130
Communist Party of India (Marxist-Leninist), 130
community defence, 175–87
Condon, Paul, 159, 181, 182
Corbyn, Jeremy, 171
Cornershop, 8, 66, 68, 69, 70, 77
Costello, Elvis, 139
Criminal Justice and Public Order Act (CJA) (1994), 156–87
Cultural Studies, 1, 3, 6, 7, 8, 17, 20, 160

D'Amour, Yusuf, 95
DCS, 225
Dar, Mukhtar, 81–104
Das, Annirudha, 32, 48, 50, 68, 77, 179, 229
Decker, J.L., 51
Deleuze, Gilles, 36
Denselow, Robin, 66, 69
Desai, A., 205
Det-Ri-Mental, 42, 145
Devonshire, Alan, 120
Dhondy, Farrukh, 143
diaspora, 8, 9, 16, 18, 19, 20, 21, 25, 185, 193, 194, 207
Disco, 82, 104
DJ Paul, 70
DJ Ritu, 72, 76
Dog-Tribe, 156, 161–7, 176, 184, 187; censorship of, 159, 164, 165, 166, 167, 175, 186
Douglas, Brian, 184
Dub, 34
Duffield Street 4, 149
Duggal, Rohit, 194, 196
Dyer, Brigadier General Reginald, 194–204, 210, 212

East 17, 210
Eastern Eye, 220
Echobelly, 8, 72, 74, 147, 166
Edwards, Greg, 116, 120
Electro, 83
ethnicity, 20, 22, 25, 28, 41, 62, 74
Euro-Beat, 10

Fanon, Frantz, 203
Farrakhan, Louis, 51, 52, 53
film music, 26, 27, 28, 51, 71, 81, 82,
    90, 91, 224, 225
Frith, Simon, 69
Fun^Da^Mental, 5, 9, 30, 42, 43, 44,
    51–4, 66, 68, 69, 71, 127, 128, 145,
    147, 148, 149, 152, 153, 154, 156,
    157, 159, 161, 162, 164, 165, 167,
    176, 179, 180, 183, 184, 185, 195,
    227
Funk, 83, 84, 103
Fuss, D., 44

Gandhi, Mahatma, 226
Gangsta Rap, 45, 47, 54, 177, 209, 210
Garage, 212
Gardner, Joy, 184
Gates, Henry Louis, 221
Gaynor, Gloria, 82
Gelly, Dave, 66
Giddha, 222, 227–9
Gillespie, Marie, 3, 34, 63, 66, 160
Gilroy, Paul, 8, 9, 37, 54, 63, 107, 119,
    138, 140, 141, 142, 144, 182, 184,
    219, 225
Giscombe, Junior, 119, 121
Golden Star, 225
Grant, David, 110
Grech, Joyoti, 229
Grossberg, L., 55
Grunge, 8
Guattari, Félix, 36, 185
Guran Ditta, 199

Hall, Stuart, 7, 19, 20, 34, 39, 41, 54,
    184
Hamed, Prince Naseem, 205, 208
Hans, Surjit, 130, 135
Hardt, Michael, 174, 185
Hebdige, Dick, 226
Heera, 38, 104
Hip-Hop, 9, 23, 42, 44, 45, 47, 48,
    53, 76, 83, 112, 127, 167, 178, 185,
    202, 207, 208
Hollywood Records, 103
Honeyford, Ray, 206
hooks, bell, 184, 204, 210
Horizon radio, 116
Hot 'n Spicy club, 33, 76
House, 9

Housee, Shirin, 81–104
Hucknall, Mick, 63
Hussain, Zakir, 211
Hussein, Imtiaz, 229
Hustlers HC, 5, 33, 38, 42, 43, 45–7,
    52, 70, 145, 147, 149, 150, 151,
    152, 153, 178, 183, 198
Hutson, Leroy, 113–14, 118
hybridity, 20, 21, 29, 33, 207, 230

Ice Cube, 53
Impi D, 165
Indian Workers Association (IWA), 5,
    129, 131, 133, 134, 136, 139, 141,
    145, 149, 153, 166
International Sikh Youth Federation,
    229
Irving, Miles, 195
Islam, 24, 52, 68, 164, 165, 230
Island Records, 77
ITV, 165, 166

Jallianwala Bagh, 193–214
James, C.L.R., 202
Jamiroqai, 63
Jaye, Miles, 120
Jazz Fusion, 212
Jeep Beats, 112
JFM, 116, 119
Johal, Ranjit, 109, 110, 111, 114, 119,
    121
Joi Bangla, 33, 64
Jones, Simon, 200
Julien, Isaac, 206
Jungle, 5, 7, 16, 33, 41, 62, 76, 79,
    103, 198, 202, 205, 208, 209, 211,
    212

Kaliphz, 5, 32, 41, 52, 66, 70, 145,
    147, 149, 152, 153, 157, 161, 175,
    177, 179, 180, 207, 208, 227
Kapoor, Raj, 92
Kapur, Steve, 208
Kashmir Liberation Front, 230
Kashmiri Workers Association, 131
Kaufman, Gerald, 169, 176
Kaur, Ranjit see Radical Sista
Kerouac, Jack, 210
Kershaw, Andy, 95
Khaled, Cheb, 21
Khan, Nusrat Fateh Ali, 24, 25, 29

Khazanchi, Deepak, 224
King, Rodney, 152, 183
Kirtan music, 208
Kirton, Lew, 118
Kiss FM, 72
KK Kings, 42, 71, 97
Knowles, C., 140
Kureishi, Hanif, 67

Labour Party, 140, 145, 148
Langdale 4, 181
Lawrence, Errol, 144
Lawrence, Sir Ivan, 169–73, 182
Lawrence, Steven, 146, 150, 196
Les Têtes Brûlées, 21
Levidow, Les, 206
Limelight club, 33
Lloyd, Peter, 168
Lock, Graham, 143

Madonna, 210
Maestros club, 88
Mailer, Norman, 210
Maina, 95
Malcolm X, 51, 53, 163
Malik, Anwar Abdel, 205
Mambo club, 89
Mangeshka, Lata, 82, 211, 217
Mann, Jas, 29
marginality, 16, 17, 18, 19, 20, 28
Maria, Tania, 119
Mary Jane Girls, 119
Mason, Al, 118
Mason, Barbara, 121
Mason, James, 110
Maxi Priest, 63
Mayfield, Curtis, 112
McCann, Ian, 108, 109, 114
Mercer, Kobenda, 39
Metal, 8
Mian, Qawwal Aziz, 15, 29
migrancy, 16, 19, 21, 25, 27
Militant, 148, 174, 175, 181
Modood, Tariq, 7, 40, 44
Mohabhat club, 75
Monsoon, 79
Morley, Paul, 141
MTV, 9, 165, 166, 167
Multitone, 77
Musafirs group, 82
Musicians' Union (MU), 99

N'Dour, Youssou, 21
Naidu, Sarojini, 213
Naked City, 166
Naraj, Prem, 84
Nation of Islam, 51, 52, 53
Nation Records, 179
National Front (NF), 98, 113, 132,
    133, 134, 136, 137, 138, 141, 143,
    177
Nawaz, Aki, 69, 71, 147, 148, 157,
    162, 163, 164, 165, 166, 176, 182,
    195
Naxalbari Movement, 130
Nazral, Kazi, 50
Neeru, Kamaljit, 228
Negri, Antonio, 5, 174, 185
Nehru, Jawaharlal, 111
Neiyyar, Dil, 35
New Asian Dance Music, 32, 33, 34
Newham 7, 149
Newham Monitoring Project, 146,
    153, 179, 180
Nicholson, General, 210

O-Jays, 110
Oliver, P., 62
Operation Eagle Eye, 159, 181, 185
Orientalism, 2, 10, 15, 16, 29, 46, 206;
    neo-, 19, 36, 160, 161, 165
otherness, 16, 19, 22, 23, 28, 29, 36,
    71, 120, 139
Outcaste, 75, 76

Pakistani Workers Association, 131
Pammi, Parmjit, 228
Pandit, John, 69, 77, 79, 179
Pardesi, 84
Parsons, Tony, 138
Peach, Blair, 129, 133, 134
Peel, John, 95
Phoenix Risin', 110, 112, 114, 121
post-Bhangra, 3, 8, 33, 34, 36, 40, 41,
    43, 51, 53, 54, 55, 130, 185
post-colonial theory, 17, 18, 20, 21
Powell, Enoch, 132, 137
Public Enemy, 53, 68
Punjabi MC, 161
Punk, 8, 82, 138, 139, 141, 142

Qawwali music, 24, 25, 29, 51, 208

Race Today, 144
Radical Sista, 4, 72, 81–104, 229
Rafi Mohammed, 211
Rafiq, Amer, 184
Ragga, 41, 79, 96, 202, 226
Ram, Satpal, 184
Rani, Ranjeeta, 136
Rap, 41, 42, 43, 44, 48, 50, 53, 71,
    79, 101, 103, 149, 152, 222, 227,
    228
Rastafari, 9, 138
Rattansi, Ali, 182
Rave, 6
RCA Records, 77
Red Action, 148
Reed, Lou, 63
Reggae, 9, 34, 35, 38, 45, 83, 84, 90,
    91, 138, 139, 141, 142, 201, 226
Revolutionary Communist Party, 148,
    175, 177
Revolutionary Communist Tendency,
    144
Revolutionary Internationalist League
    (RIL), 159, 180, 181
Reynolds, Simon, 67, 119, 120, 212
Robinson, Tom, 139
Roche, Barbara, 172
Rock Against Racism (RAR), 69, 133,
    134, 137, 138, 139, 140, 141, 142,
    144, 147, 149, 153, 179
Rosaldo, Renato, 115
Rose, Cynthia, 42, 78
Rotten, Johnny, 137
Ruddock, Joan, 168, 171
Rushdie, Salman, 116, 165, 184

Sadique, Avtar, 131
Safri Boys, 71
Sagoo, Bally, 4, 9, 16, 25, 26, 27, 28,
    33, 66, 67, 68, 71, 75, 81–104, 226
Sahotas, 225
Said, Edward, 10, 213
Sakamoto, Ruichi, 21
Sangeeta, 228
Sasha, 229
Satrang, 71
Sanders, Pharaoh, 120
Savage, Jon, 138
Sawney, Nitin, 66
Sayyid, Bobby, 38
Scott Heron, Gil, 106

Screwdriver, 135
Sex Pistols, 71
Shakti group, 37
Shankar, Ravi, 143
Shankeys Soap, 33
Sidran, Ben, 119
Singh, Malkit, 94
Singh, Tejinder, 70
Smith, Robert, 120
Socialist Workers Party (SWP), 133,
    134, 136, 137, 138, 139, 140, 141,
    142, 143, 144, 145, 148, 152, 174,
    178, 179, 181
Sony, 9, 25, 27, 99, 103
Soul, 8, 34, 84, 96, 106, 107, 108,
    112, 113, 114, 115, 117, 119
Soul Sonic Force, 83
Soul Weekenders, 108, 109, 117
Southall Black Sisters, 146
Southall Youth Movement, 133, 134
Southern Death Cult, 71
Spartacist League, 137, 143, 144, 175,
    177, 181
Spivak, Gayatri, 8, 19, 44, 218
Streetsounds, 116, 117
Stubbs, David, 176
Sullivan, Caroline, 66
Sumberg, David, 169, 170
Sunrise radio, 94
Swedenburg, Ted, 43

Taussig, Michael, 196
Techno, 6, 8, 103, 212
Time Recordings, 103
Toop, David, 79
Tower Hamlets 9, 149
Transl-Asia, 6, 8, 223, 224, 227
Two-Tone, 138
2Phaan Da Alien, 32, 70, 207

UB40, 139
Uddin, Mushtaq, 127
UK Apache, 208, 209, 212
United Black Youth League (UBYL),
    135
Unity, 146

Vaz, Keith, 169
Vincent, Robbie, 116
Voodoo Queens, 8, 70, 72, 73–4, 77,
    153

Wag Club, 65, 76
Walia, Mandeep, 46, 151
Watergate, 112, 114, 121
Watts, Dave, *see* Blacka-D
West End Records, 121
West, Cornel, 222
Widgery, David, 138
Williams, Linda, 115
Workers Against Racism (WAR),
    175
Workers Power, 181
World Council of Hindus in Britain,
    229
World Music, 3, 6, 21, 22, 23, 24, 26,

    32, 63, 96, 161
World Wide Web, 61, 78

X-Ray Specs, 72, 139
XLNC, 38, 161

Young Muslims (UK), 229
Youth Against Racism in Europe, 146,
    175
Youth Connection, 146

Zee TV, 78, 222
Zephaniah, Benjamin, 65
Žižek, Slavoj, 28, 38